AF575972

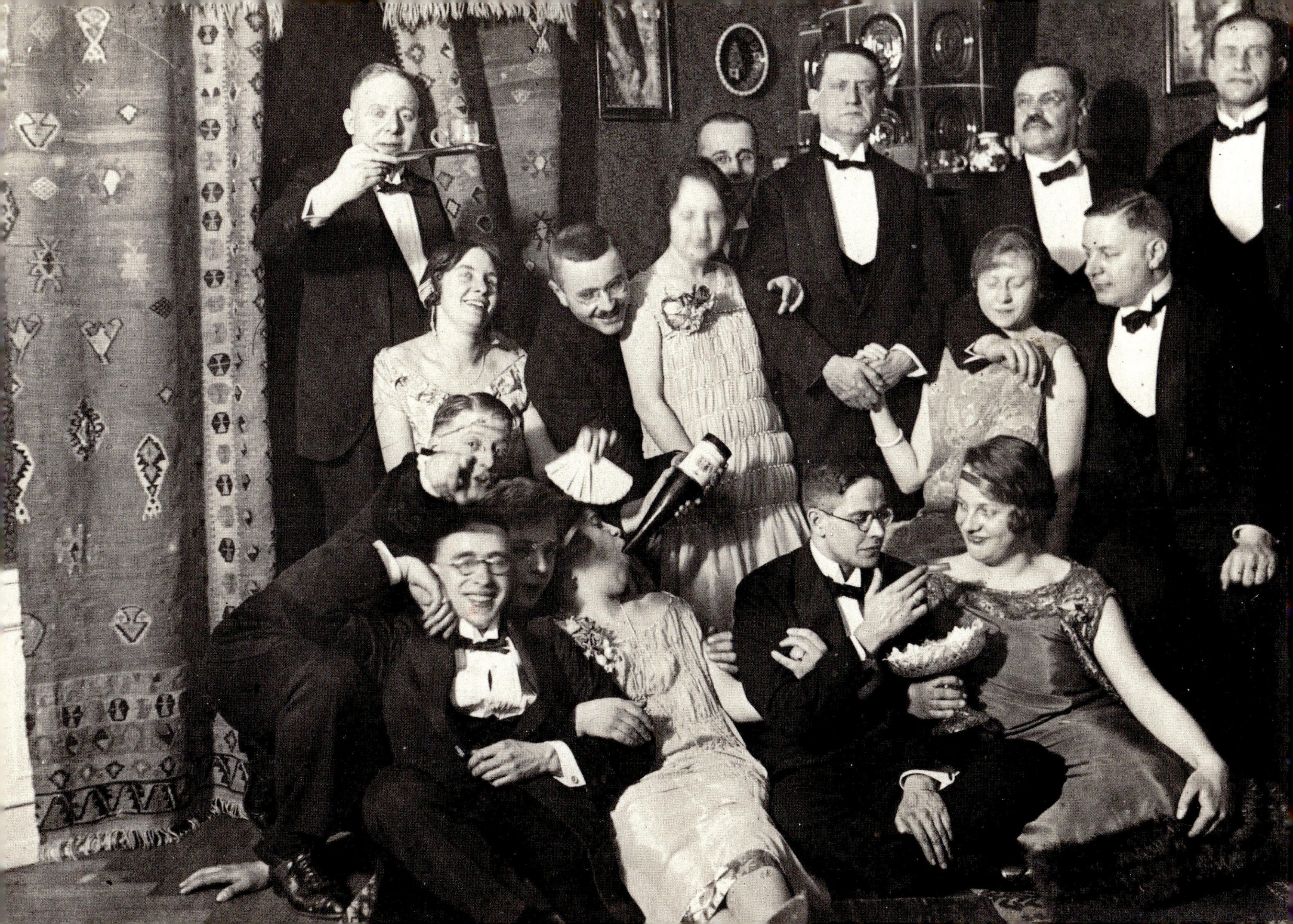

party! party!! party!!!

In Germany the war winter of 1916–17 was long and harsh. Many resorted to eating the turnips grown as animal fodder, earning the period its *Steckrübenwinter* (Turnip Winter) epithet. Long lists of casualties on the Western Front made stalemates on the Somme and at Verdun feel like defeats. In the East, however, revolution in Russia would soon end the war there, and as German troops began to return home, hope that the years of suffering might soon be over was kindled. That hope was dashed the following summer, when a plan for German U-boats to isolate Britain in the Atlantic and force a surrender failed, and the entry of the United States into the war created a very different reality. The noose of the Allied blockade grew tighter, leading to even greater shortages, even more suffering, and even longer casualty lists.

In the spring of 1918, the German military made a last-ditch attempt to achieve victory in the West. Troops freed up by the collapse of Russia were thrown against the Allies and came almost within reach of Paris, but were eventually repulsed. A slow retreat ensued, followed in November 1918 by revolution in Germany. On the battlefield it was capitulation – total surrender dressed as an armistice. The Allies' only concession was that Germany would not be occupied by foreign troops. Alsace-Lorraine, won from the French in 1871, became French again. Germany's empire and its emperor were gone, and the Weimar Republic was proclaimed.

The so-called Paris Peace Conference opened in January 1919 with the intention of redistributing the colonies of the defeated countries and deciding what Germany was to forfeit. The conference dragged on as nations waited to learn what their new status and size would be after they had been picked over by the victors. Cartoons showed the delegates feasting, or with beards grown long during endless negotiations. US President Woodrow Wilson's League of Nations promised to replace global conflict with universal diplomacy, but in fact humiliated Germany by imposing reparations so large it would have no hope of paying them.

The German economy was shattered. Any lingering self-confidence was in danger of being stamped out entirely as the Republic reeled from this economic assault. Demonstrations, recriminations, and the plotting and planning of coups ensued as a power vacuum sucked the country towards civil war. All traces of economic recovery were smothered by outstanding debt. The banks printed money feverishly, irresponsibly, until it became worthless. And with never-before-seen inflation rates came new illnesses. A condition dubbed 'zero-stroke', a neurotic compulsion to write endless zeros, hit bankers and bookkeepers – caused, it was said, by minds overloaded with calculations involving thousands of millions.

As one generation had watched Germany transformed by the war, another had come of age during wartime and now lived with its consequences – including half a million widows and more than a million orphans. Signs of discord were everywhere. Demobilised and haggard soldiers joined the *Freikorps*, right-wing paramilitary units that were formed to keep order but had political agendas of their own. Men maimed in the trenches sold matches or begged on the streets, and prostitutes were everywhere. It was perhaps inevitable that in the face of all this and after the years of uncertainty and hardship, an irrepressible desire for fun and adventure would emerge to take hold of the country's youth in the 1920s.

Despite its troubles and factions, despite the constant push-and-pull of right- and left-wing extremism, the Weimar Republic was Germany's first democracy, which in itself was a kind of revolution. Women had comprised more than a third of the labour force during the war and, although this proportion decreased as men returned home, there was no disguising the fact that women were as capable as their male counterparts, and in 1919 they won the right to vote. The expectation of equality together with the elimination of so much of social normality led to a rise in the numbers of women indulging, alongside men, in decadent pastimes revolving around sex and drugs. Others reacted to the changes by becoming more conservative, styling their hair in long braids and clinging to the traditional values of *Kinder, Küche, Kirche* (children, kitchen, church).

Cameras were now readily available, and press photography was entering a period of unprecedented coverage. Looking at the consequently extensive documentation of the Weimar era, it is tempting at first glance to see it as one long period of debauchery. The truth, however, is more subtle. While writers and artists from all over the world sought out the breaking of Germany's taboos and documented its crime, drug culture, extreme sexuality and lewdness, the overwhelming majority of the country's populace was concerned only with making ends meet, enduring long hours of work and living with the constant fear of unemployment and the deadly Spanish flu. Temptation was, however, omnipresent, even for those who lived by codes of behaviour precluding the wild excesses of the cabarets – people like Immanuel Rath, the moralistic teacher in Josef von Sternberg's *The Blue Angel* who chastises his students for their obsession with cabaret artiste Lola Lola (Marlene Dietrich) before falling in love with her himself. It would take no more than a moment of weakness, a sudden desire to break from convention and the humdrum routines of poverty, to embrace the raucous and euphoric spirit of the time.

Clashing ideologies driven by people who were determined, one way or another, to stamp their authority on society would eventually bring this singular period to an end; but for a while the peculiar circumstances of time and place brought many ordinary people into close proximity with modes of behaviour usually reserved for those who live their lives after midnight.

All of the photographs in *party! party!! party!!!* come from private sources that have been brought together over many years. Little or nothing is known about most of the people who appear in them, although some would have been public figures in their day. It is the places that are remembered better than the people; establishments that were infamous enough for tourists to come and gawk, and be quietly despised by streetwise locals.

Aside from the Kirchner family album, few of the pictures published here originally had accompanying captions. In some cases locations were available and have been incorporated as captions. Further information is included in the form of a commentary alongside the photos, which provides an overview of events contributing to the cultural and political climate of the time and occasionally offers further insight into individual images. None of the pictures in this book have been published previously.

part I

1917
1925

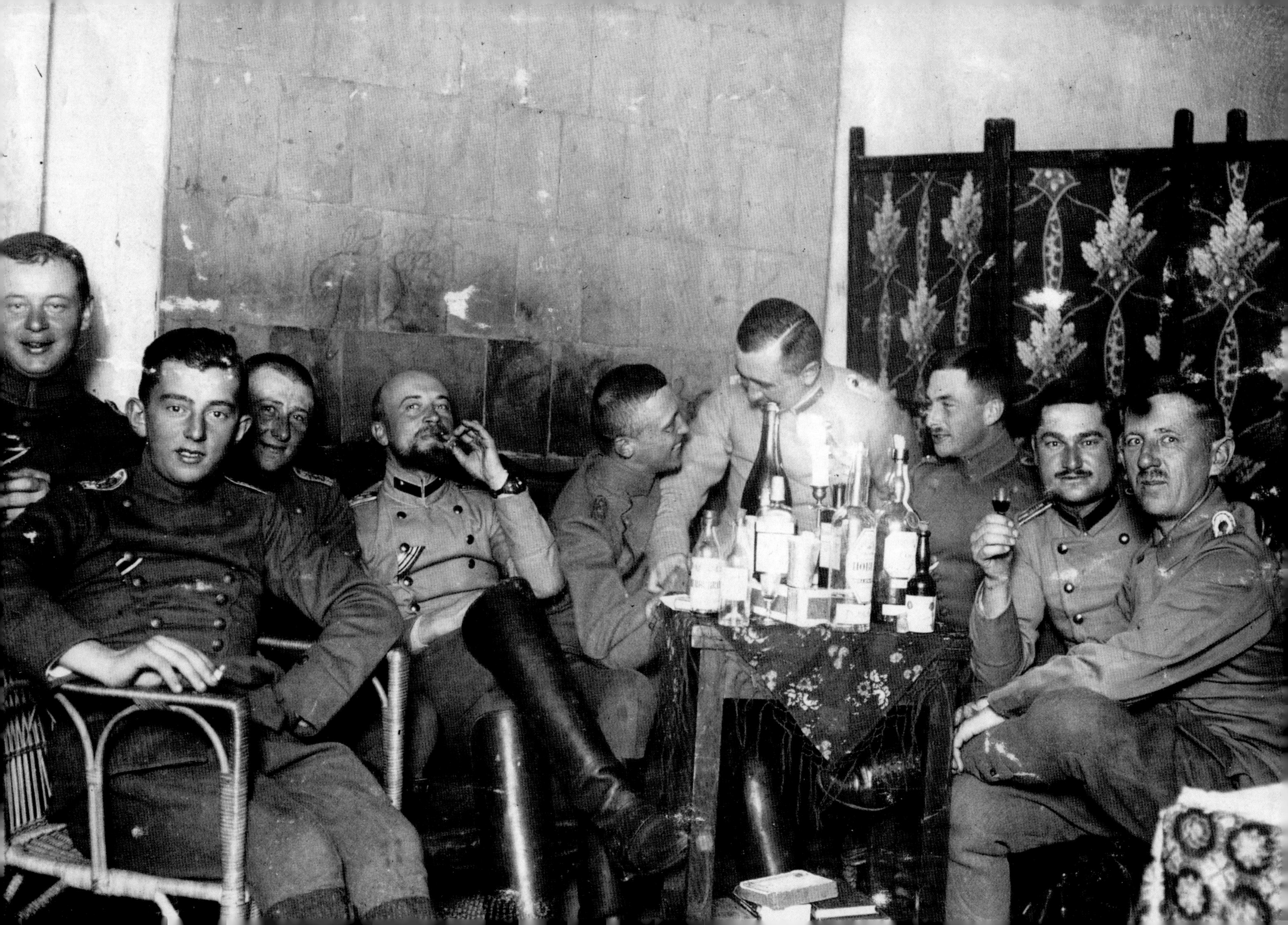

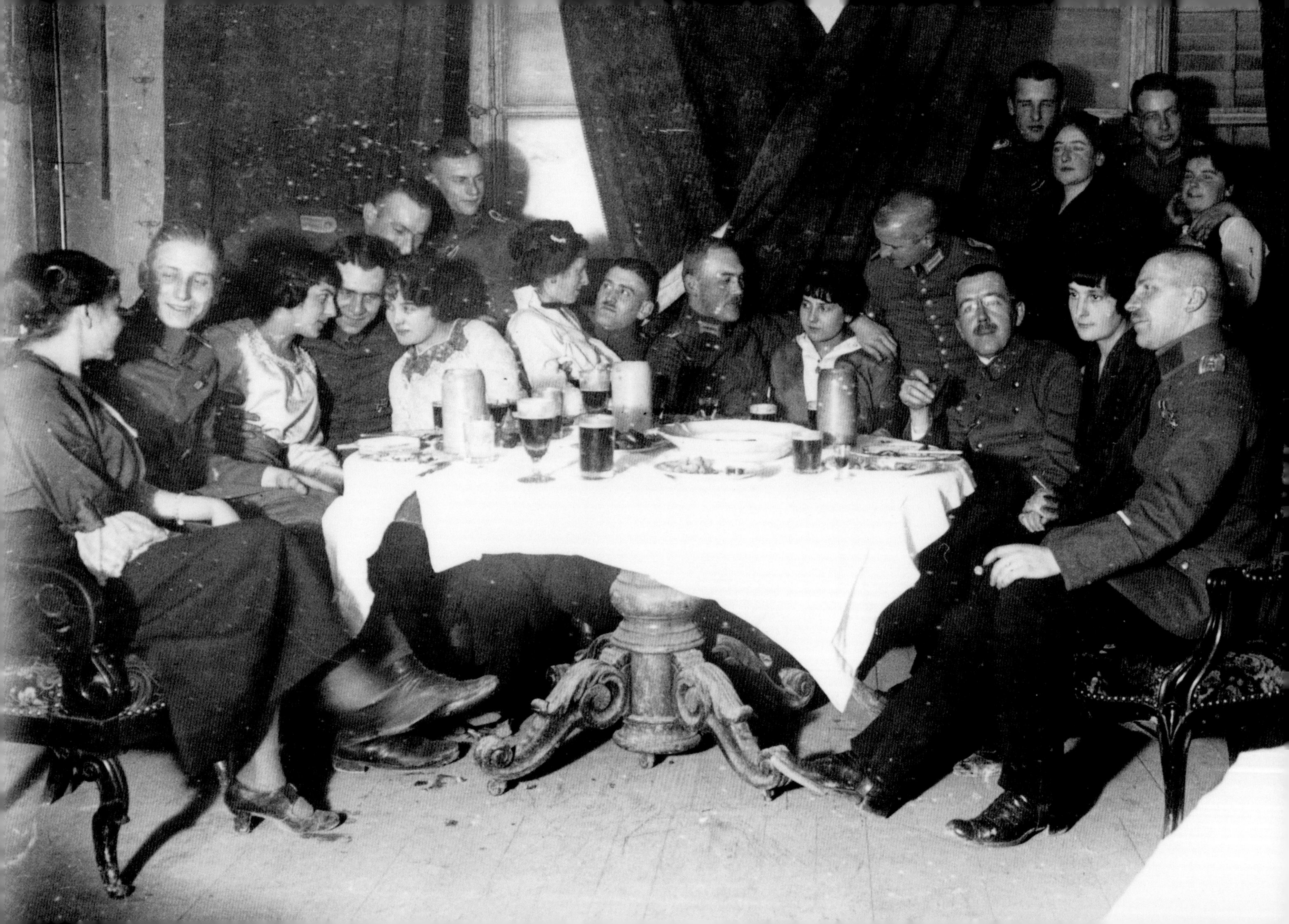

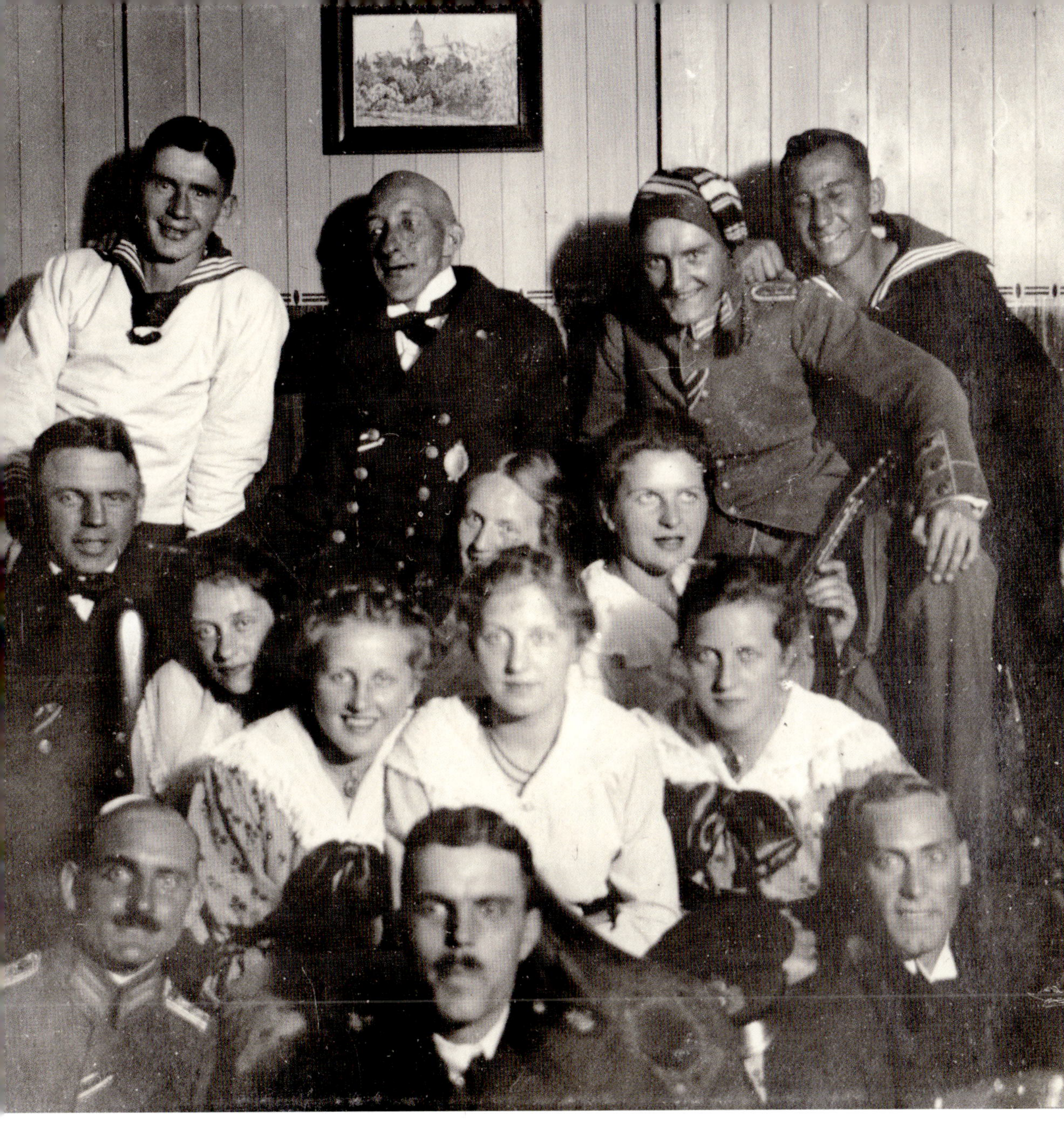

Far left: A party on the Western Front near Arras, 1917

The table holds what appear to be glasses of Bock, a traditional dark German beer historically associated with special occasions and religious festivals.

Left: Officers with their wives and girlfriends at Nordholz Naval Airbase towards the end of World War I

Nordholz Naval Airbase, close to Nordholz in northern Germany, was home to the Zeppelin airships. In this image, the officer with the double-breasted tunic in the back row wears a pilot's badge.

The end of World War I failed to bring the stability the German middle classes had been hoping for. With the monarchy gone, the left wing pursued revolution and the right wing reacted, while inflation spiraled out of control. In a world messed up beyond hope or reason, young people gave themselves licence to indulge in pleasure where it could be found, and the art of partying entered a period of renaissance.

January 1919
The left-wing Spartacist uprising in Berlin fails, and its leaders are murdered.

April 1919
The Original Dixieland Jazz Band visits and records in London.

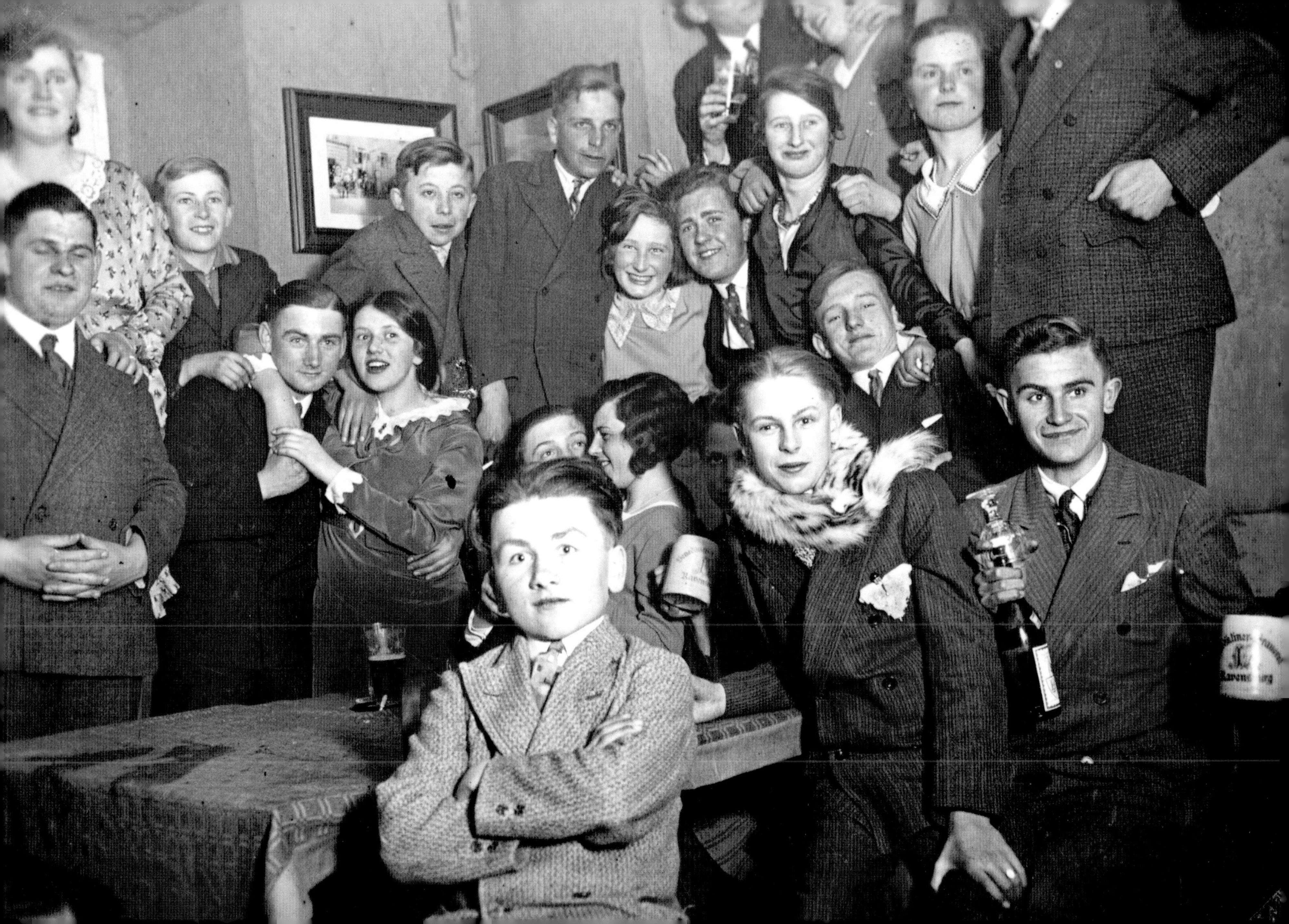

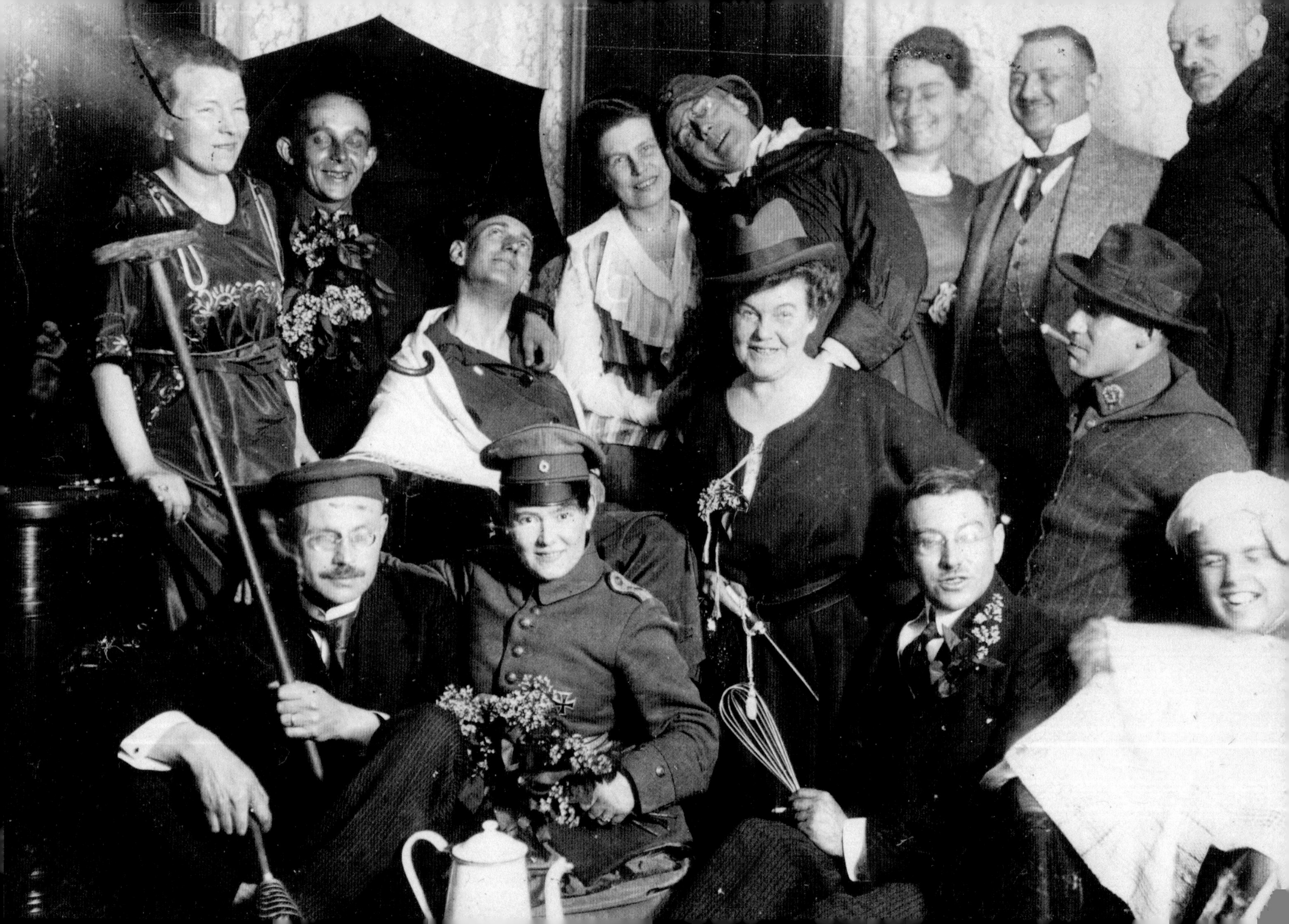

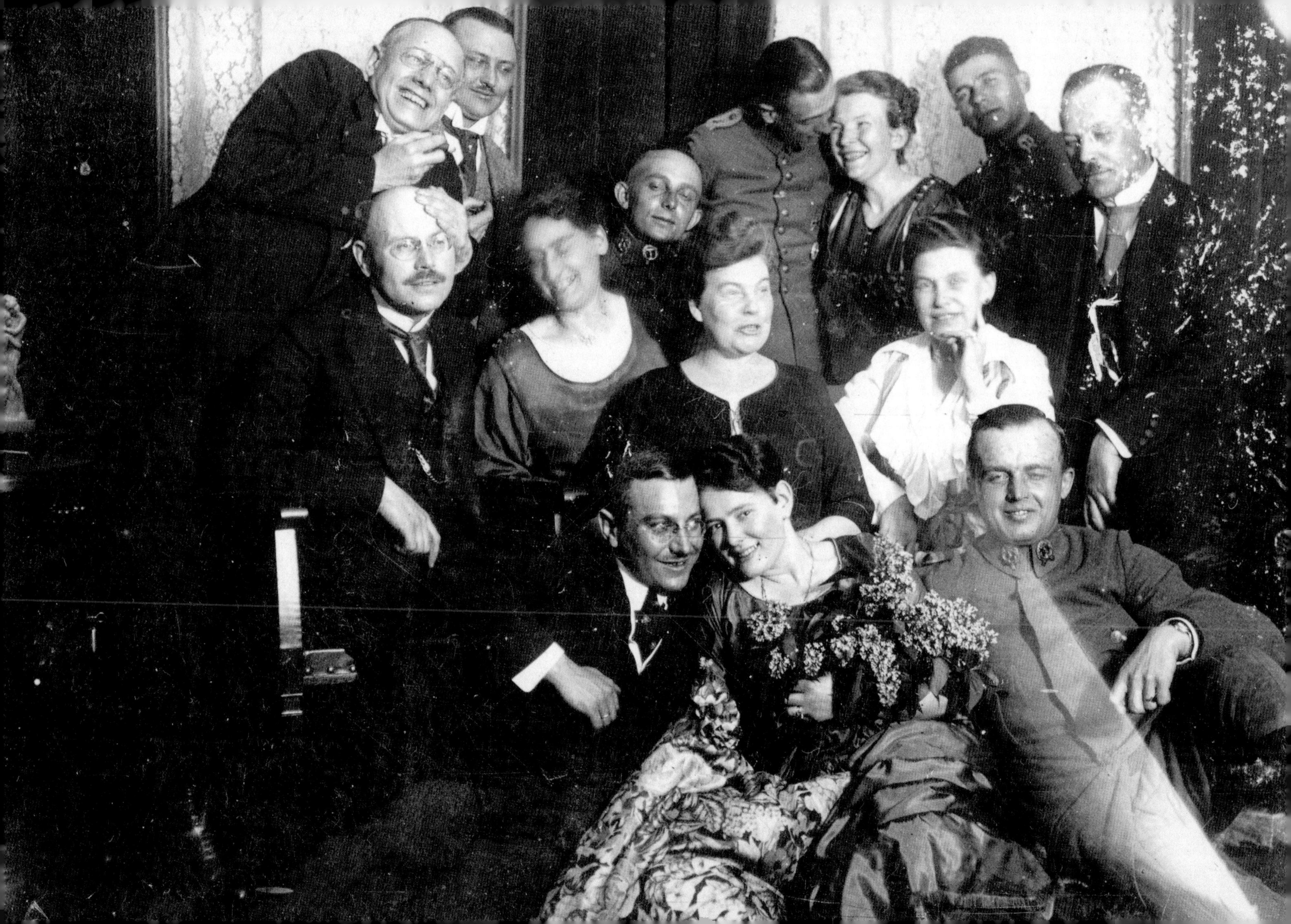

Previous pages:
Officers and civilians party together, April 1919

Some of the women in these images hold bouquets of lilacs, a spring flower associated with Easter and symbolising youth and joy. Carefully framed to the left of the group is a 19th century porcelain figurine of a child satyr carrying the infant Bacchus.

December 1919
Professor Hendrik Lorentz of Holland's Leiden University offers Albert Einstein an honorary professorship, hoping that Einstein's status will promote international scientific exchange and help improve relations between the nations. He learns, however, that Einstein not only attended the funeral of Marxist Rosa Luxembourg and read a text written in her honour, but is suspected of involvement in the bloody revolutionary activity taking place in Belgium. The professorship does not transpire. Too late, the information is found to refer to Carl Einstein, a well-known left-wing agitator with no connection to Albert. In reference to the current artistic trend, the misunderstanding is dubbed 'scientific Dada'.

January 1920
The League of Nations is founded with the intention of promoting world peace.

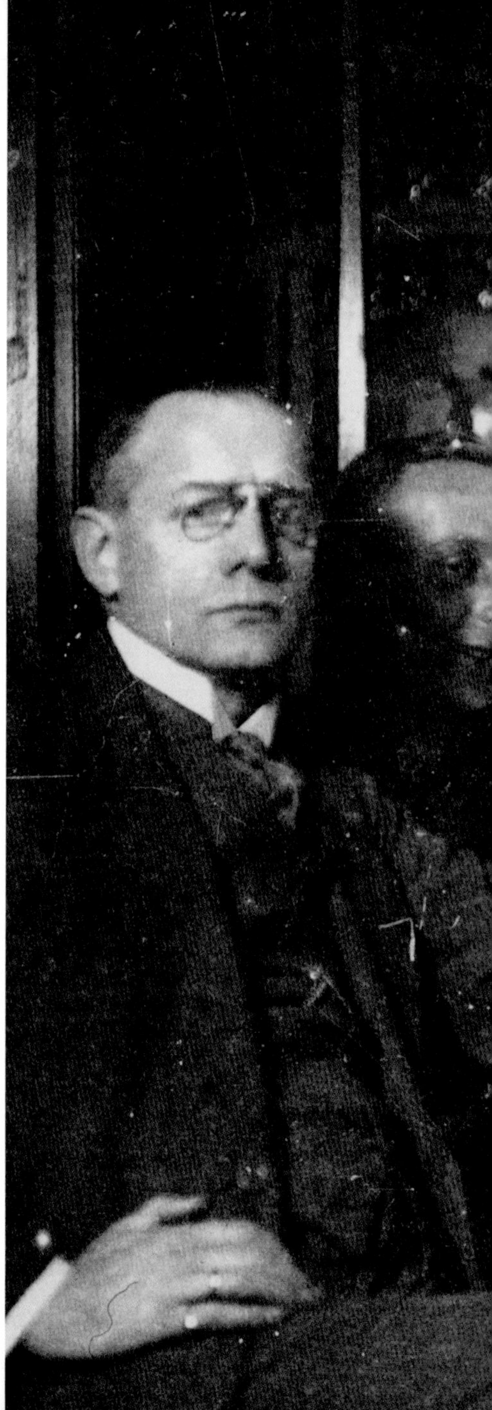

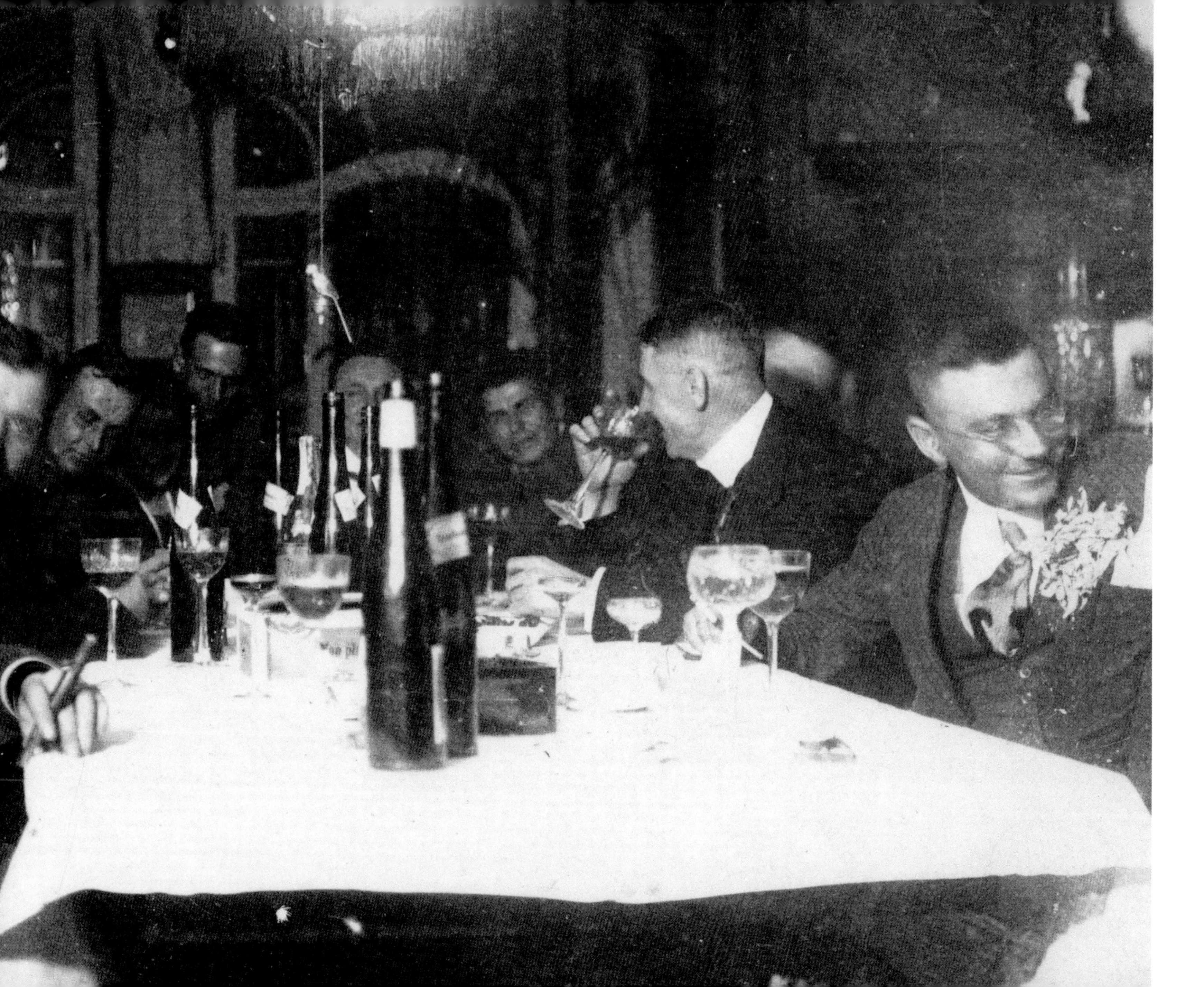

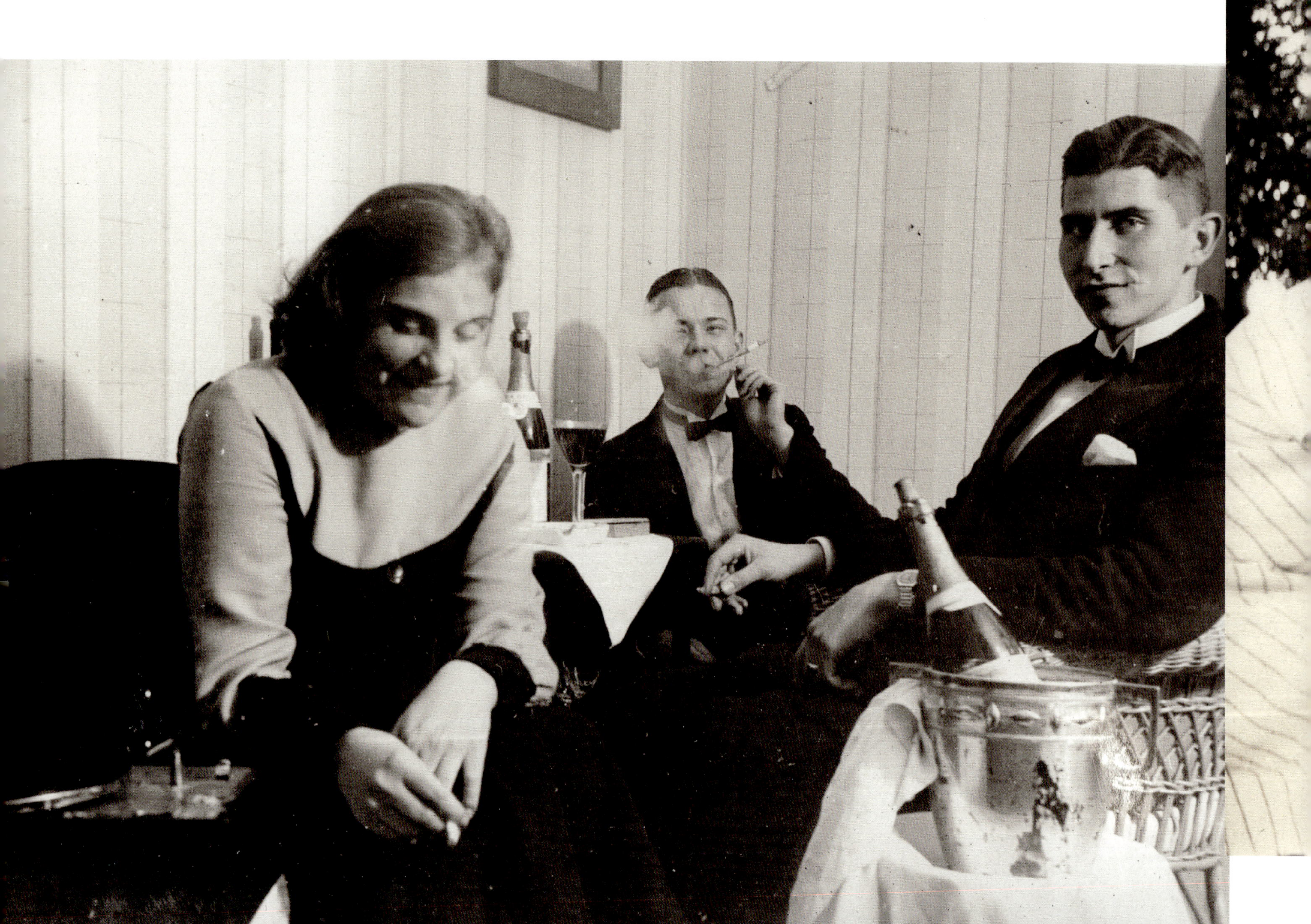

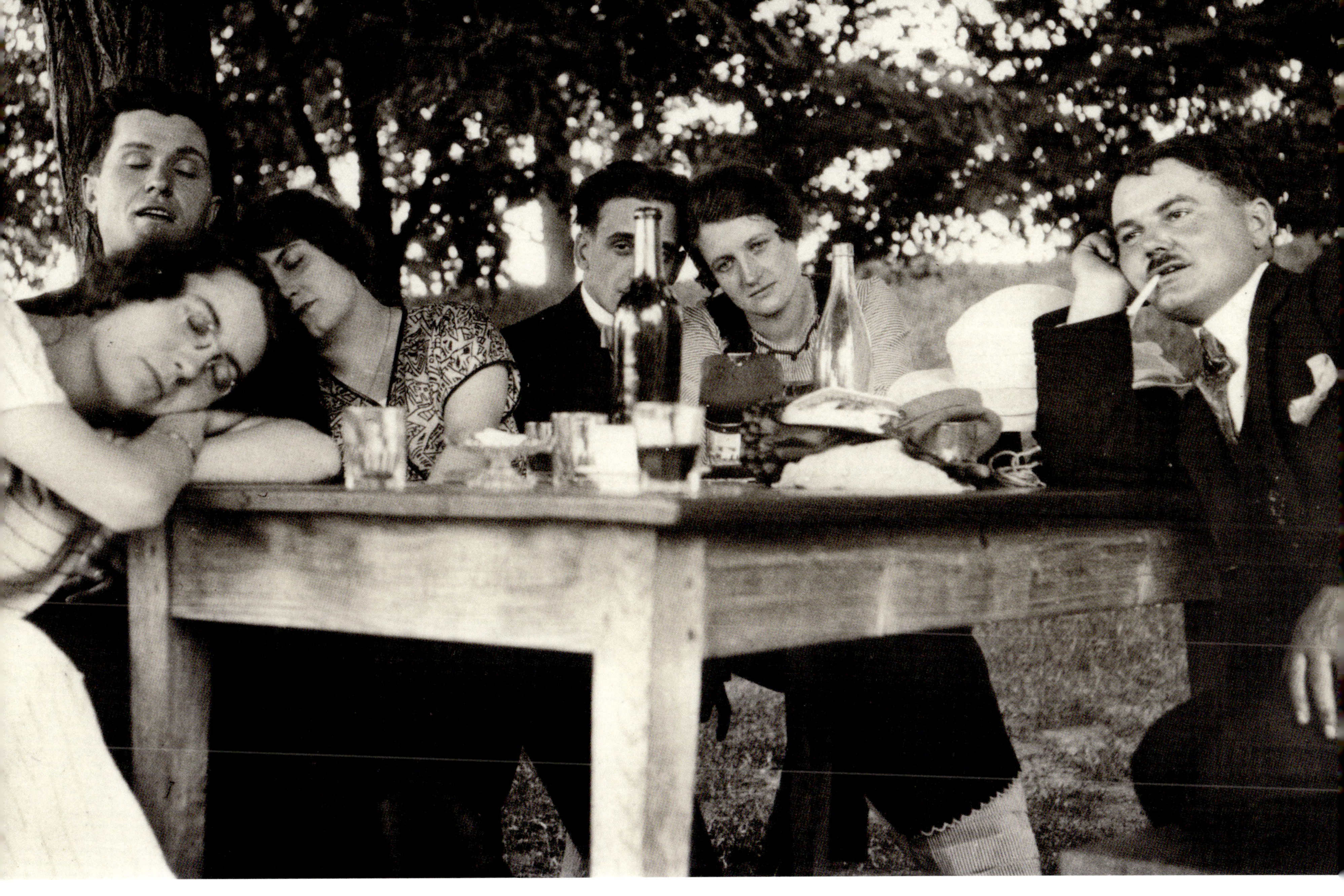

A LESSON IN HYPERINFLATION

	1914:	4 Marks	= US$1
	1919:	48 Marks	
early	1922:	320 Marks	
late	1922:	7,400 Marks	
	1923:	4,210,500,000,000	
	1924:	4 Marks	

November 1923 saw the introduction of the Rentenmark, which stabilised the currency long enough for the introduction of a law to enable the exchange of 1 trillion old paper Marks to a new Reichsmark.

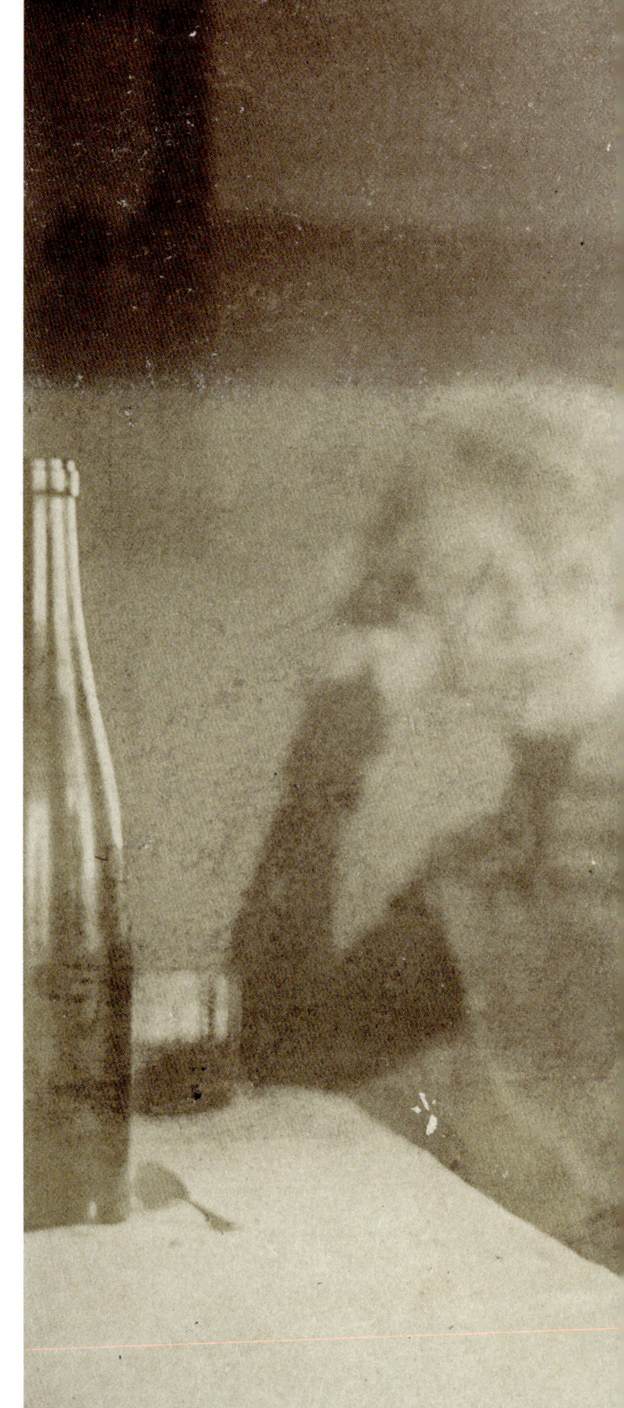

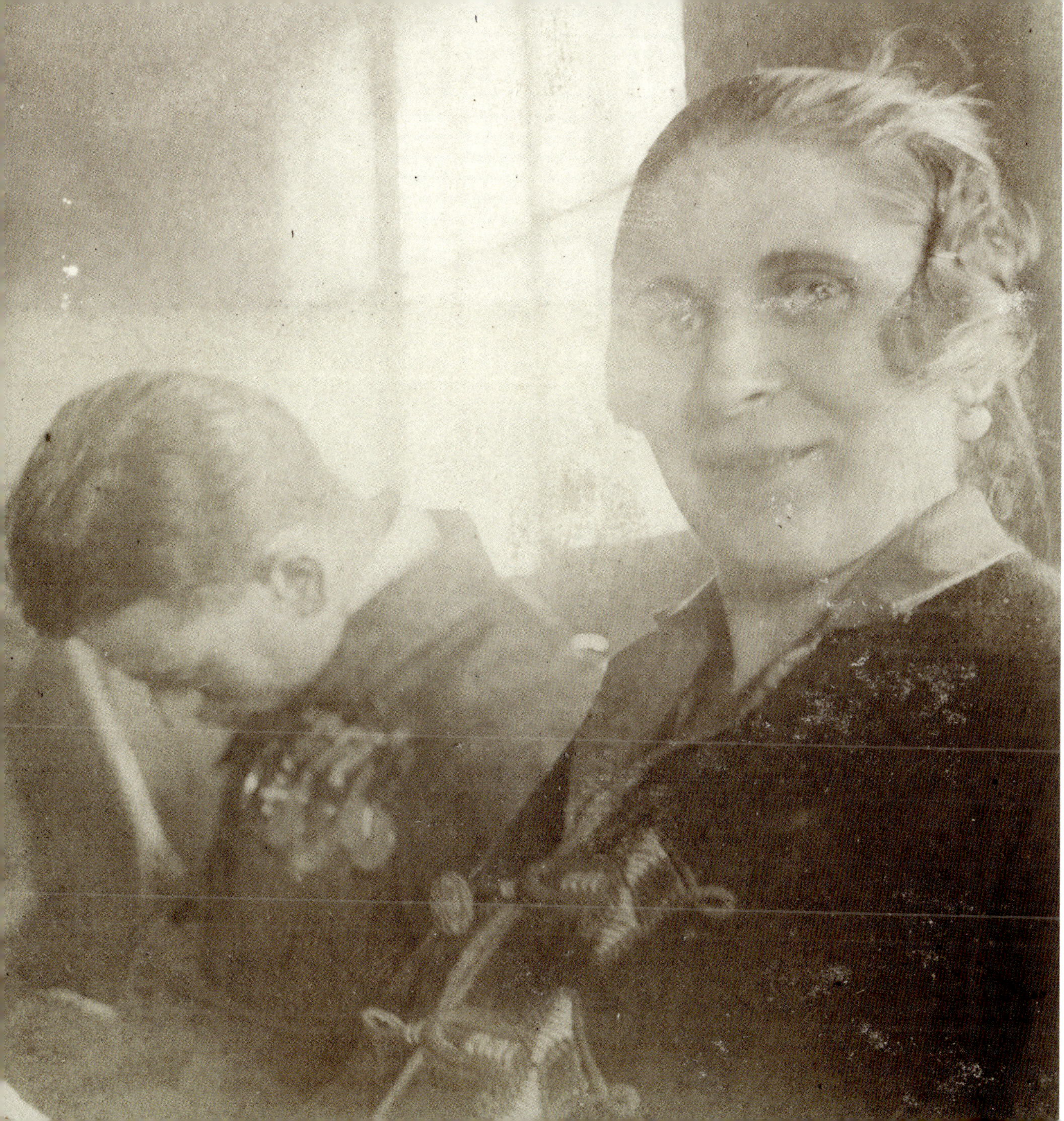

Elaborate fancy dress became a staple of Weimar parties, as illustrated by the trio at this gathering, whose costumes span three centuries of style – the woman to the left in 19th century cavalry attire, the much-decorated central figure in contemporary military costume, and the man on the right in 18th century dress complete with a fine, if dishevelled, rendition of that period's hairdressing.

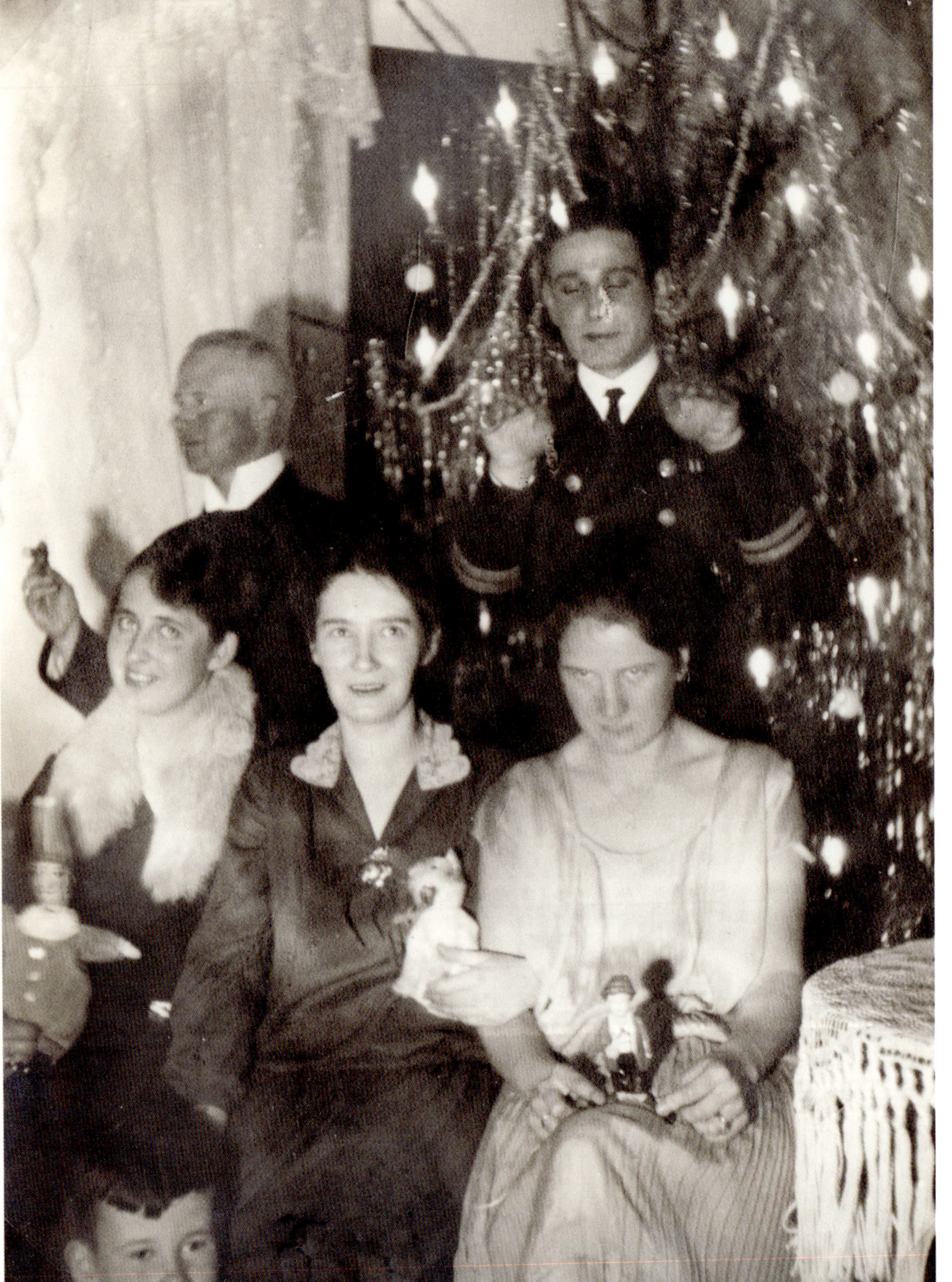

January 1920
Prohibition comes into force in the United States.

The woman to the left holds a traditional Kasper puppet, the German equivalent of Britain's Punch of Punch and Judy fame. The rise of master puppeteer Max Jacob brought renewed public enthusiasm in Germany for the art of puppetry.

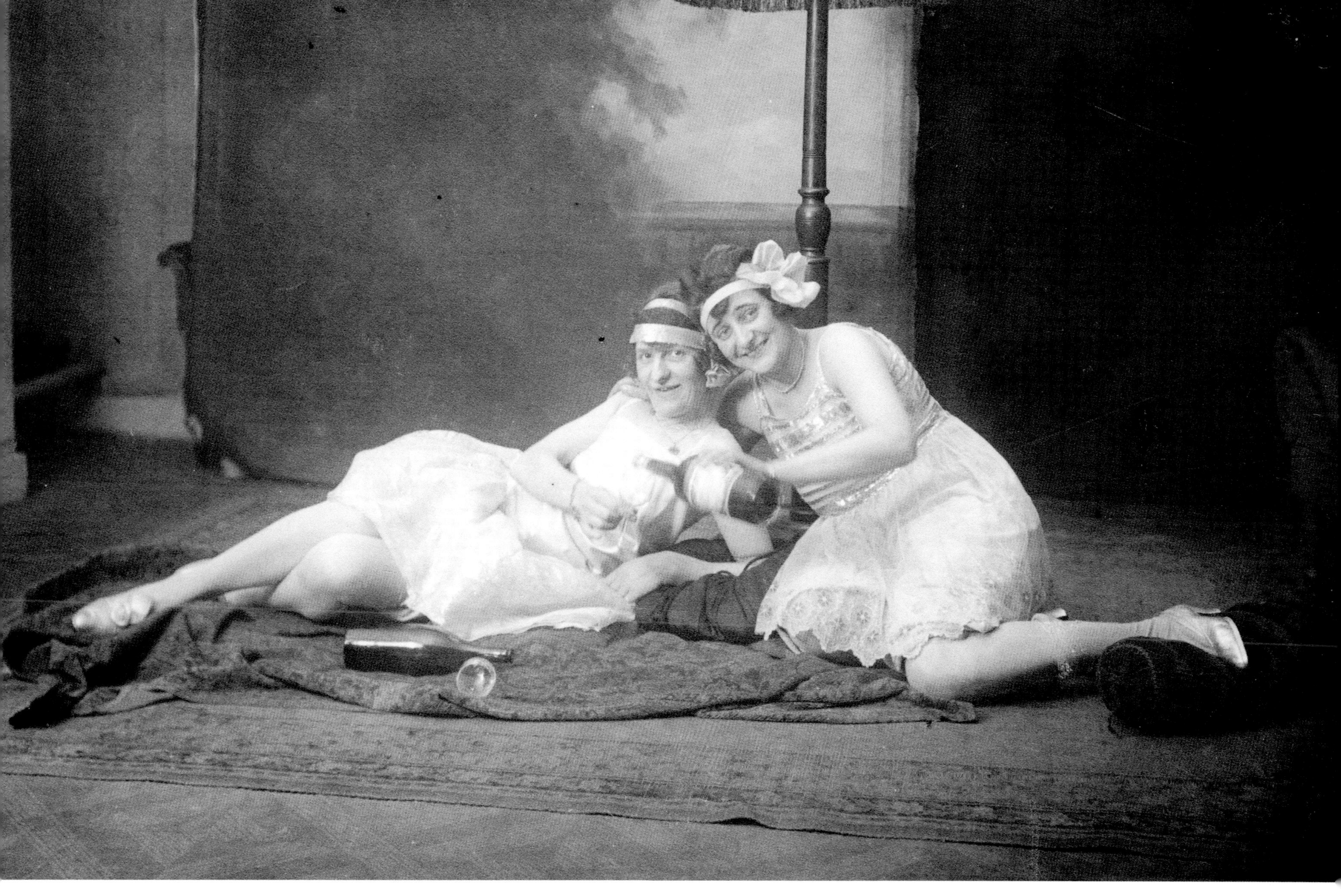

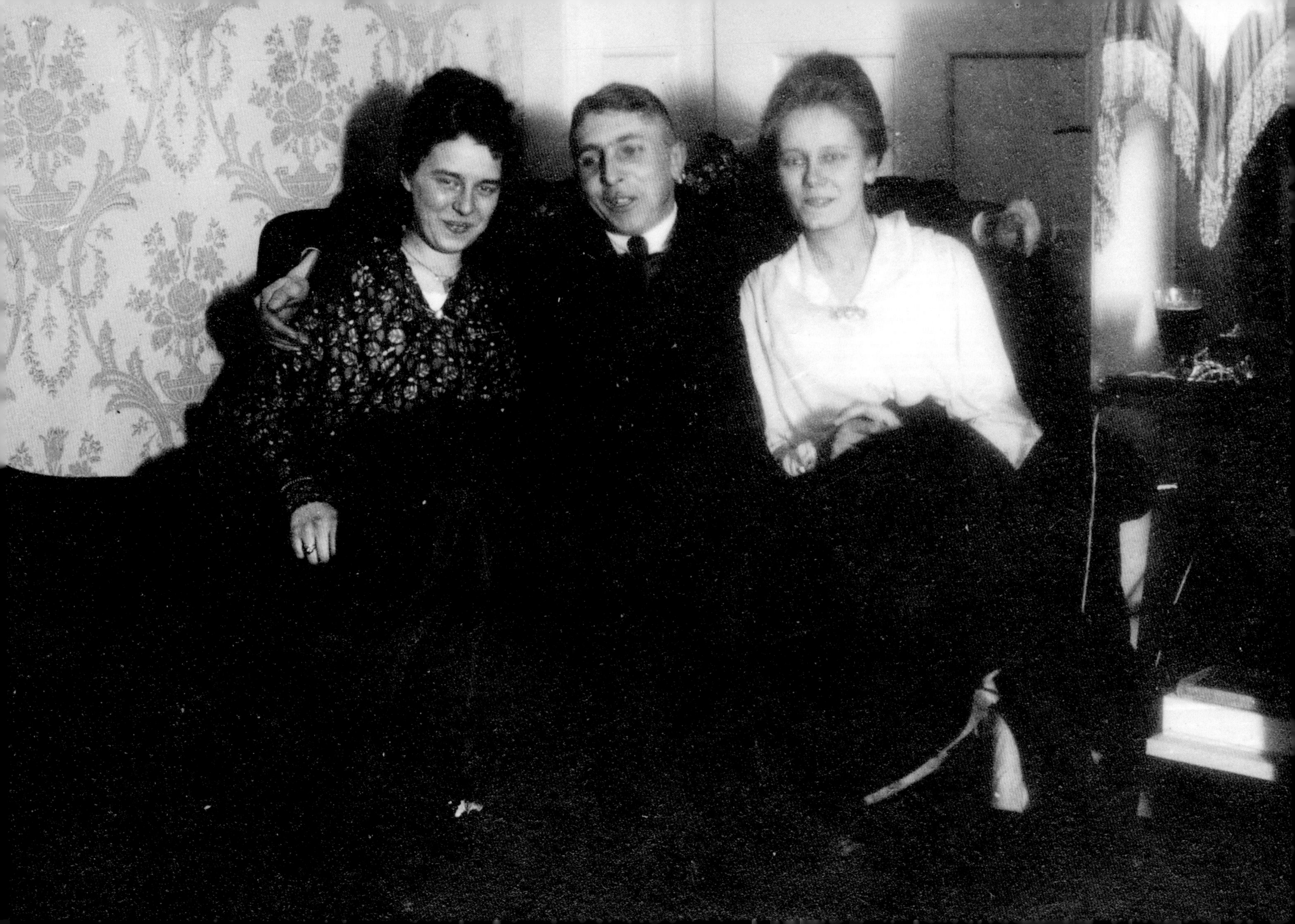

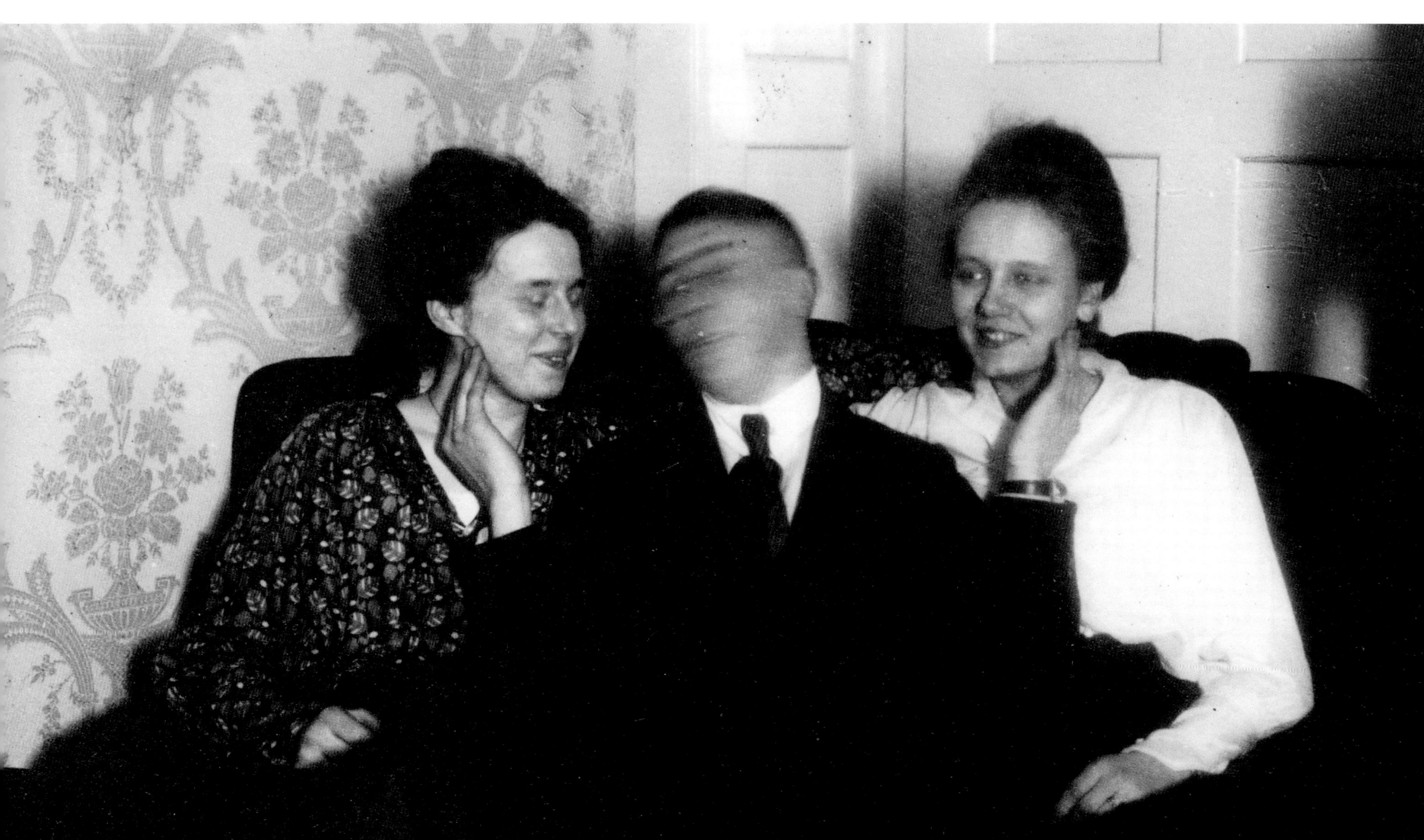

March 1920
The Kapp Putsch, an attempted right-wing coup, is ended by widespread protest and a general workers' strike. In the industrial Ruhr region, workers of the Ruhr Red Army sense an opportunity and begin an open communist revolution, which also fails.

Celebrations mark the end of the Kapp Putsch

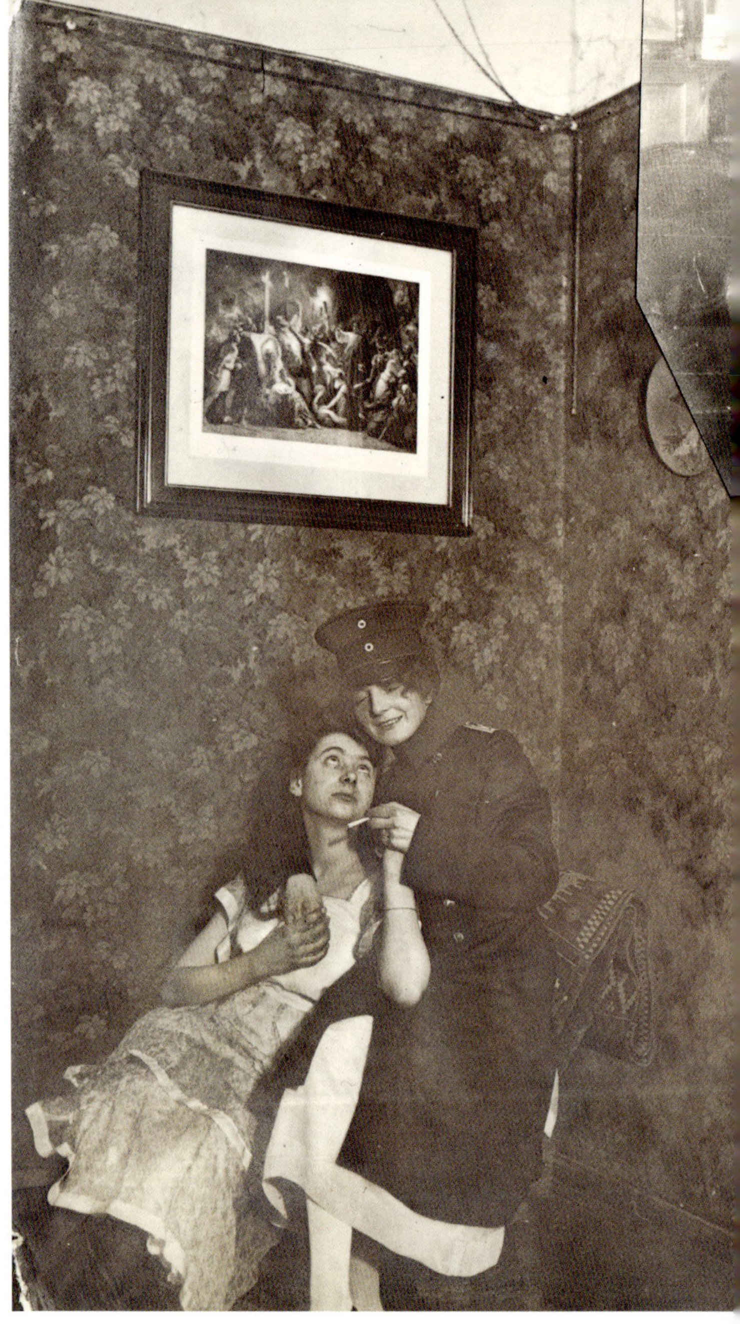

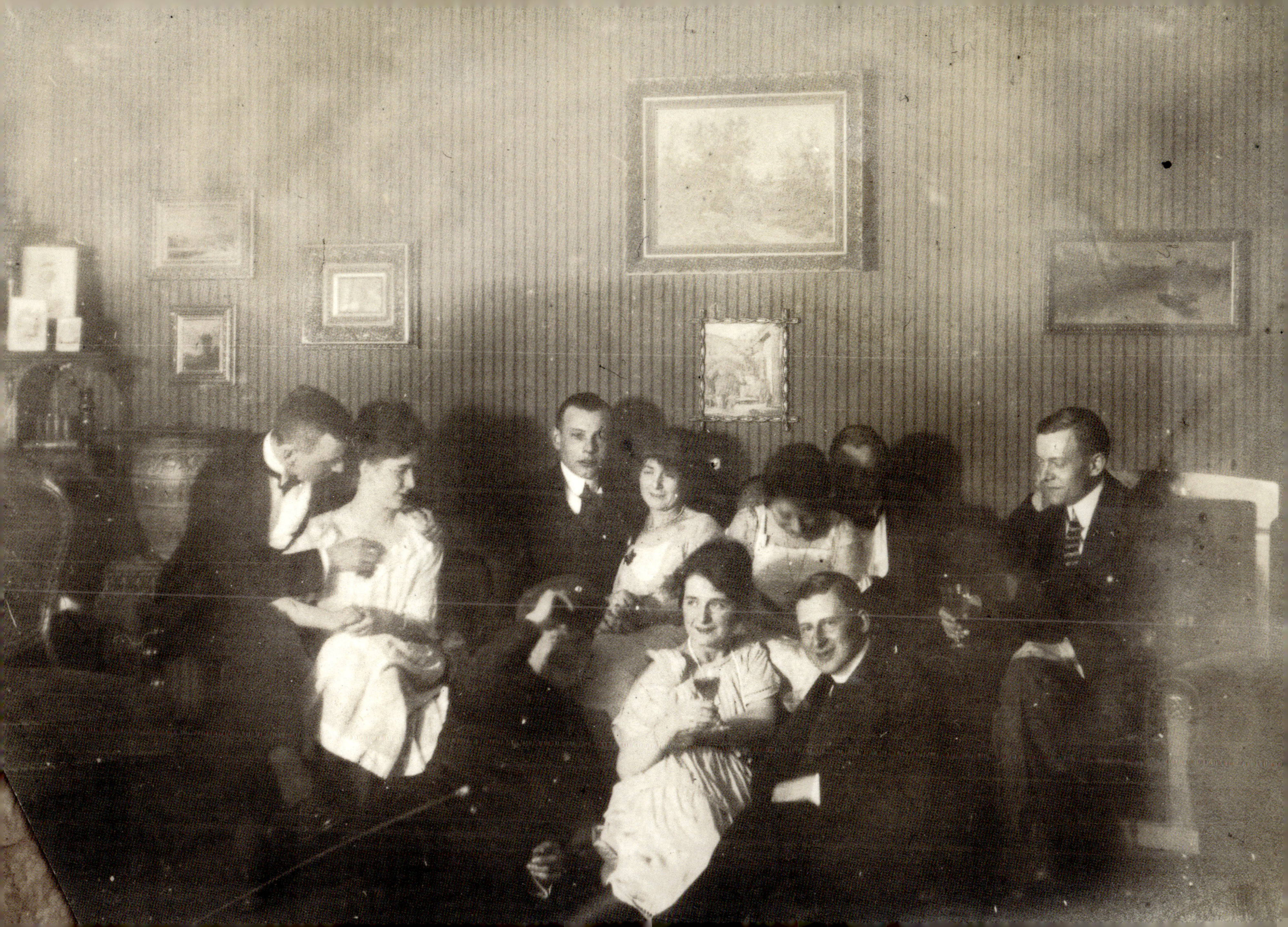

Mensur, or academic fencing, is usually performed with just eye guards, a padded vest, and razor-sharp swords. There is no winner or loser, and any resulting facial scars, known as *Schmisse*, are considered to be badges of honour.

Fencing swords grace the wall of this student fraternity in Heidelberg, a prominent centre for the practice of traditional academic fencing

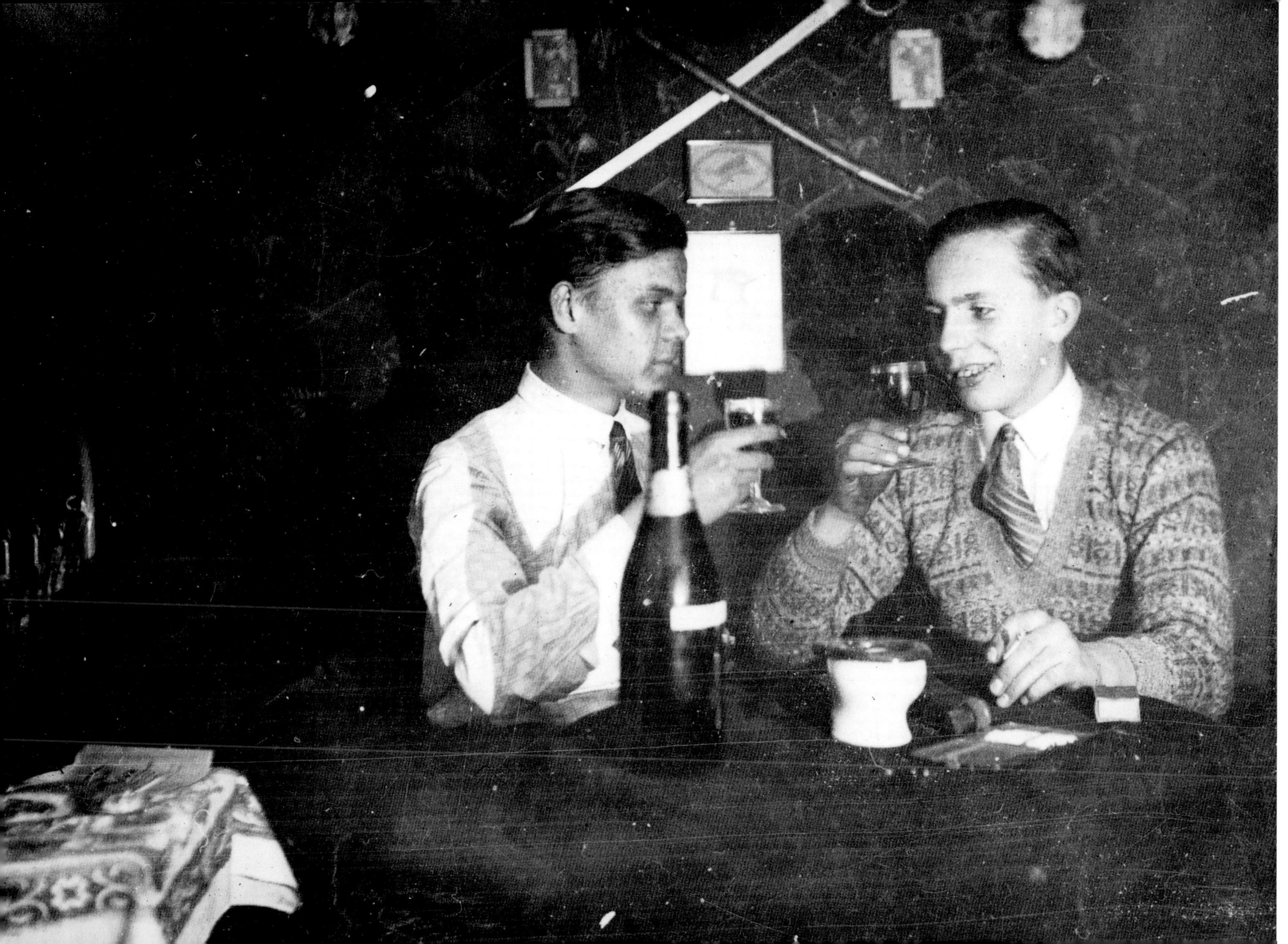

March 1922
F. Scott Fitzgerald's *The Beautiful and Damned* is published in the United States. "She was got up to the best of her ability as a siren, more popularly a 'vamp' – a picker up and thrower away of men, an unscrupulous and fundamentally unmoved toyer with affections."

November 1922
Fritz Lang's movie *Dr Mabuse the Gambler* is released in Germany. Dr Mabuse is a hypnotist and a master of disguise who swindles and murders using his special powers until he is captured and imprisoned in an insane asylum.

November 1922
After years of searching, Howard Carter discovers the entrance to the tomb of the legendary Pharaoh Tutankhamun.

1 April 1923
A German newspaper announces that the extension of an underground railway in Berlin has revealed a large cache of mummies and Egyptian antiquities. An expert named Dr Eirpa is quoted as saying that the discovery rivals Tutankhamun's tomb in significance and reveals a prehistoric Egyptian colony in Germany.

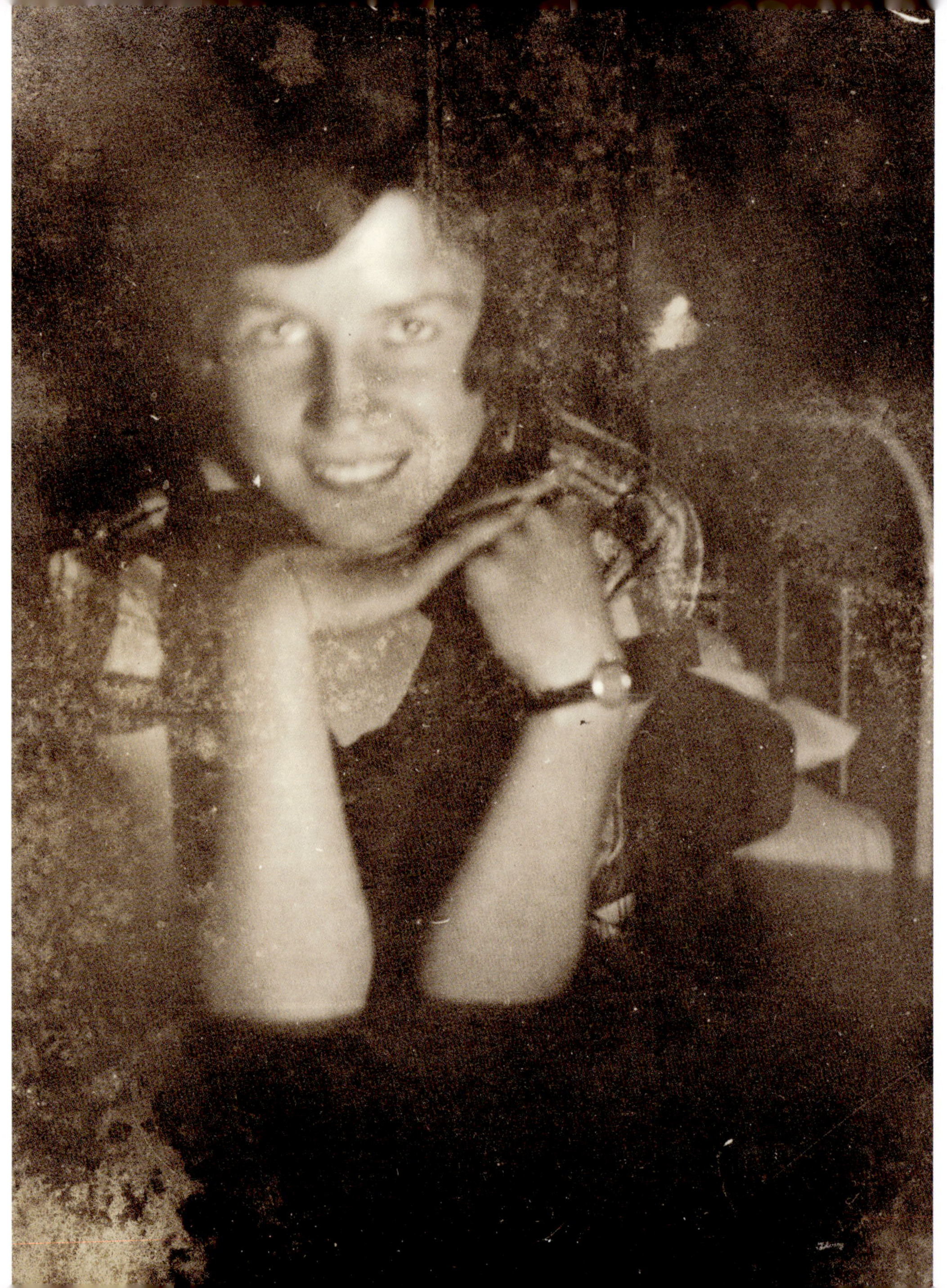

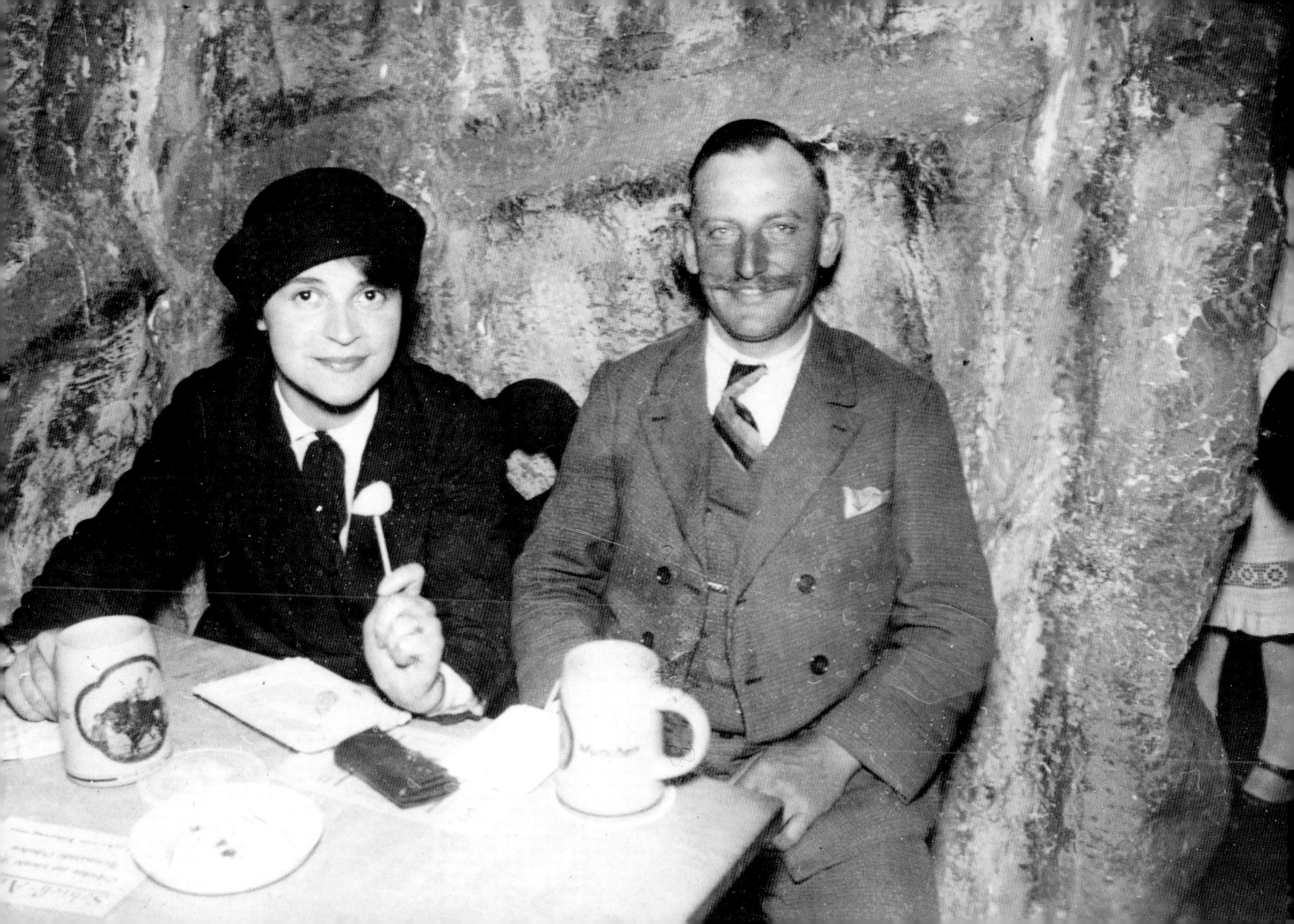

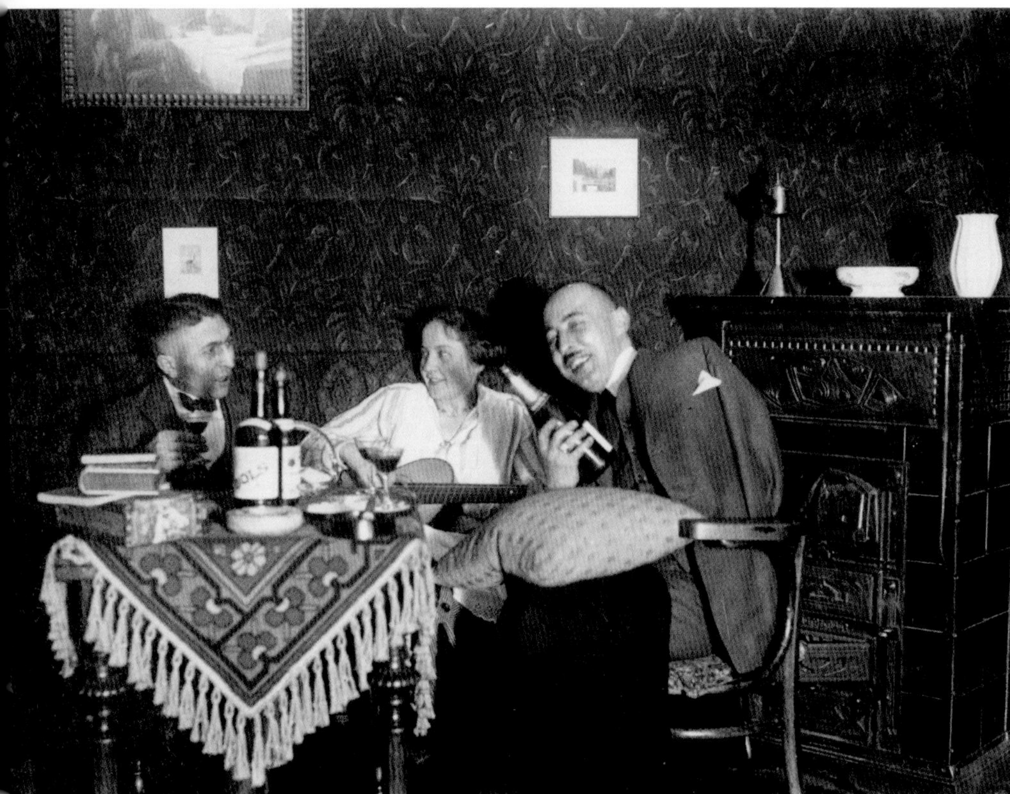

"Lingering at shop windows was a luxury because shopping had to be done immediately. Even an additional minute could mean an increase in price. One had to buy quickly. A rabbit, for example, might cost two million marks more by the time it took you to walk into the store. The packages of money needed to buy the smallest item had long since become too heavy for trouser pockets. I used a knapsack."
– George Grosz, 1923

Above and right: Wealthy industrialists the Thiel family of Essen celebrate Sylvester (New Year's Eve) in 1923 and 1924

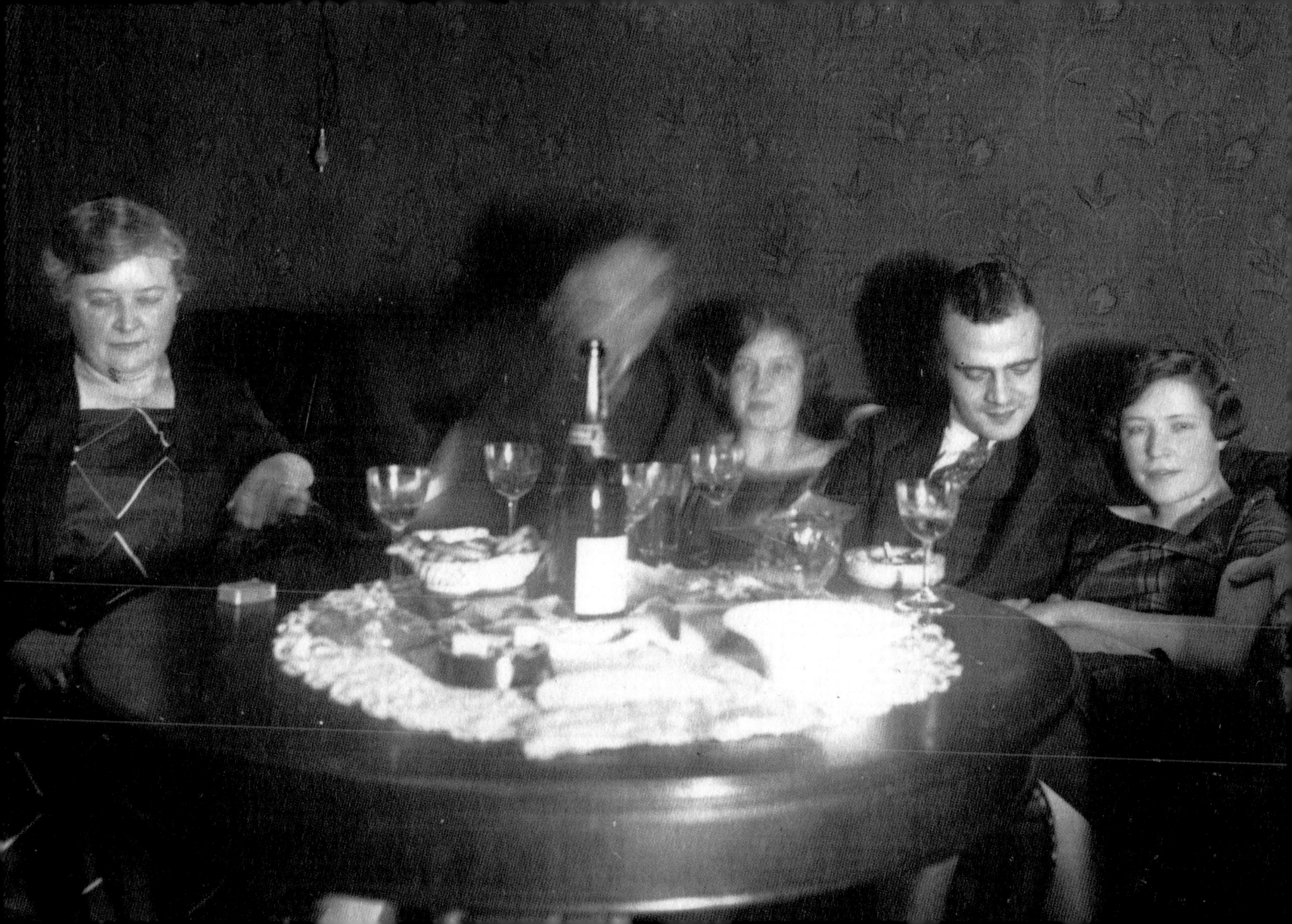

March 1924
The song 'Happy Birthday To You' is published in the United States by Claydon Sunny.

April 1924
André Gide's *Corydon*, a set of philosophical dialogues defending homosexual relations, is published in France.

October 1924
The first traffic light in Berlin is set up on the Potsdamer Platz.

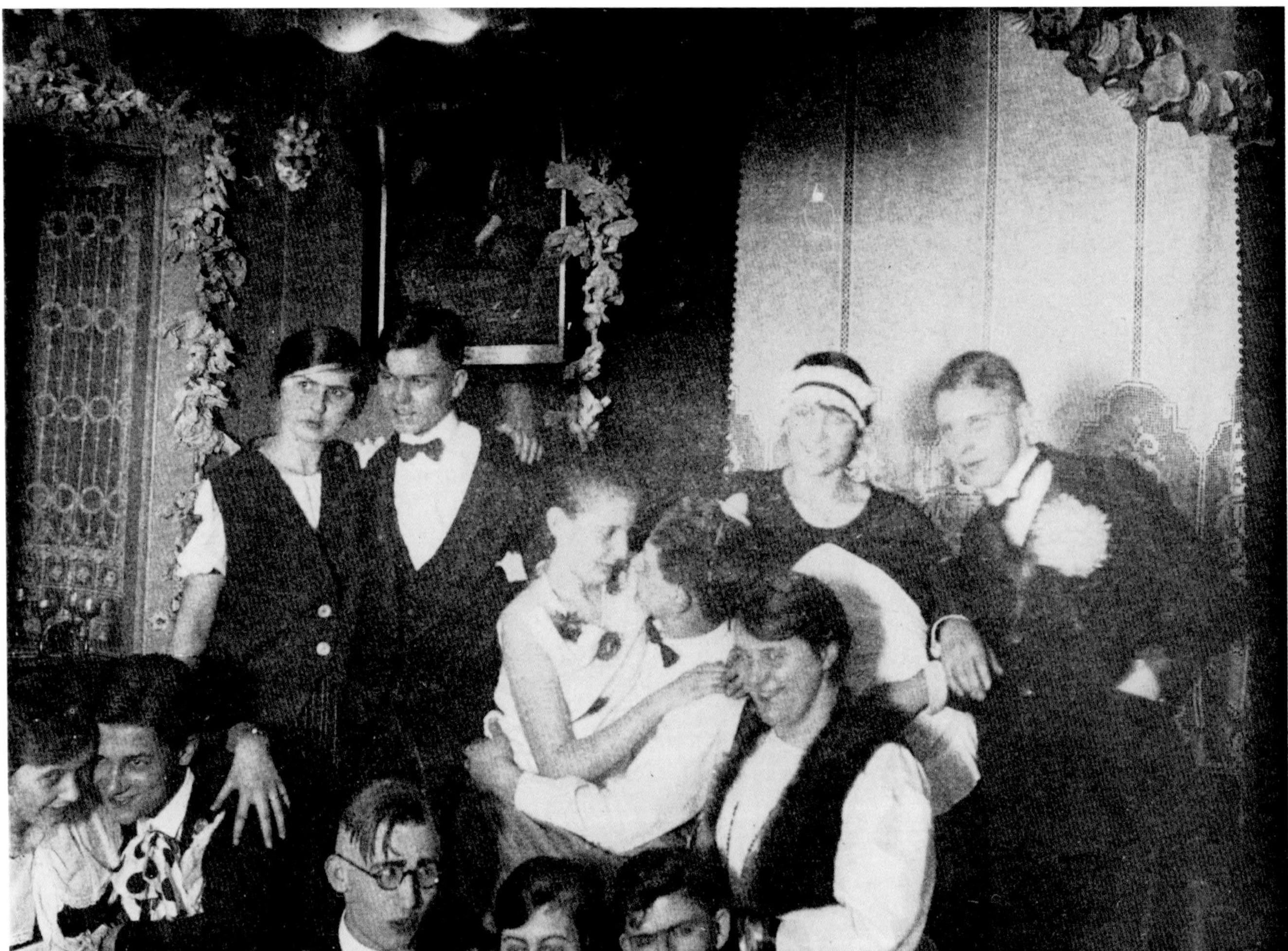

A framed print of a Prussian leader on horseback, usually Frederick the Great, was as ubiquitous in the German home as the aspidistra was in the British one

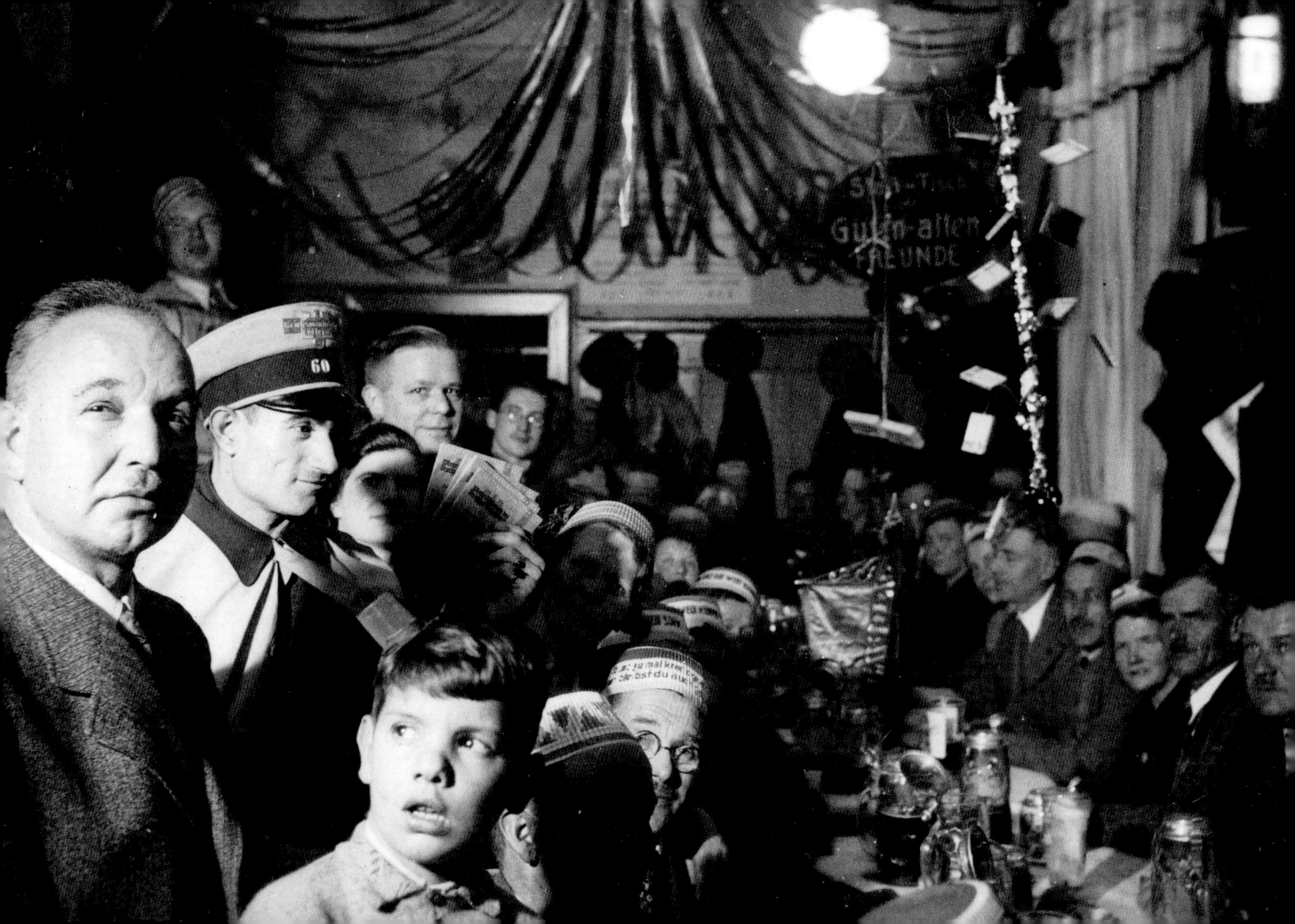
60
FREUNDE

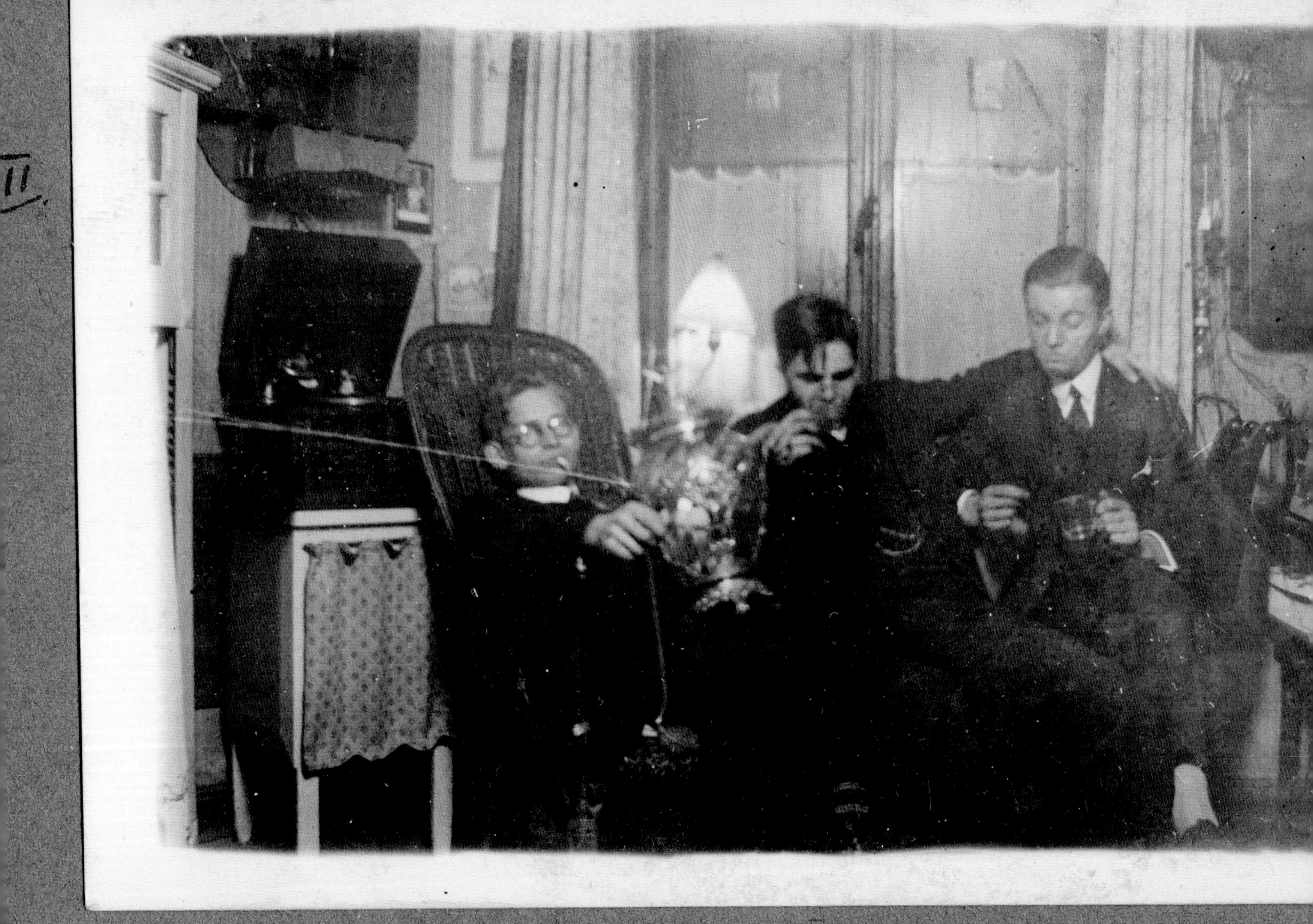

Lina Wachtelborn Meier's Weimar Republic cookbook *Aechte deutsche Kochkunst* included a recipe for *Heißer Punsch* (hot punch): "Place the punch bowl in a hot water bath and add a pint of boiling water. Add the peel of one lemon and a pound and a half of sugar. Leave it to infuse. Then add one bottle of white wine, one bottle of fine rum, the juice of two lemons, and two quarts of hot water. Stir with a wooden spoon and heat until very hot. Serves two."

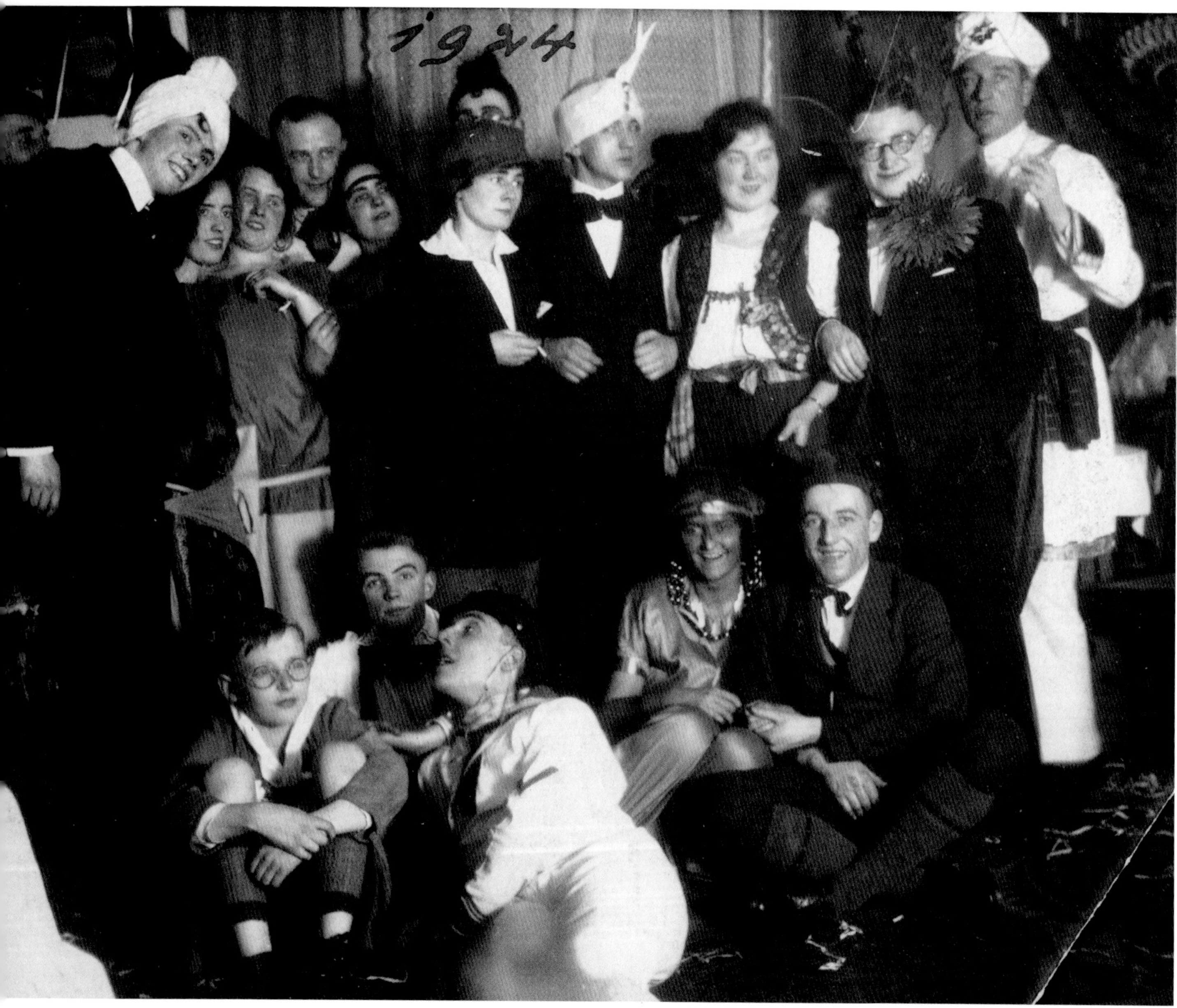

March 1924
The Thief of Bagdad, starring Douglas Fairbanks, is the Hollywood hit of the year, and its dazzling special effects make it one of the most expensive movies ever produced. Fancy dress parties take a turn for the better as the turban, in many variations, makes a comeback.

January 1925
The Leica, a compact camera invented by Oskar Barnack that uses 35mm film, goes into mass production. The Leica fits easily into a purse or coat pocket, and its sharp, fast lenses (named after Barnack's dogs Rex and Hektor) facilitate night-time photography.

October 1925
Gentlemen Prefer Blondes: The Intimate Diary of a Professional Lady by Anita Loos becomes a bestseller in the United States.

December 1925
Carl Zuckmayer's movie *Der Fröhliche Weinberg* is released in Germany to great acclaim. The culmination of the plot takes place at a wine festival where all the characters get drunk and find the one they love.

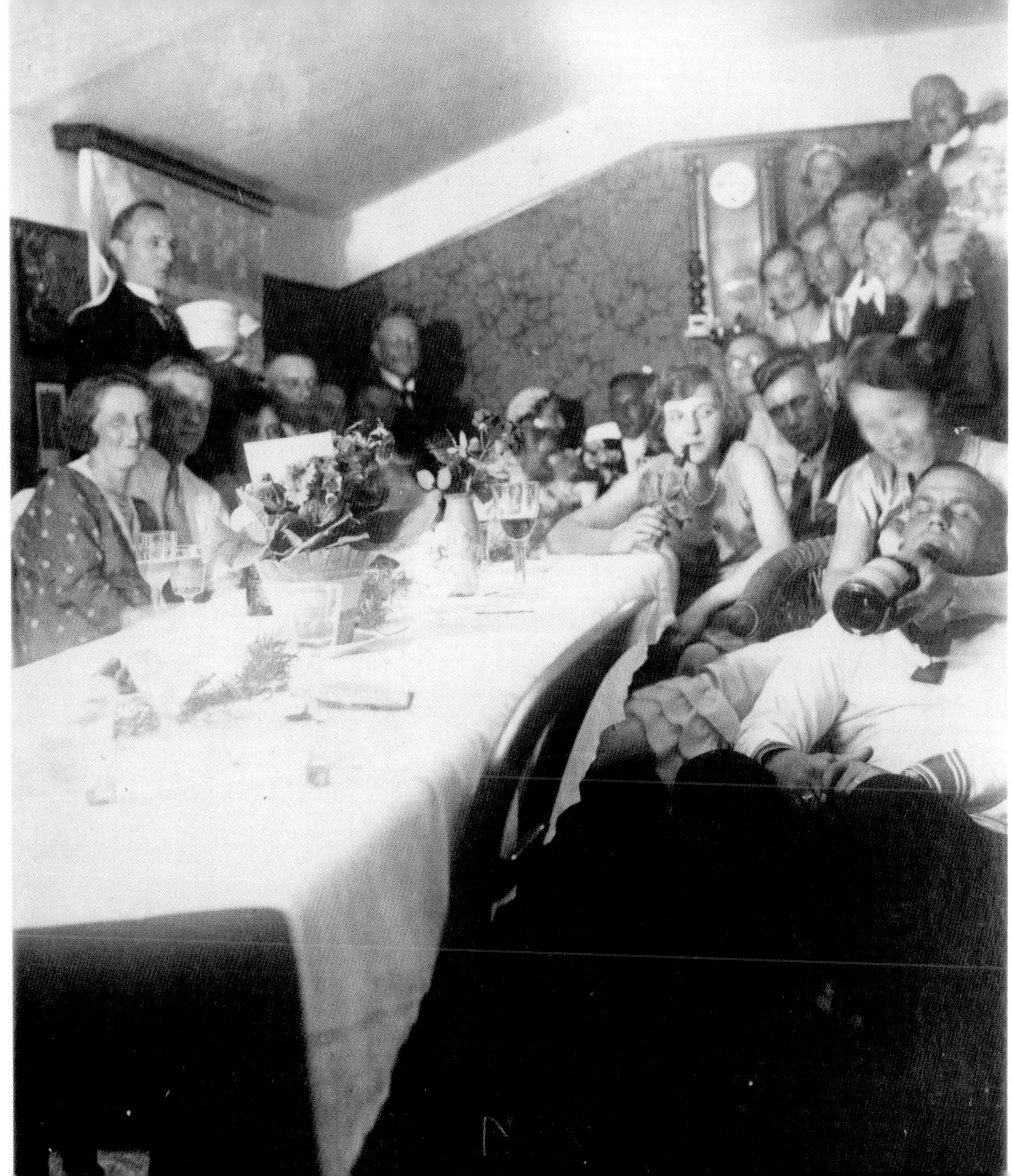

from the Kirchner family album

1924
1929

The Kirchners were a well-to-do family living in the southern German city of Mannheim. Throughout the 1920s they threw and attended parties, picnicked, skied, toured, and generally flourished. Their album ends in 1929, the year of the Wall Street crash.

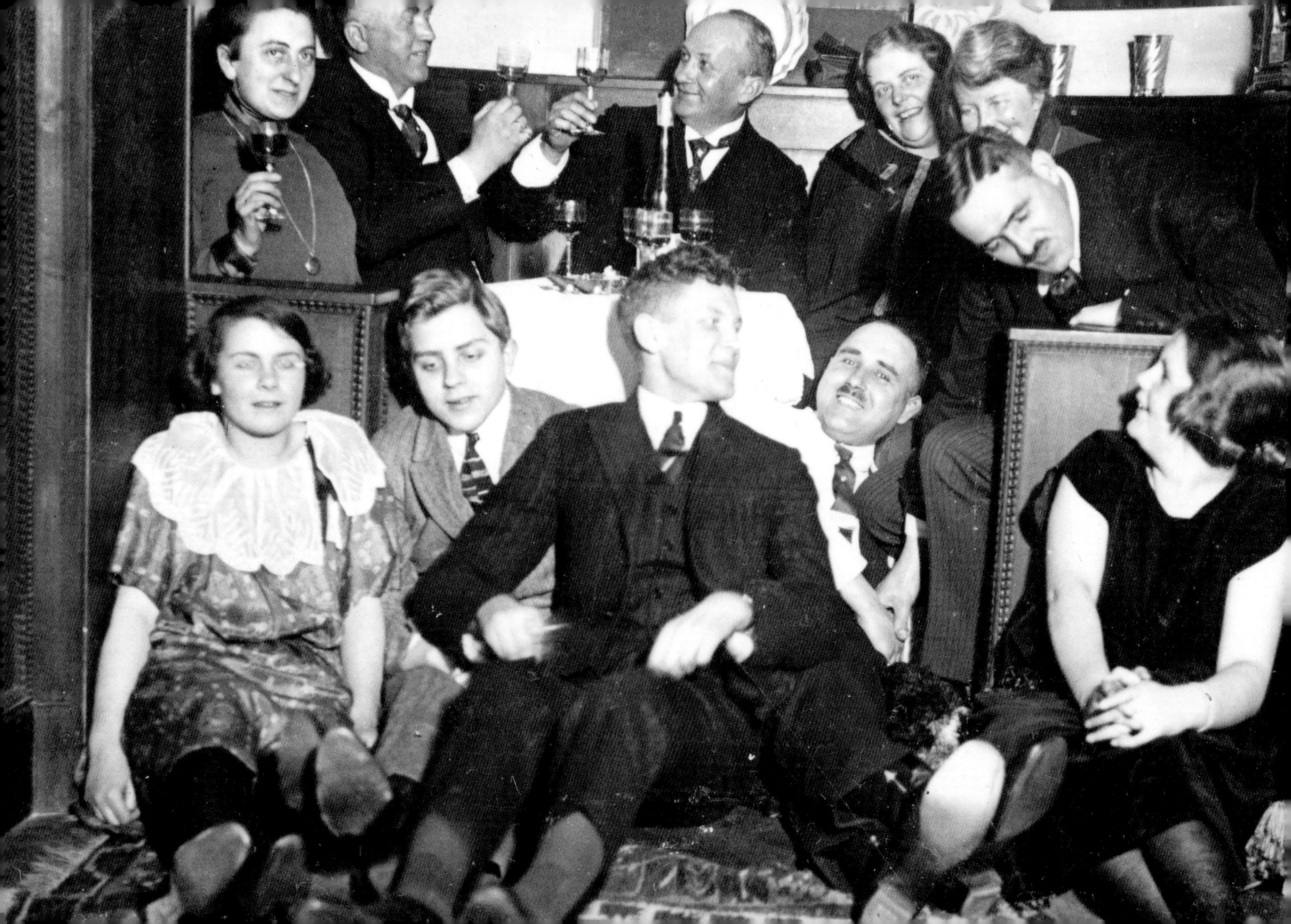

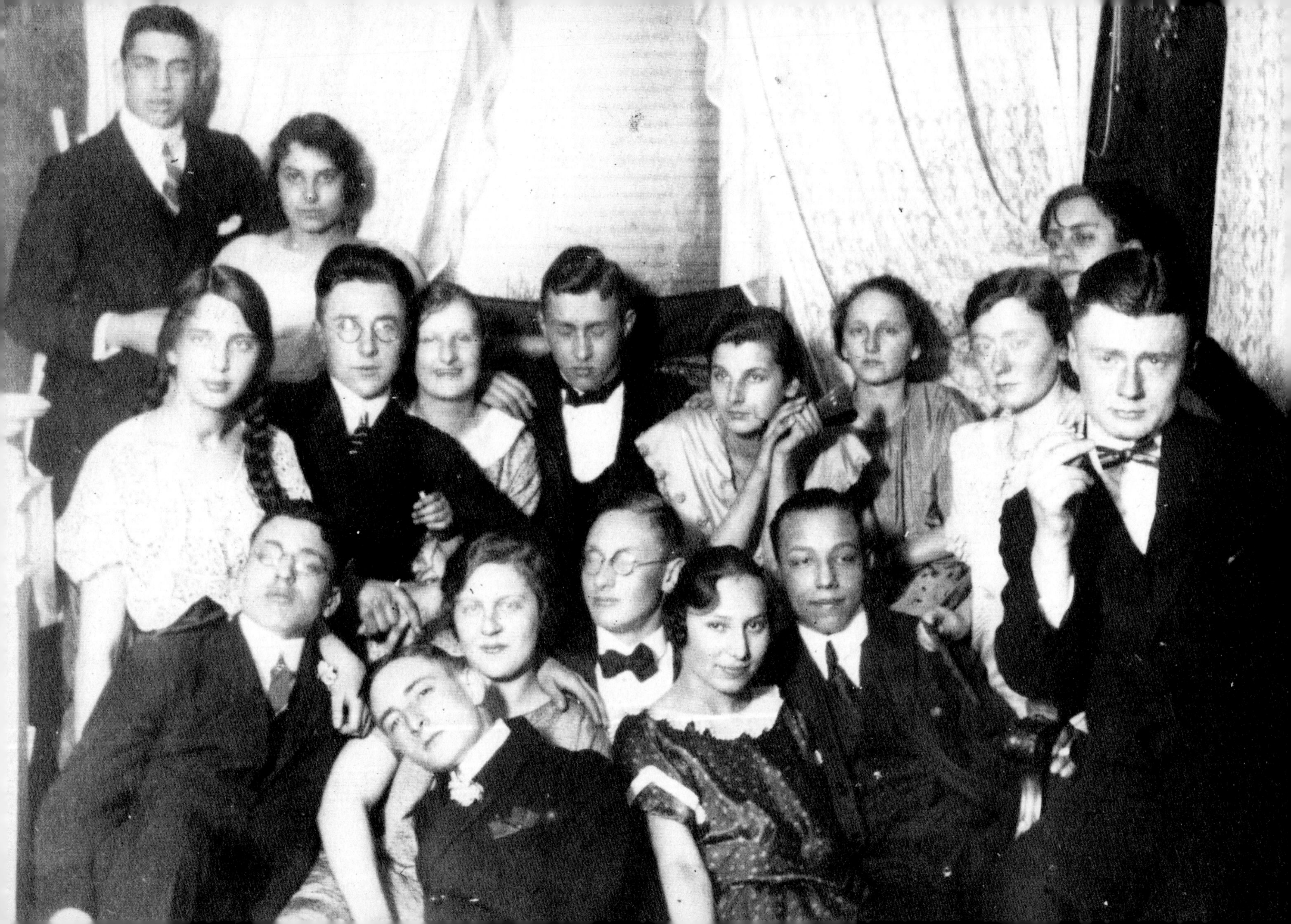

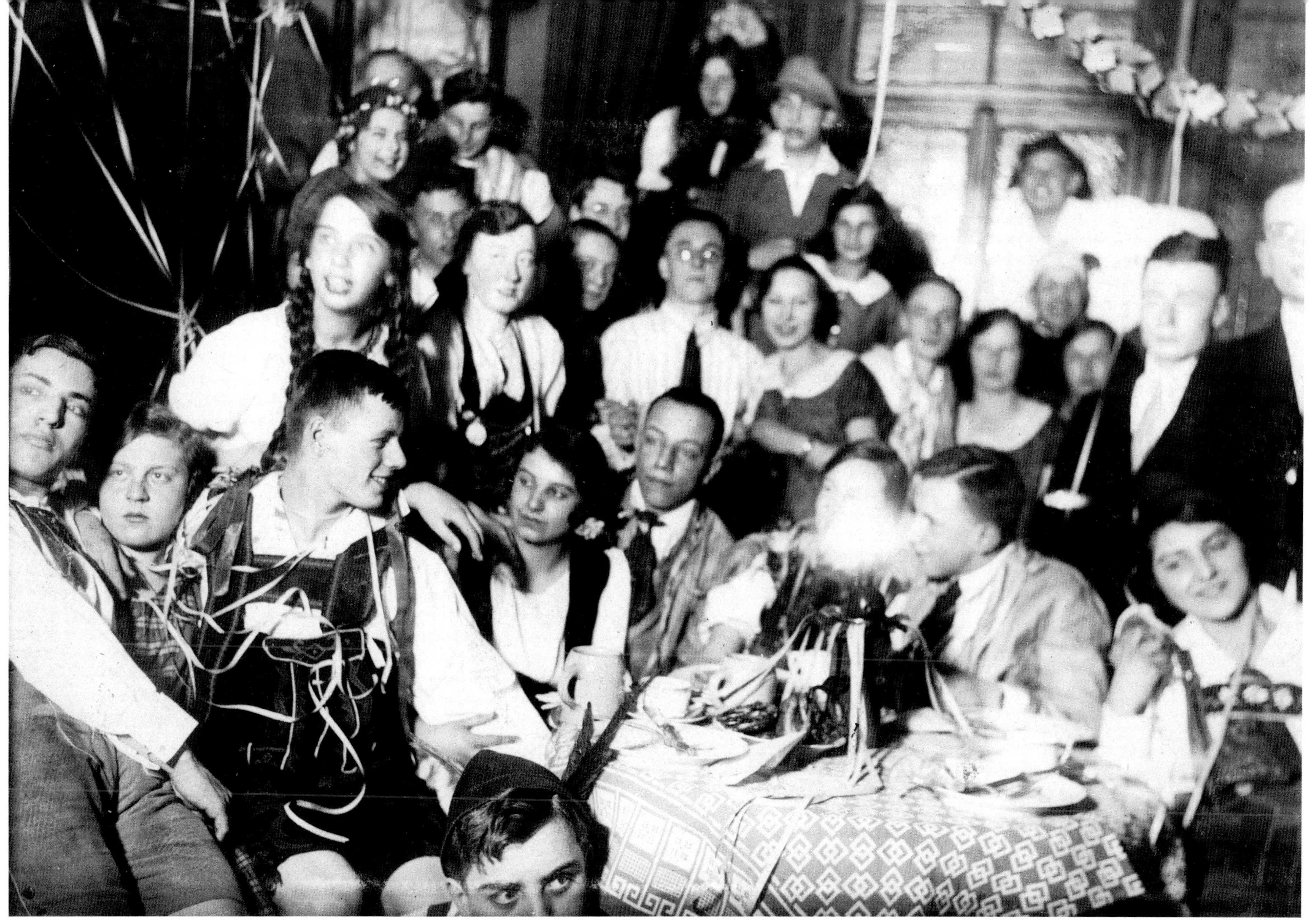

Above: At Emilie Reichert's, 16 February 1924

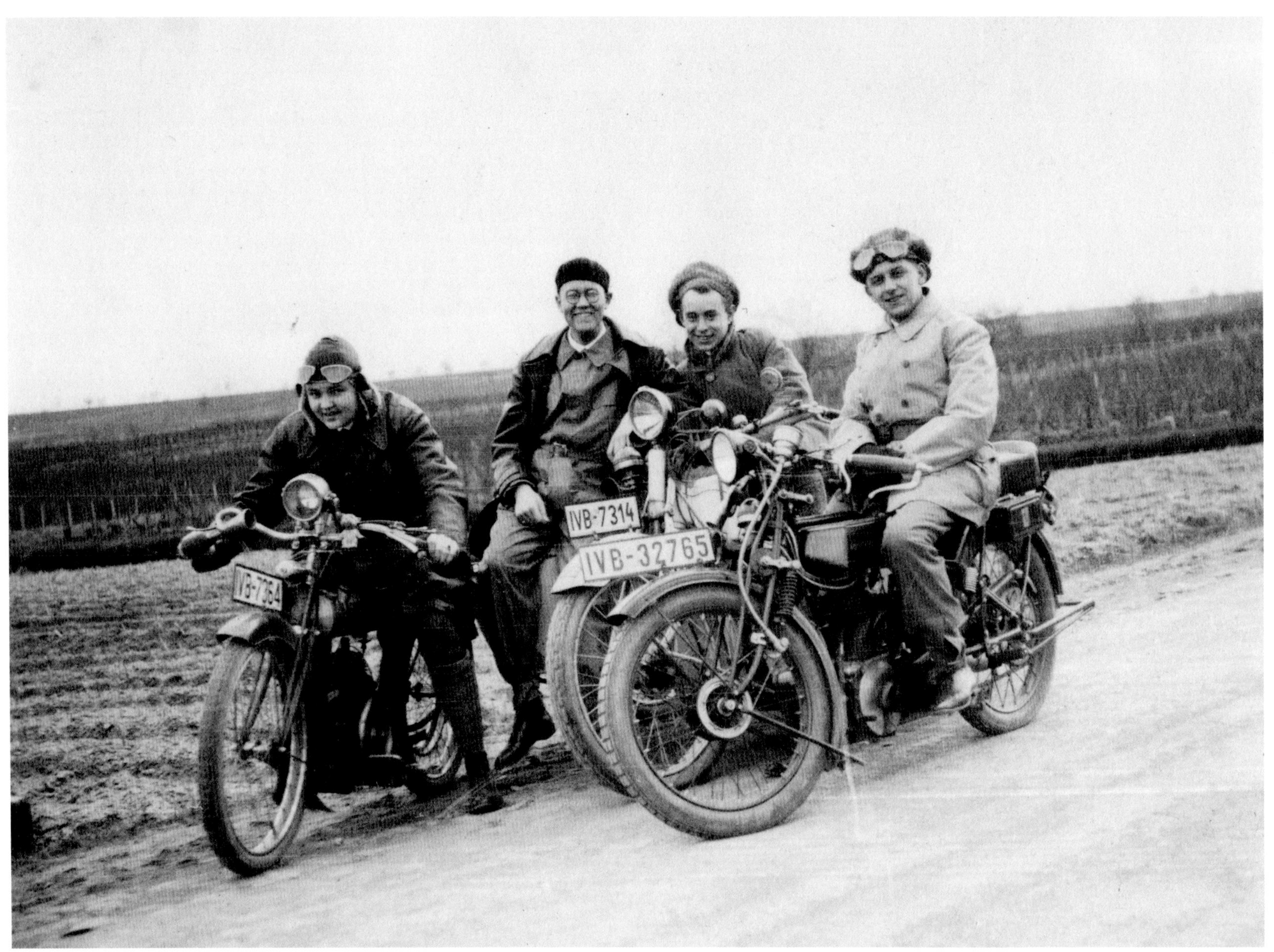
IVB-7364
IVB-7314
IVB-32765

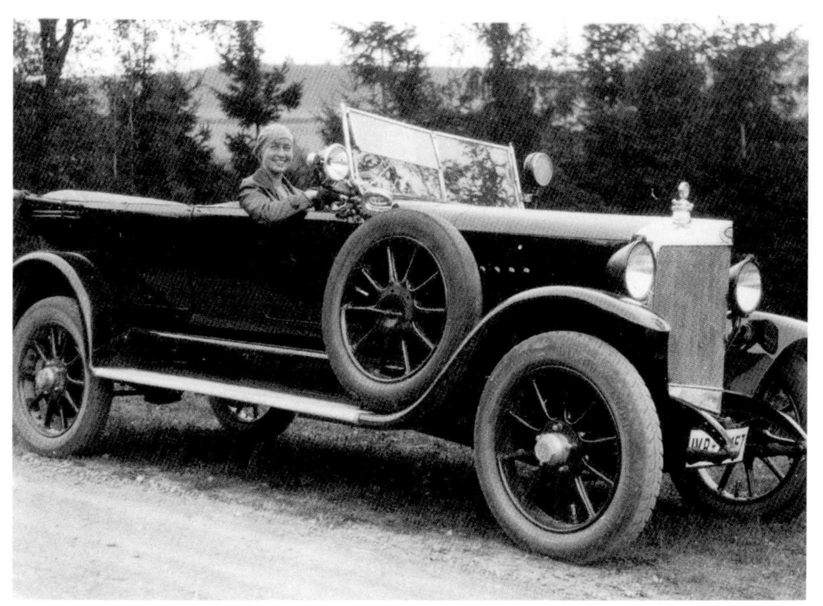

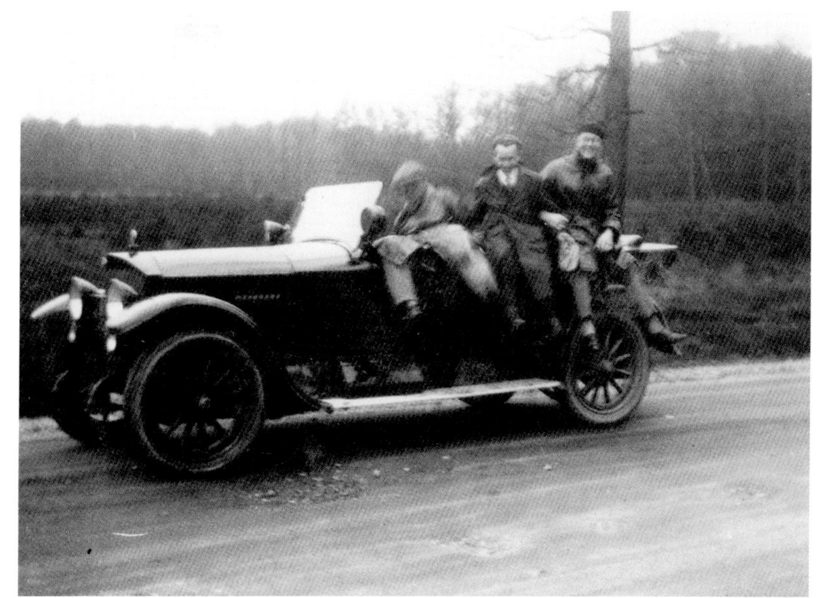

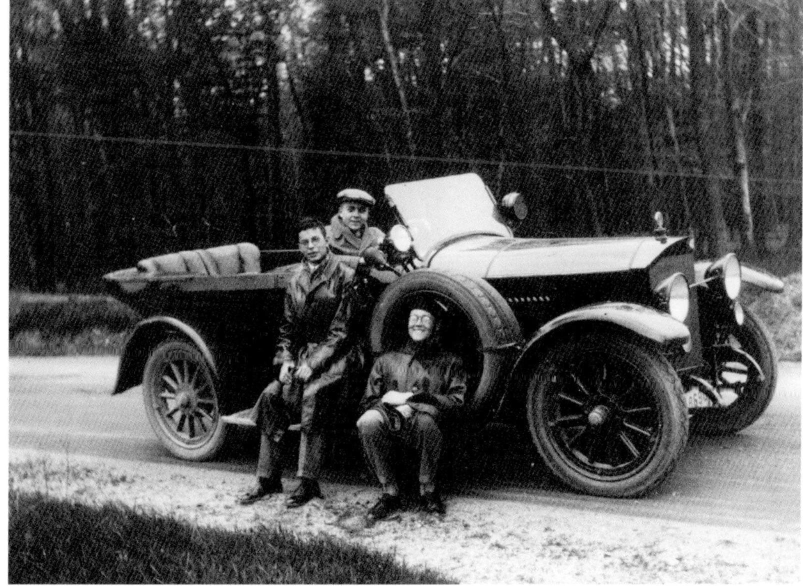

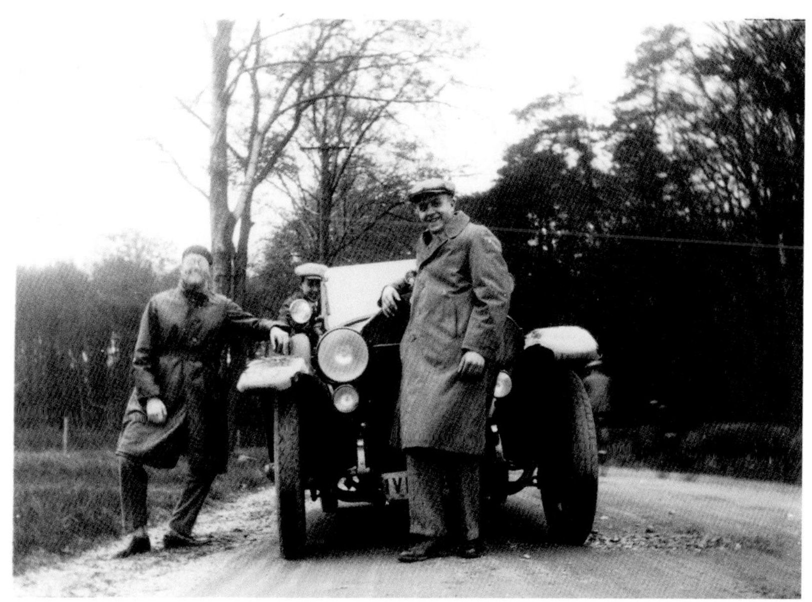

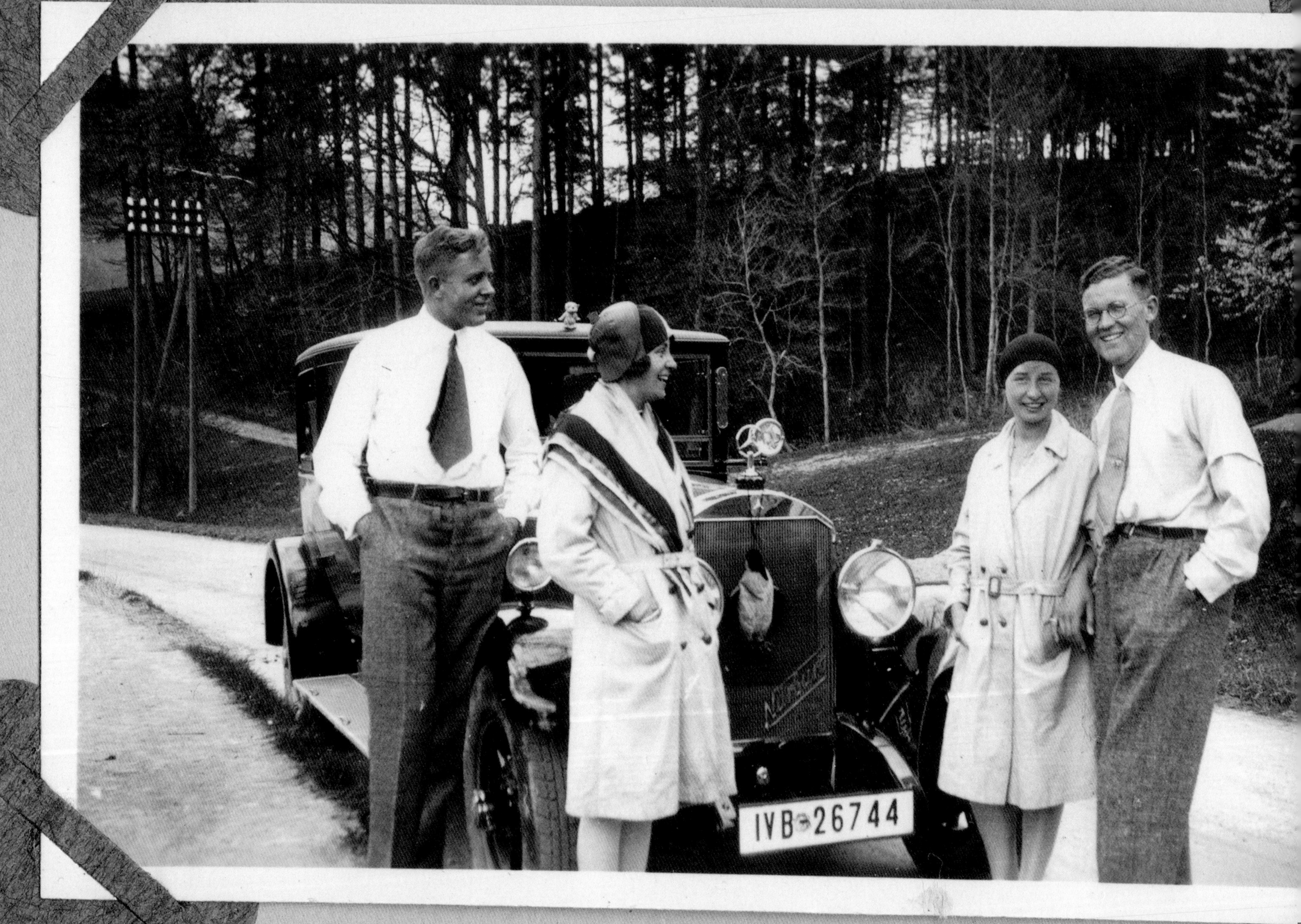
IVB 26744

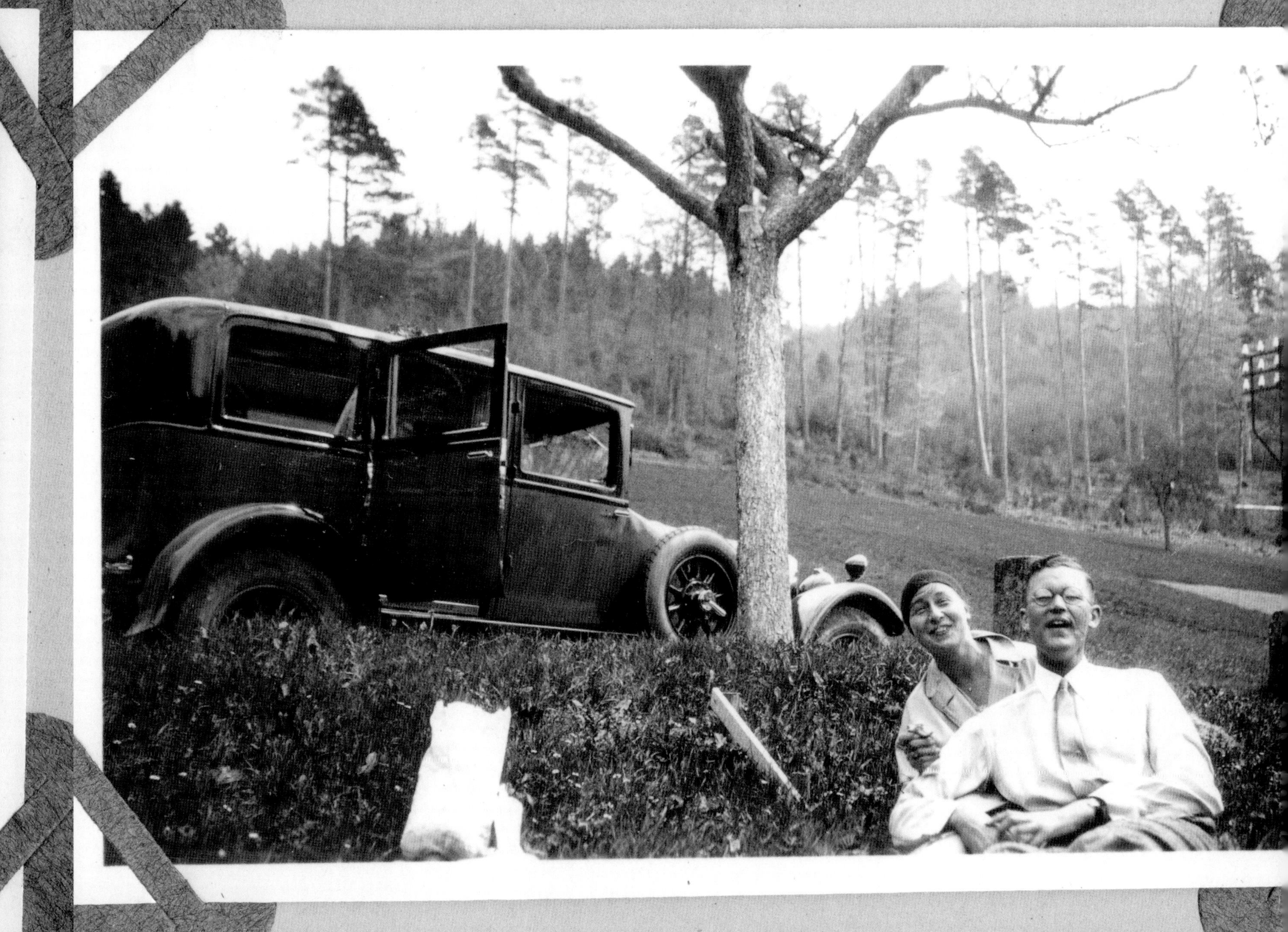

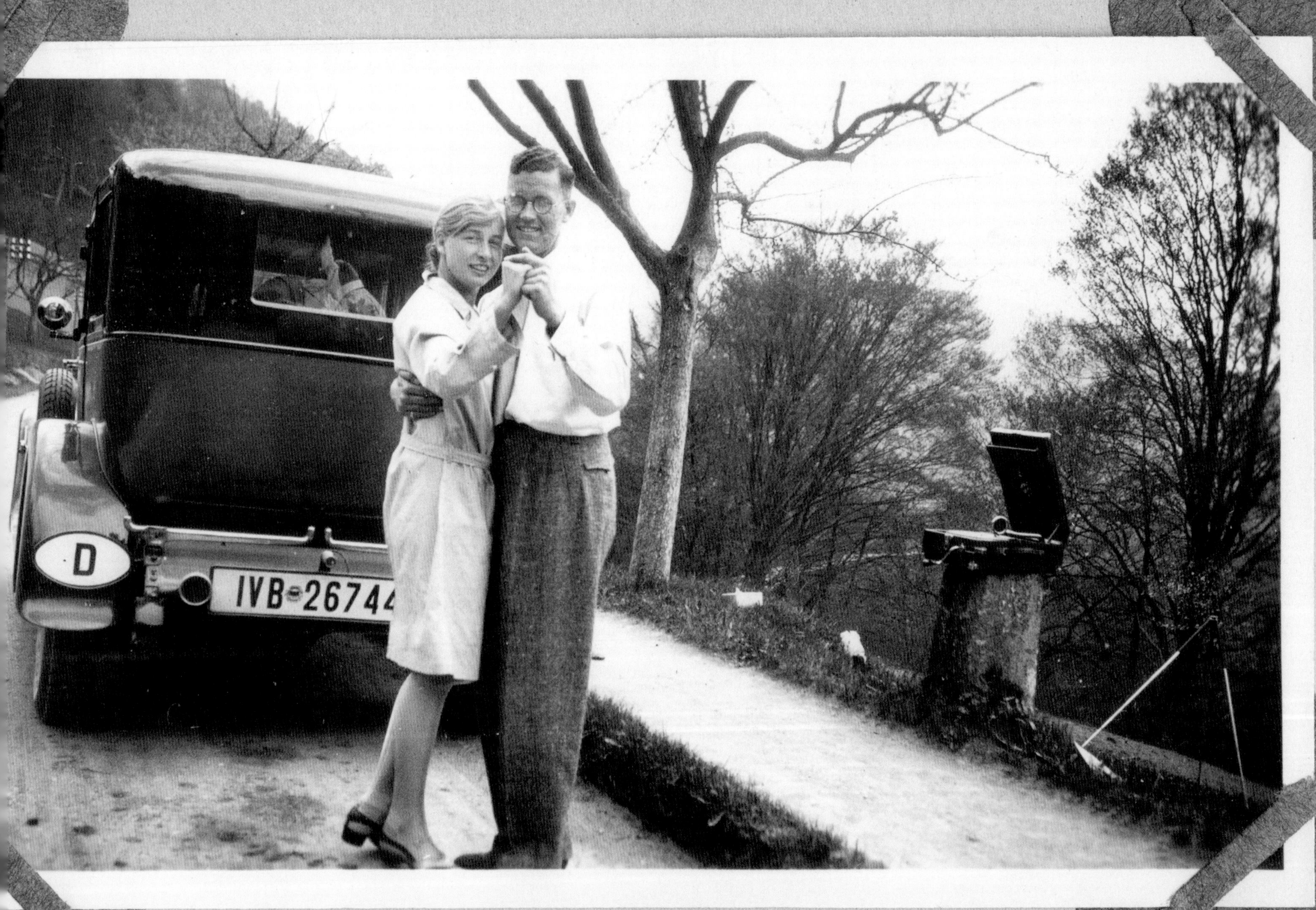
D
IVB 26744

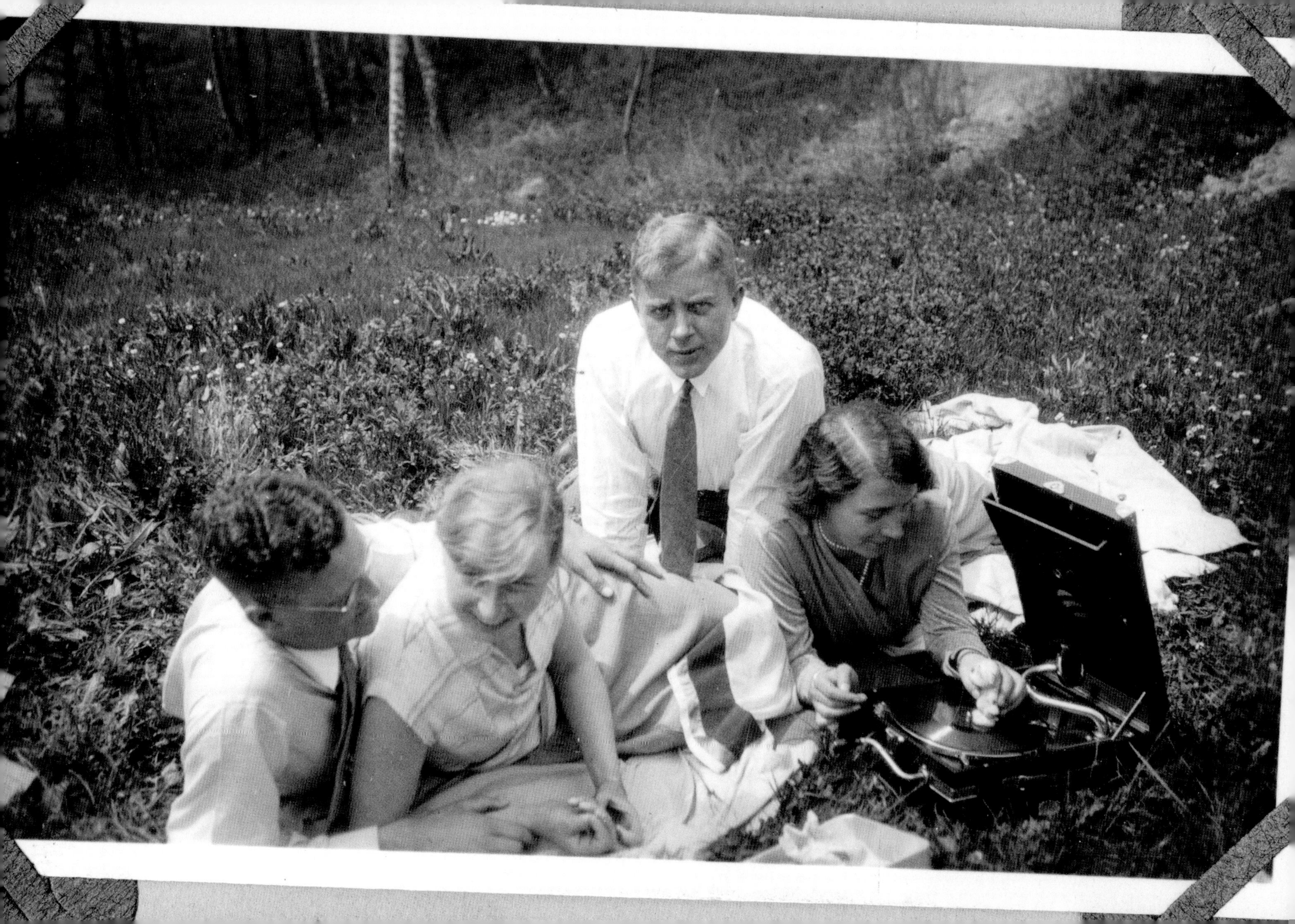

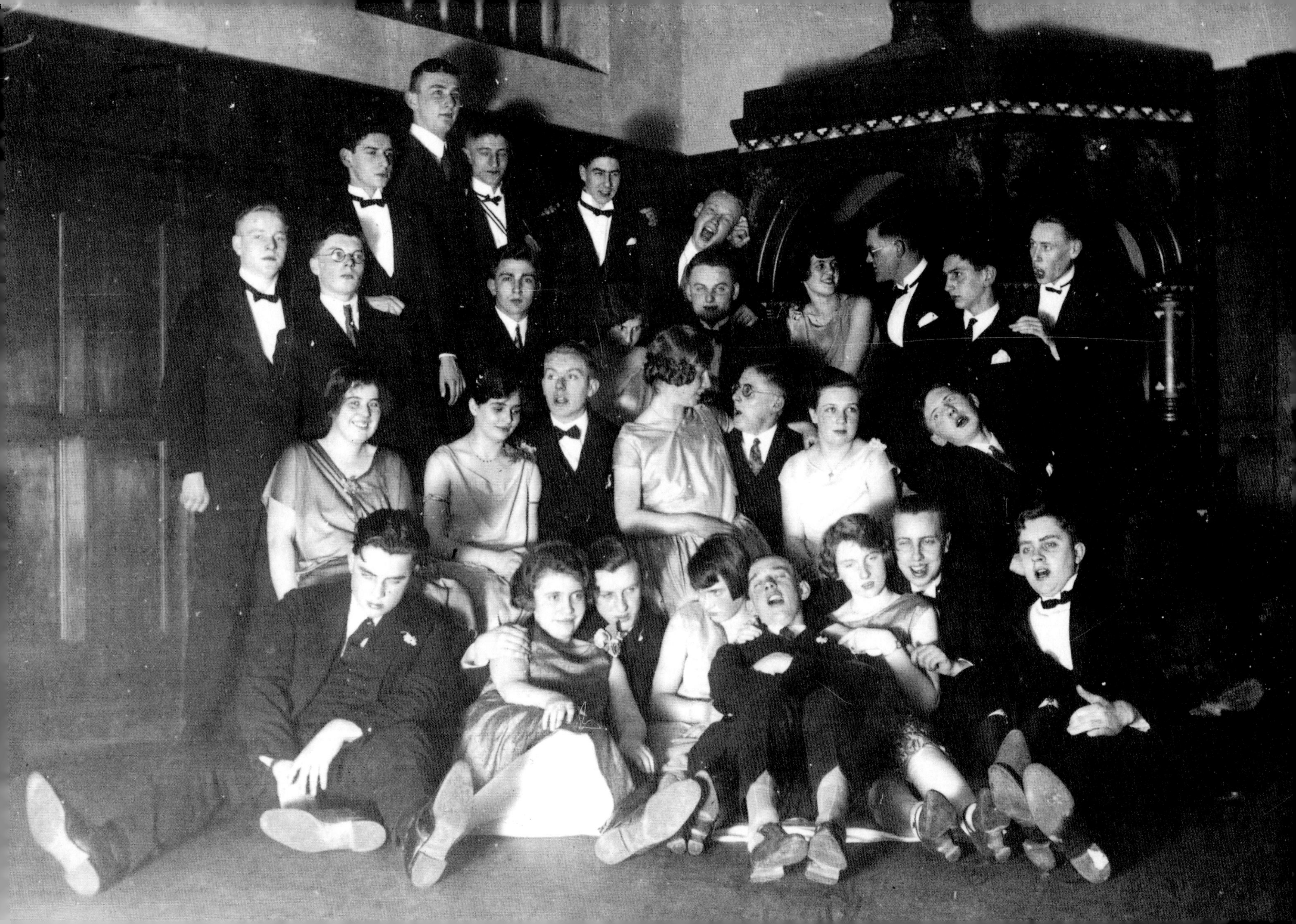

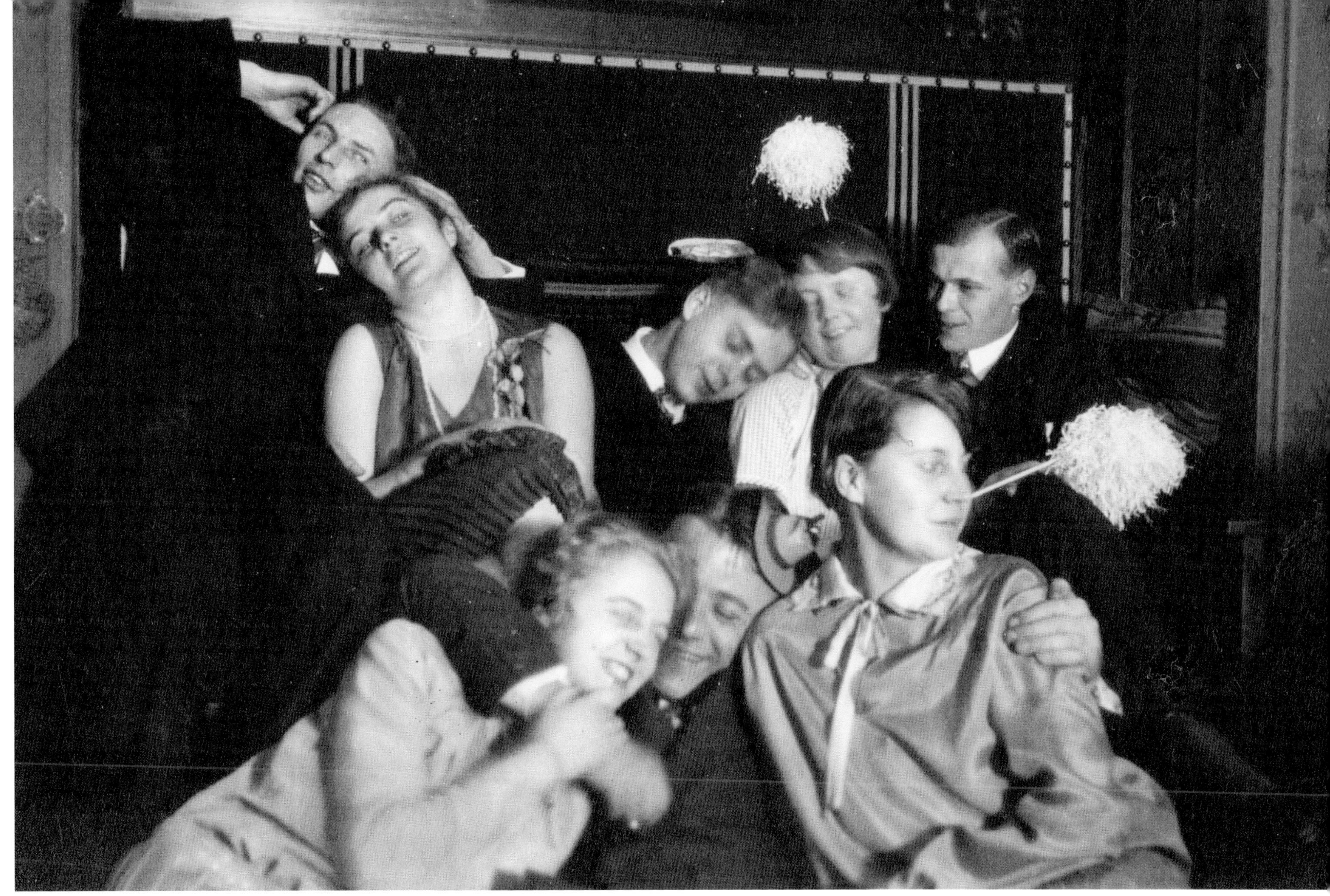

Above: Sachsenhausen, Anneli's farewell party, 13 February 1928

Opposite page: Graduation party at Kinzingerhof, 1926

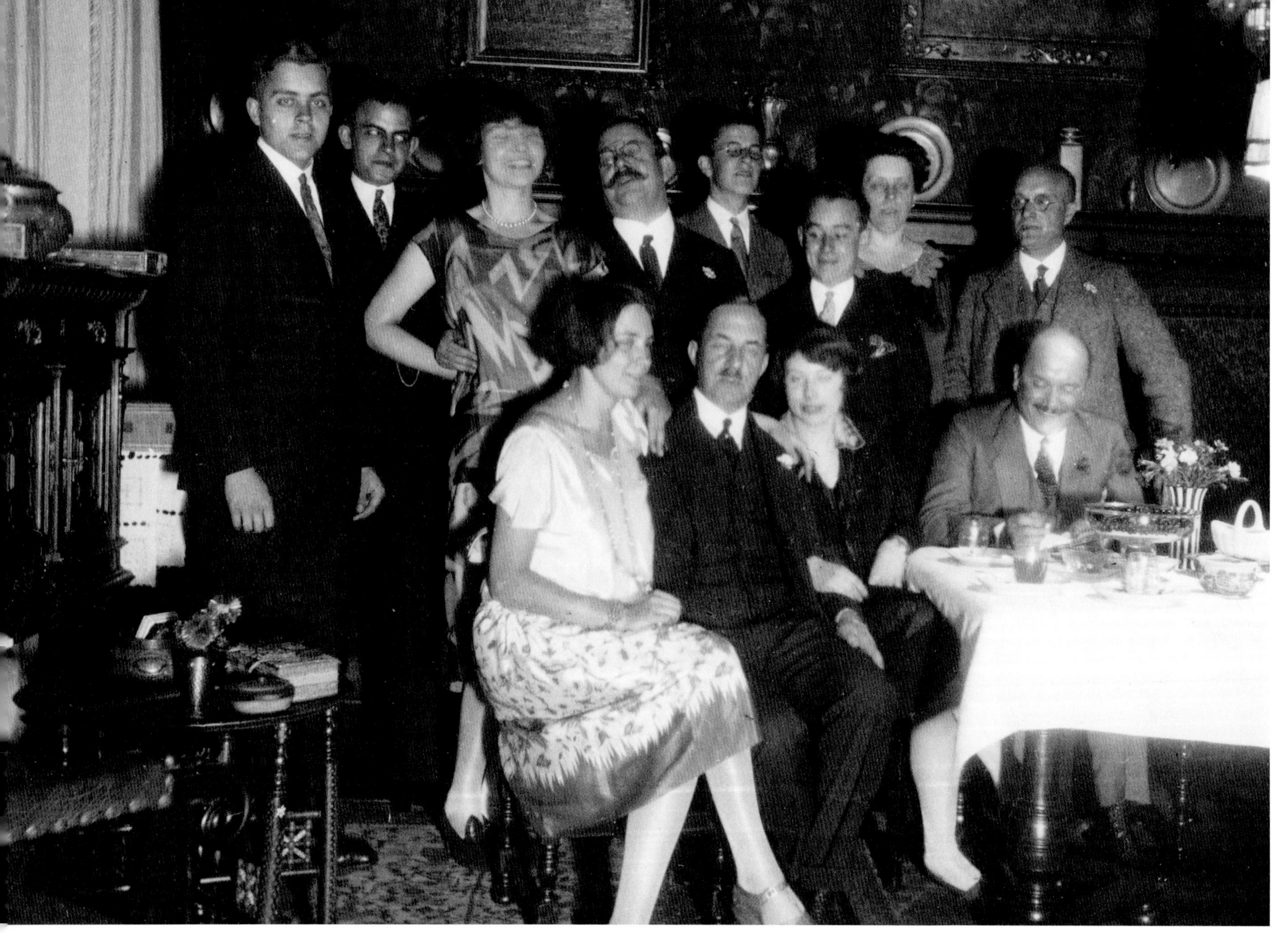

Opposite page: Hami Brod, Kinzinger, Gretel Kurst

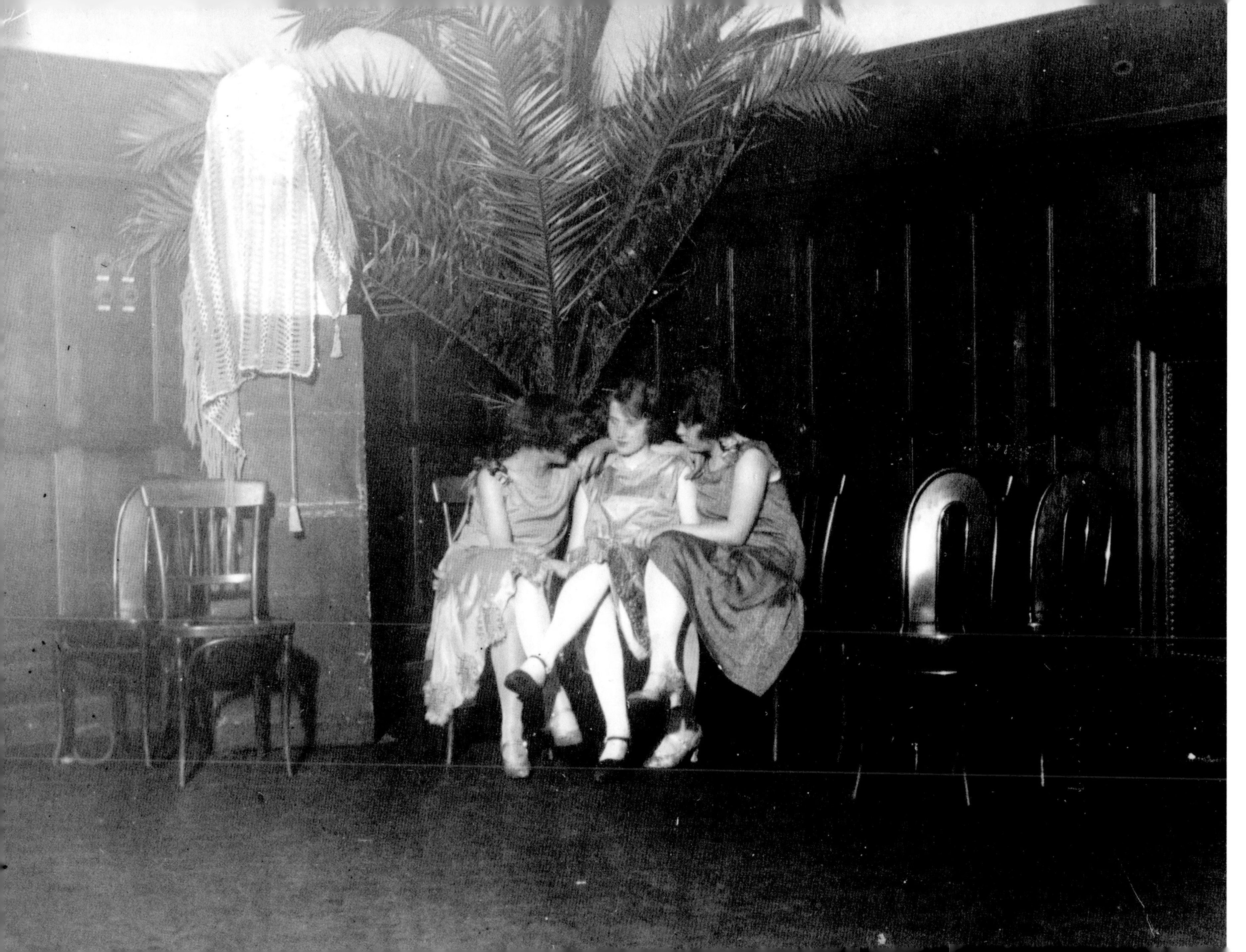

part II

1926
1929

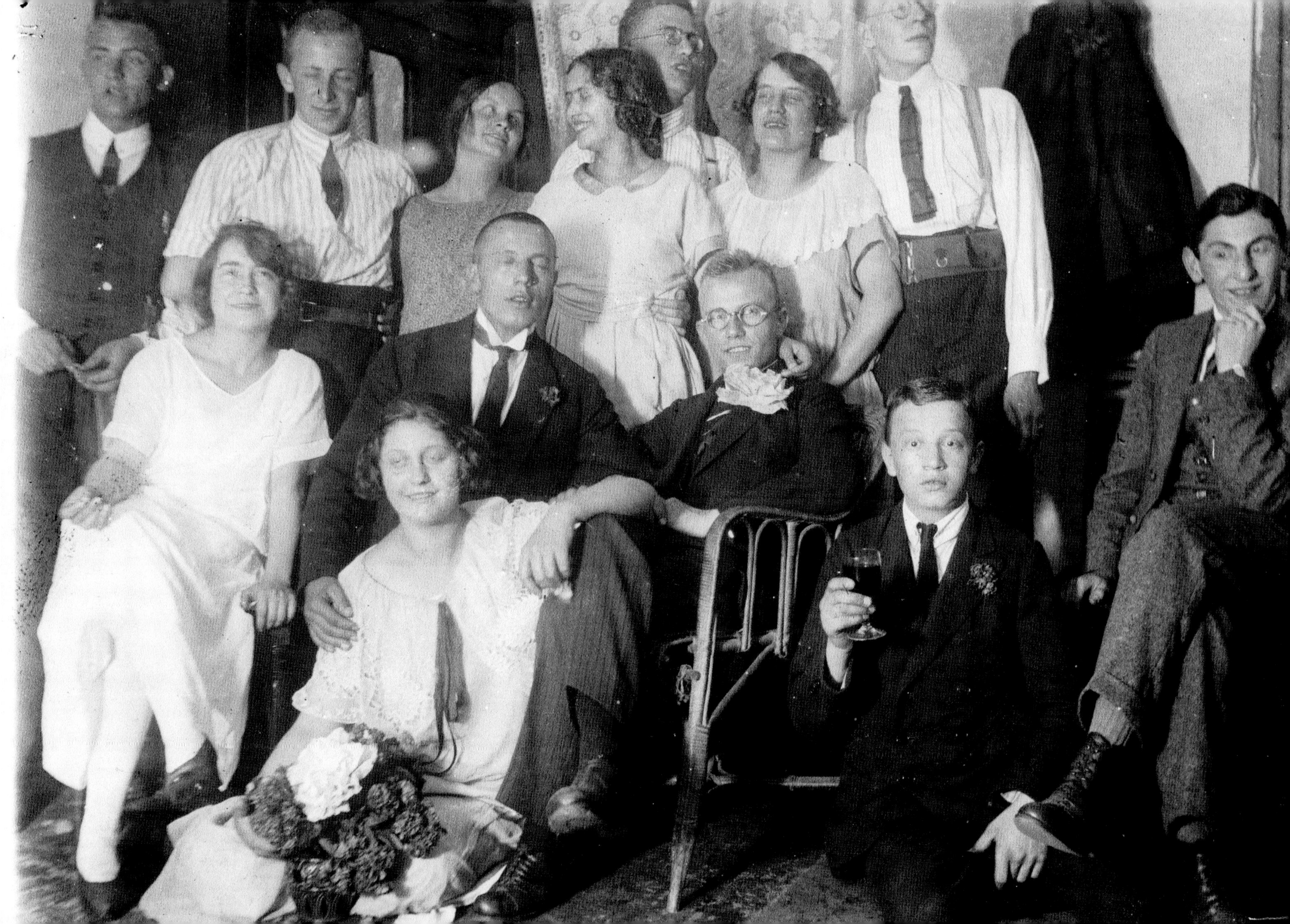

February 1926
The Committee on Evil Literature is set up in the Irish Free State to investigate publications referred to it as morally corrupting or obscene. It receives complaints about *The Daily Mail*, *Vogue*, *The Illustrated Police News*, and advertisements for hair removal cream.

A legal loophole exempting foreign languages from obscenity laws results in Paris emerging as the unofficial obscene book capital of Europe.

November 1926
American biologist Dr Raymond Pearl publishes *Alcohol and Longevity*, which claims that moderate consumption of alcohol can be beneficial. Dr Pearl is renowned for his Prohibition-era parties and heavy drinking.

May 1926
American "King of Jazz" Paul Whiteman and his Orchestra visit Berlin.

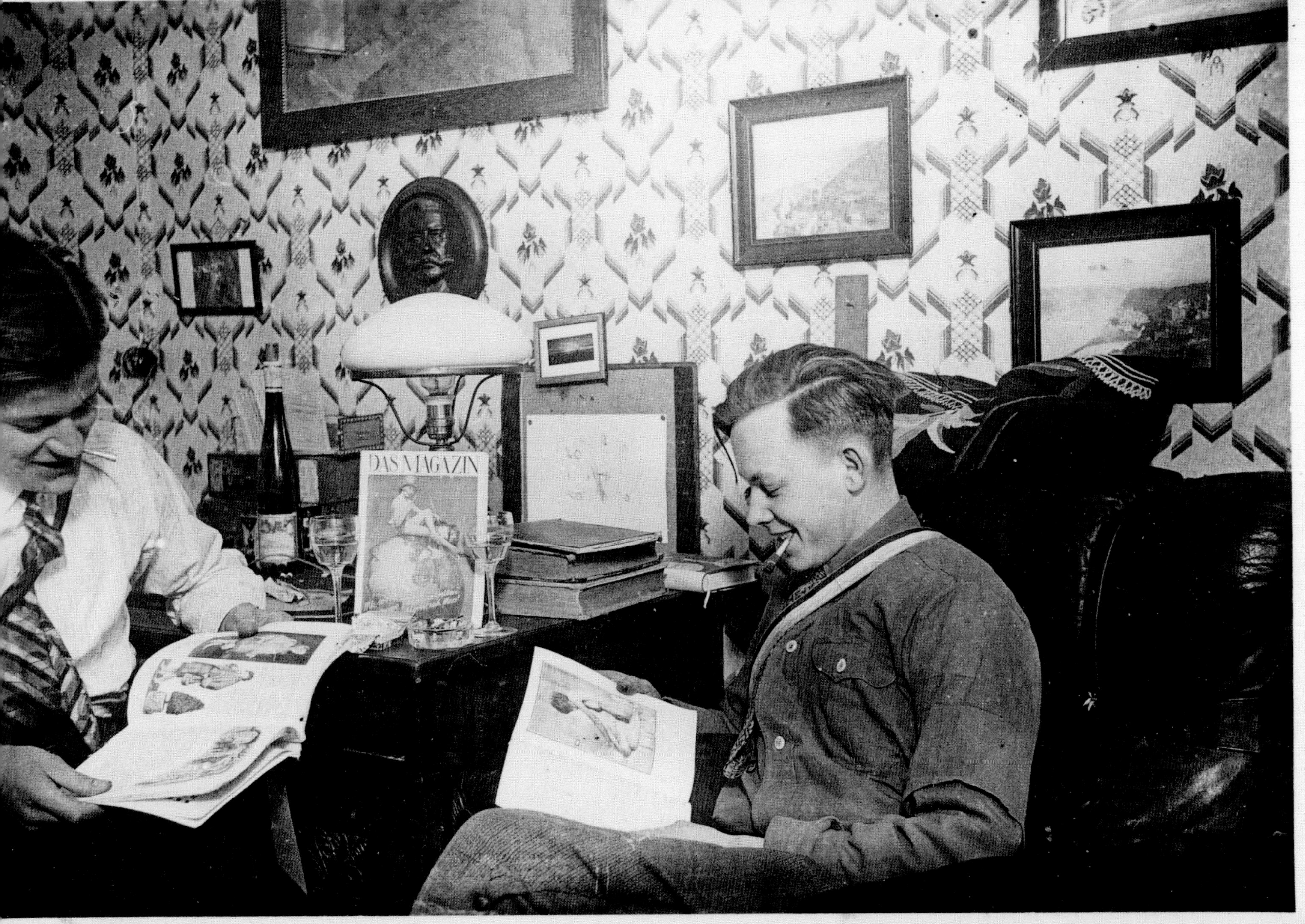
DAS MAGAZIN

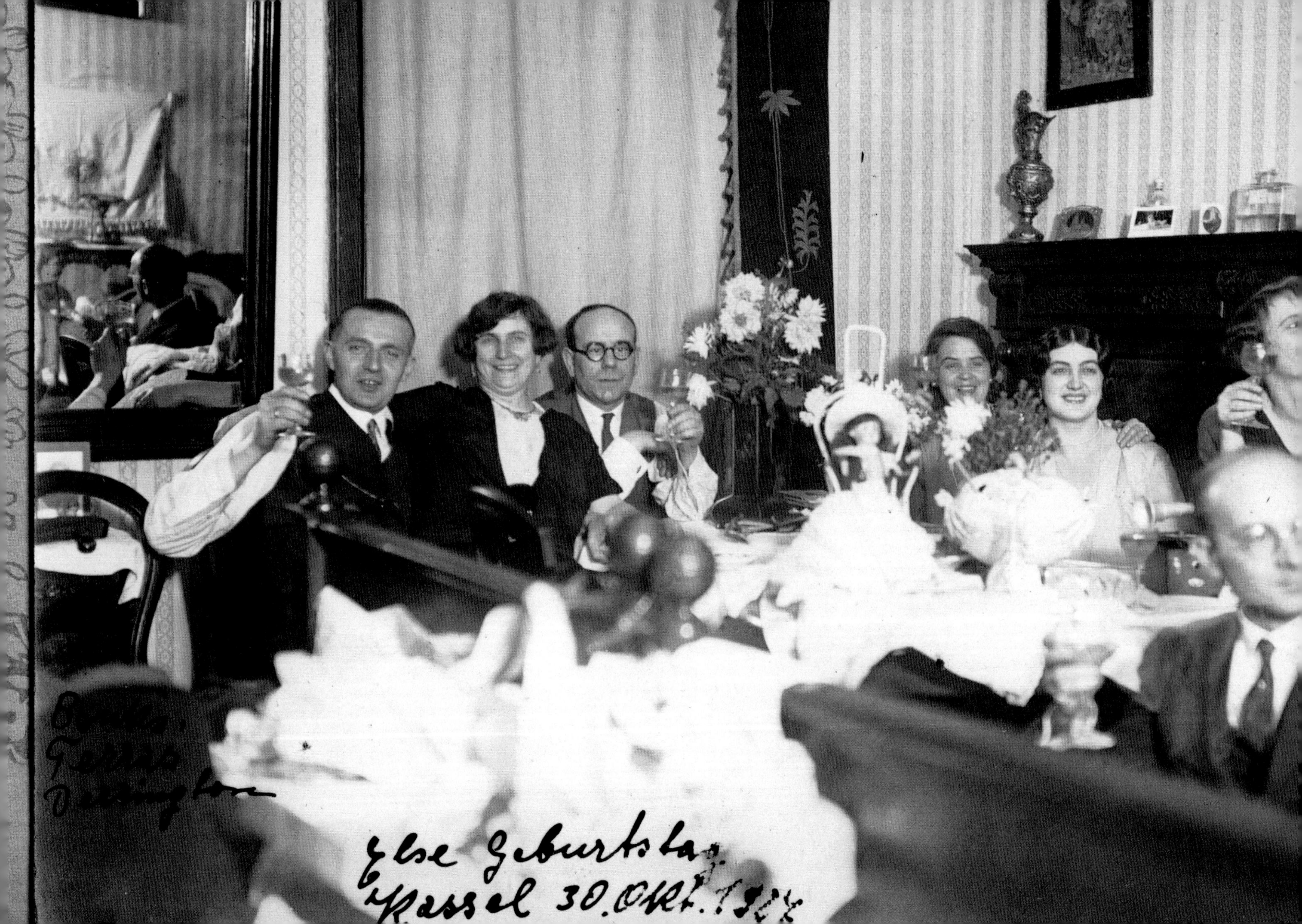
Else Geburtstag
Kassel 30.Okt.

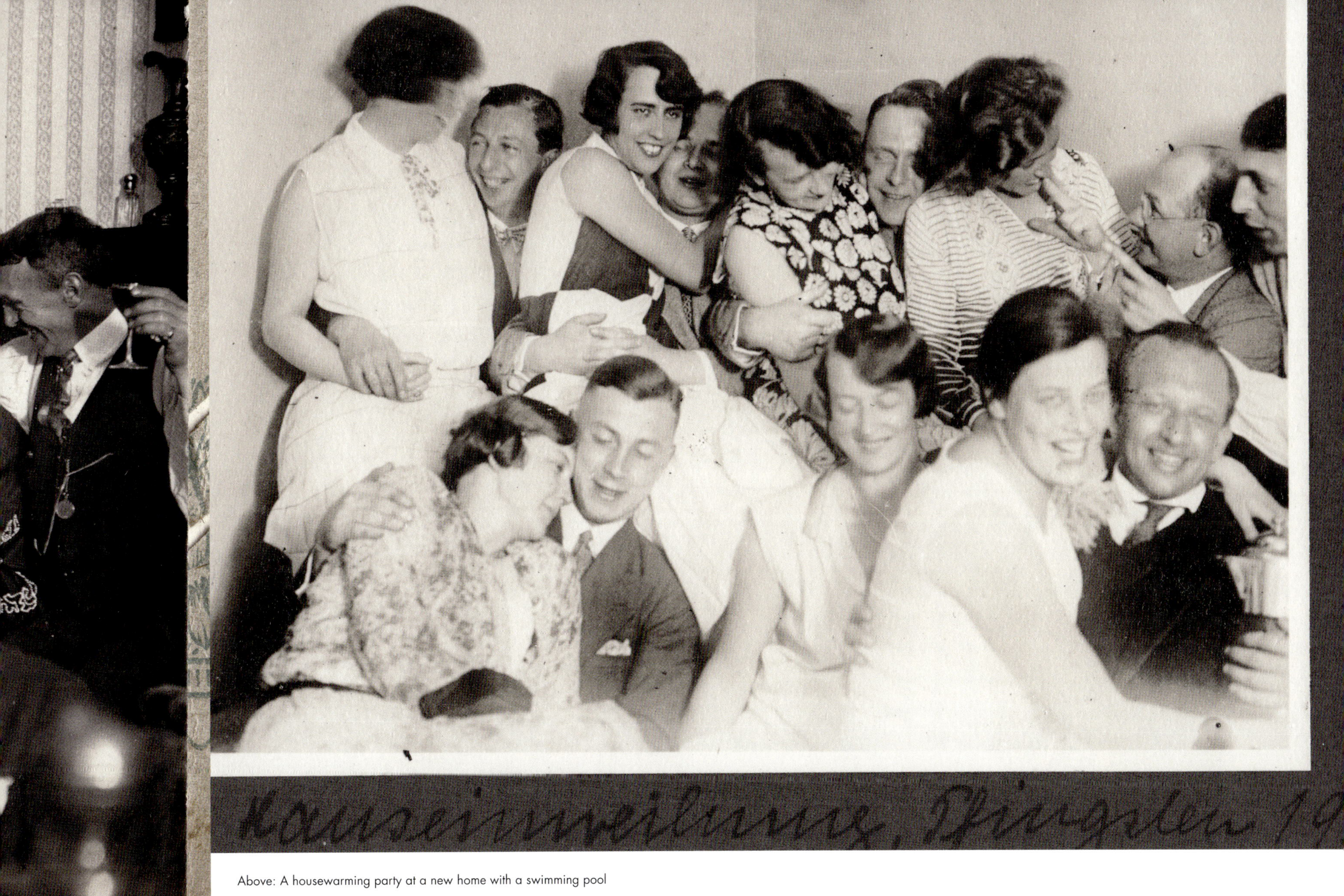

Above: A housewarming party at a new home with a swimming pool

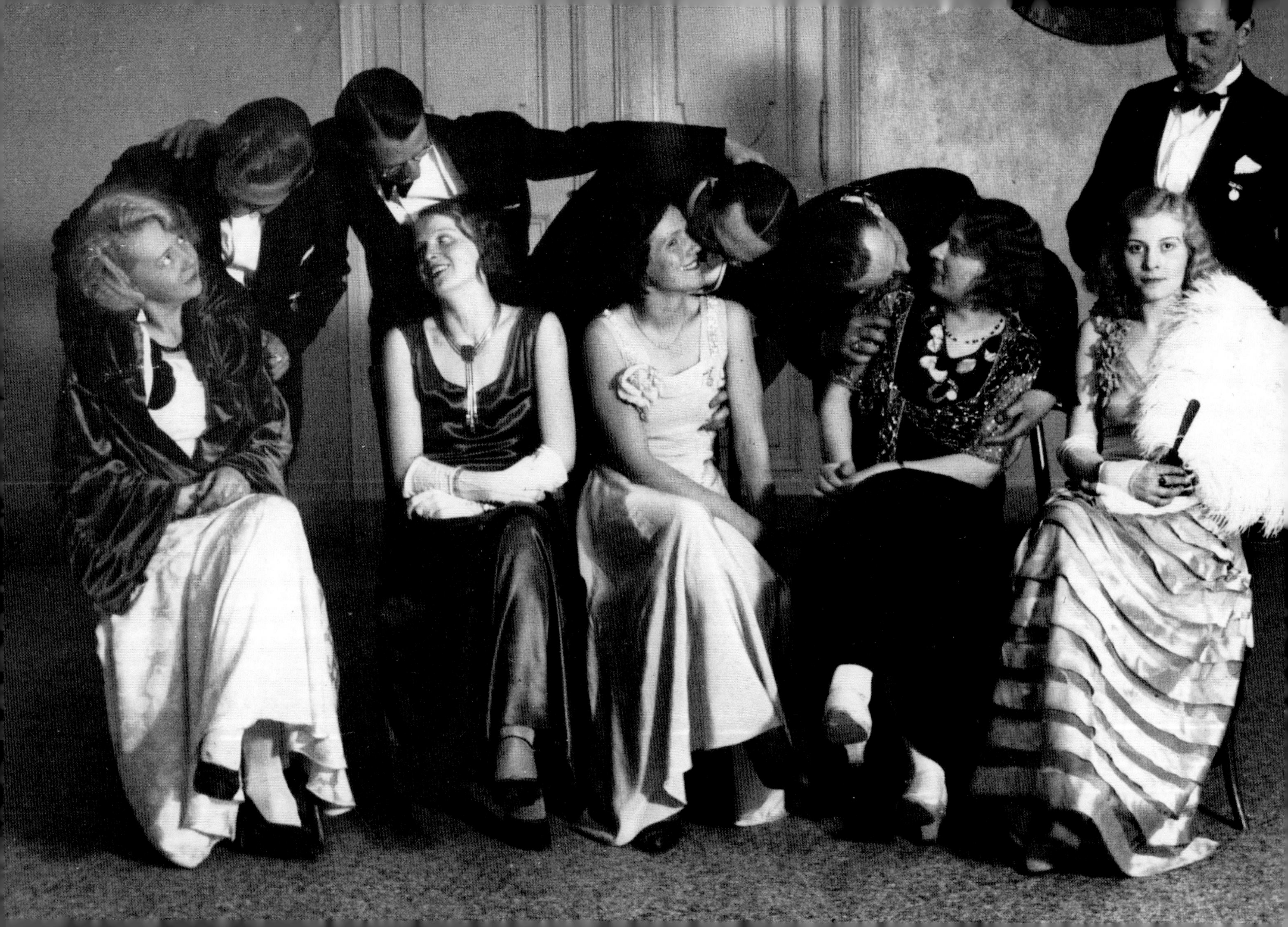

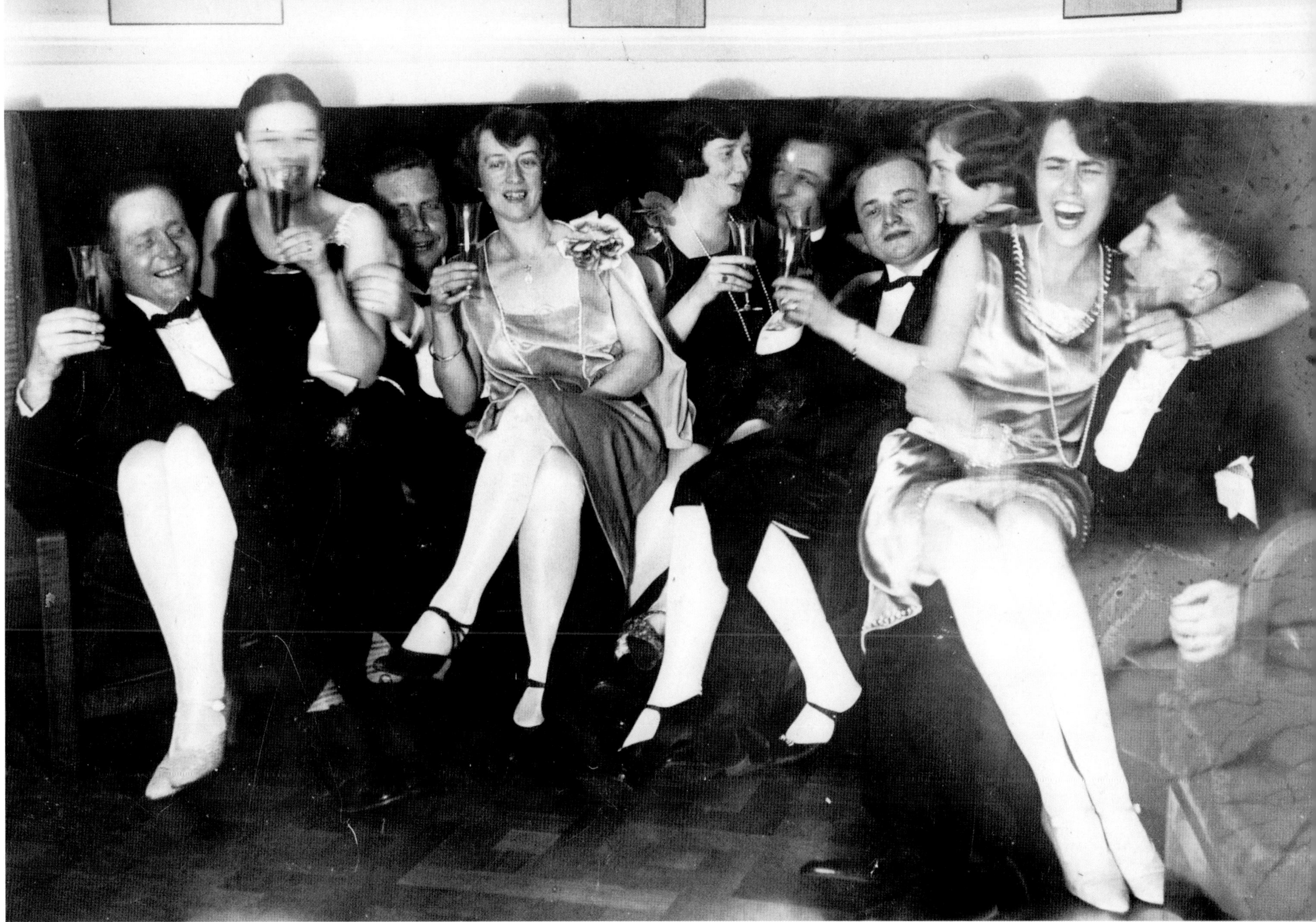

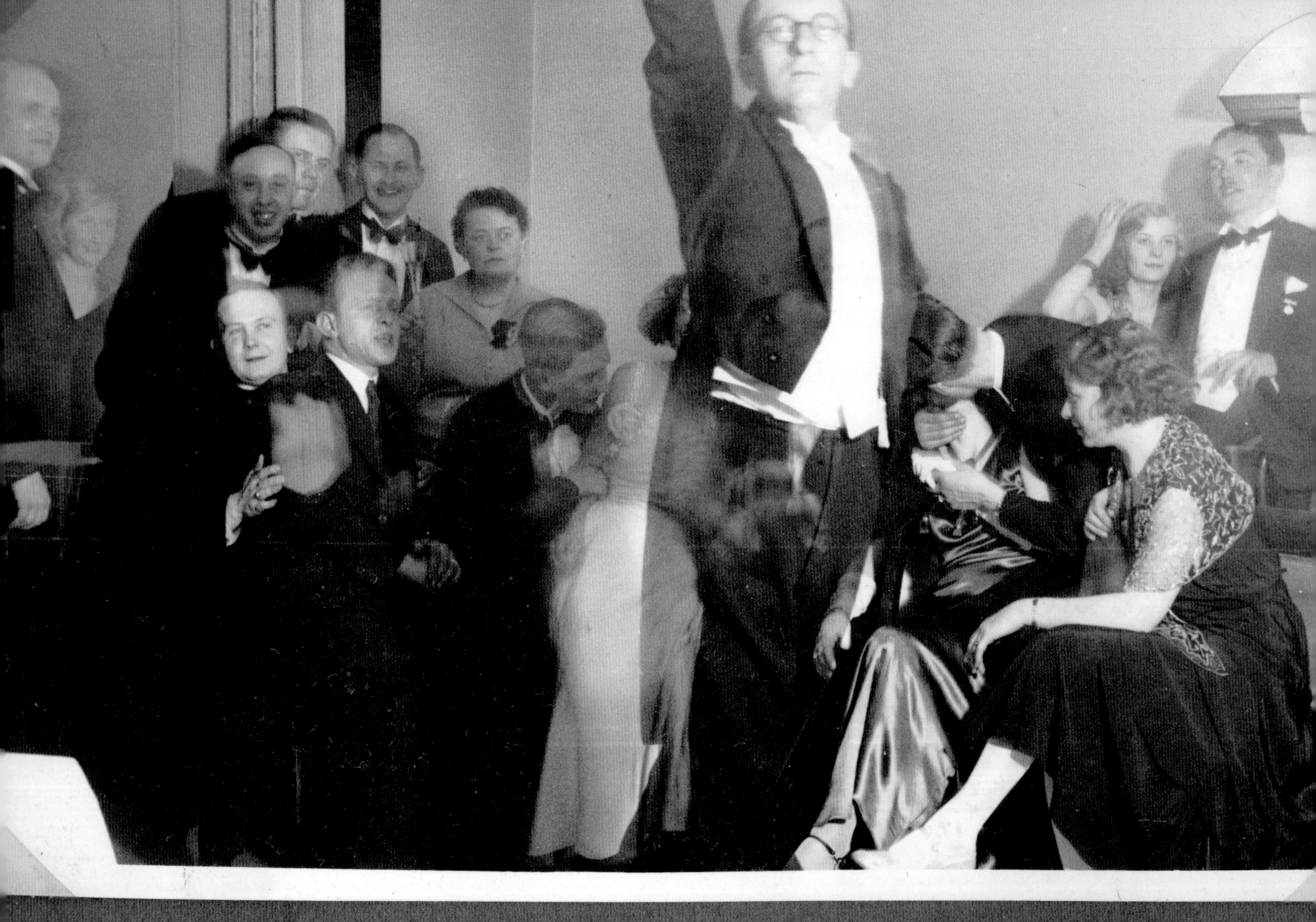

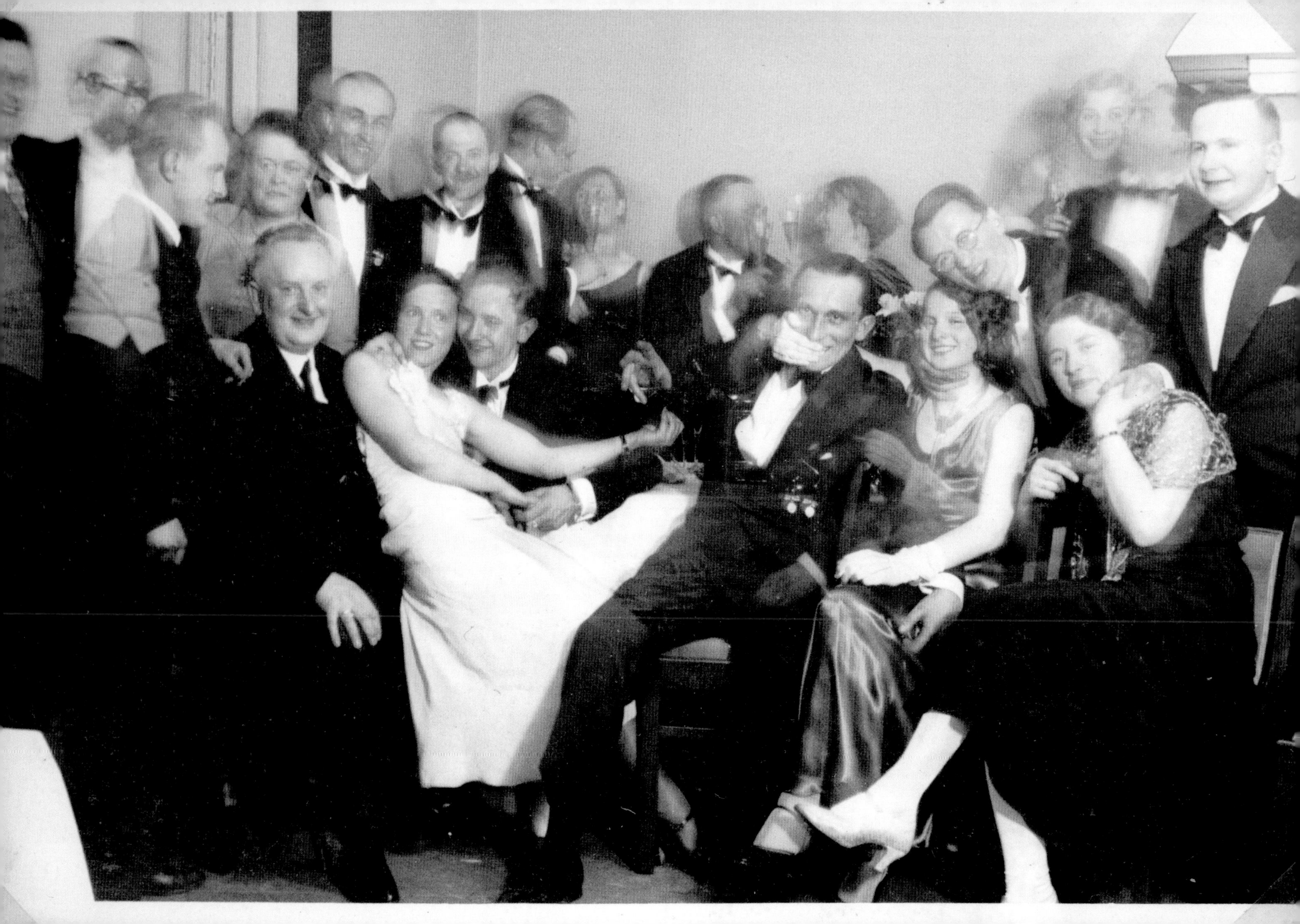

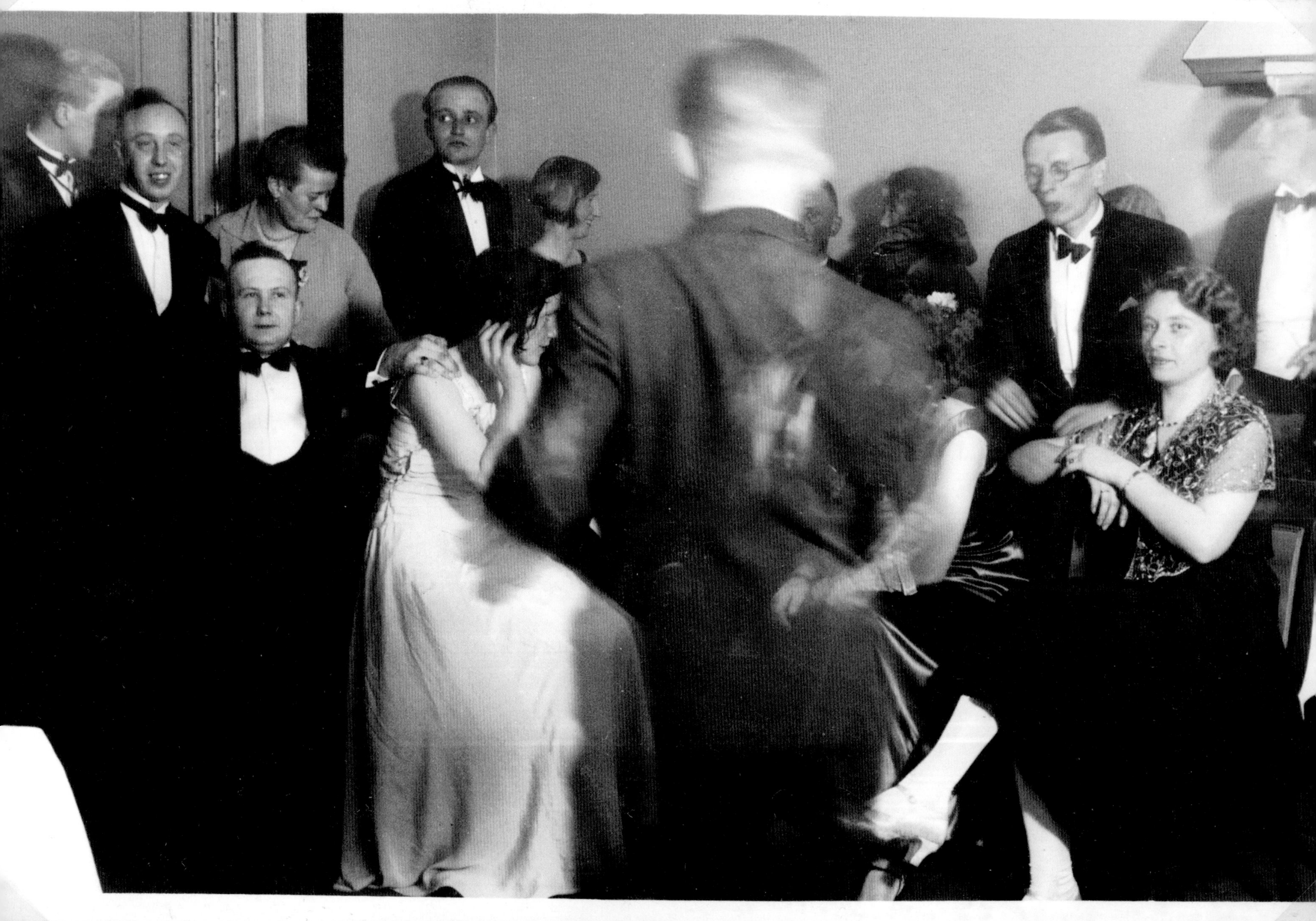

January 1928
Jack Hylton and his Jazz Orchestra visit Weimar Germany.

October 1928
The first transatlantic passenger service begins as the LZ 127 Graf Zeppelin flies from Friedrichshafen in southern Germany to Lakehurst, New Jersey, in the United States.

January 1929
Georg Pabst's melodrama *Pandora's Box*, starring Louise Brooks, is released in Germany. Although the fashion for short hair is already on its way out, Louise Brooks's severely bobbed hair comes to define the age.

A craze for yo-yos emerges in the United States.

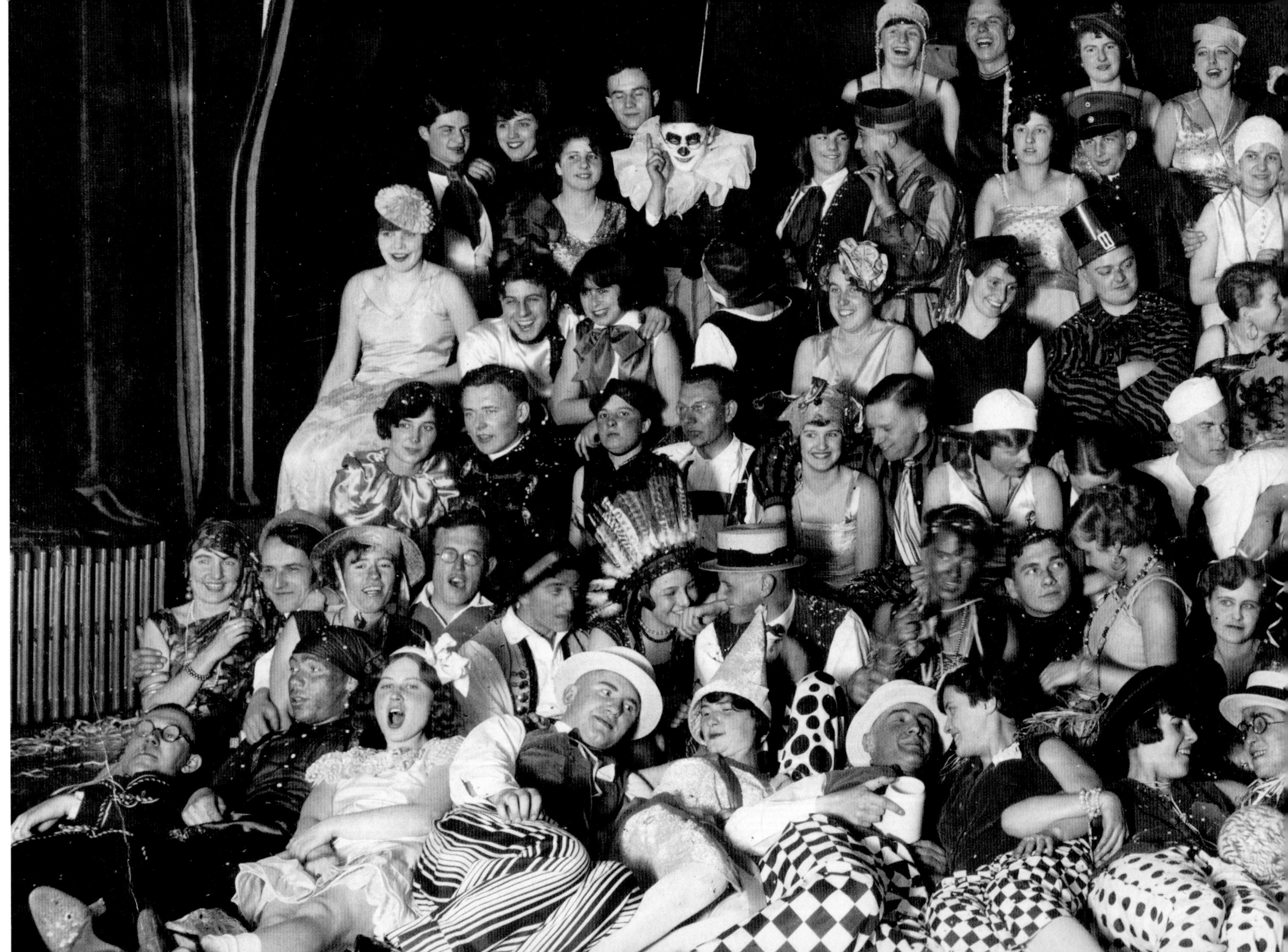

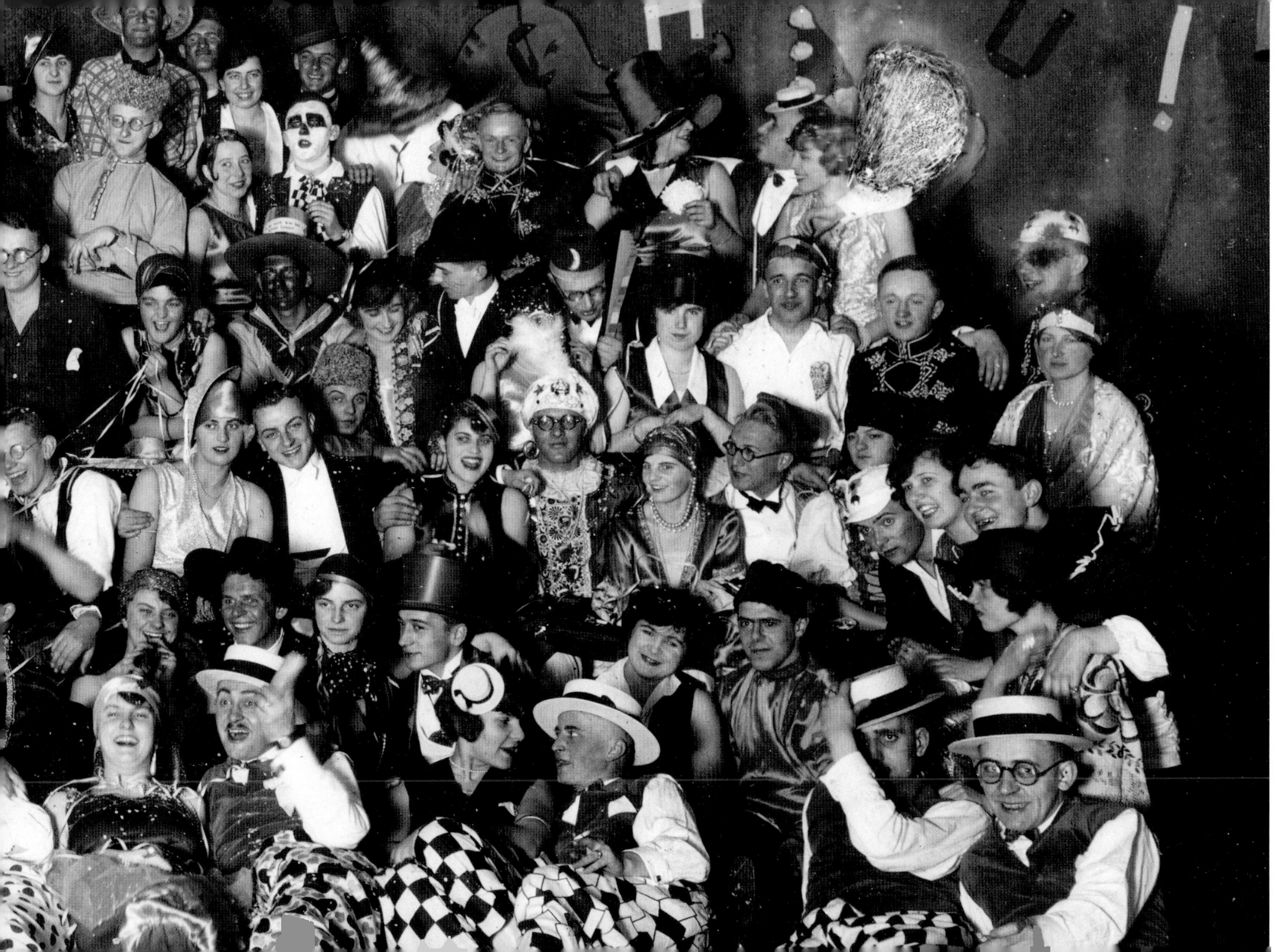

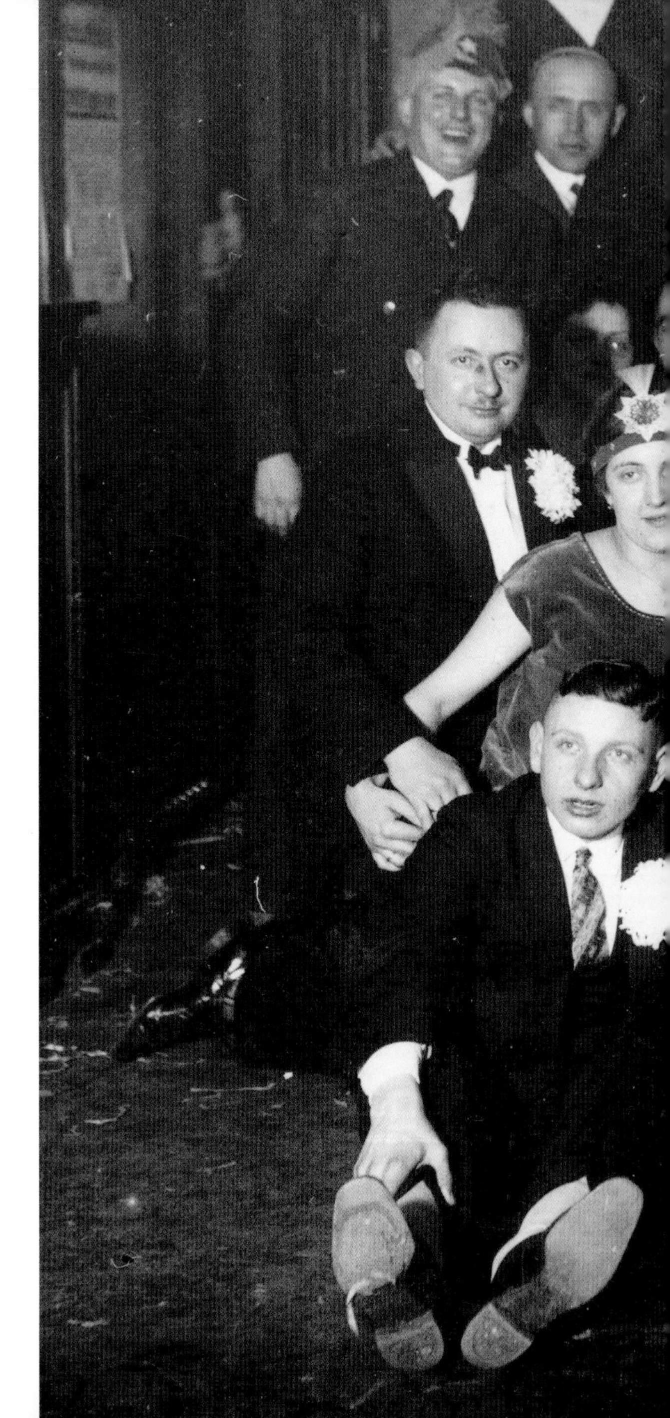

A party at a bowling club

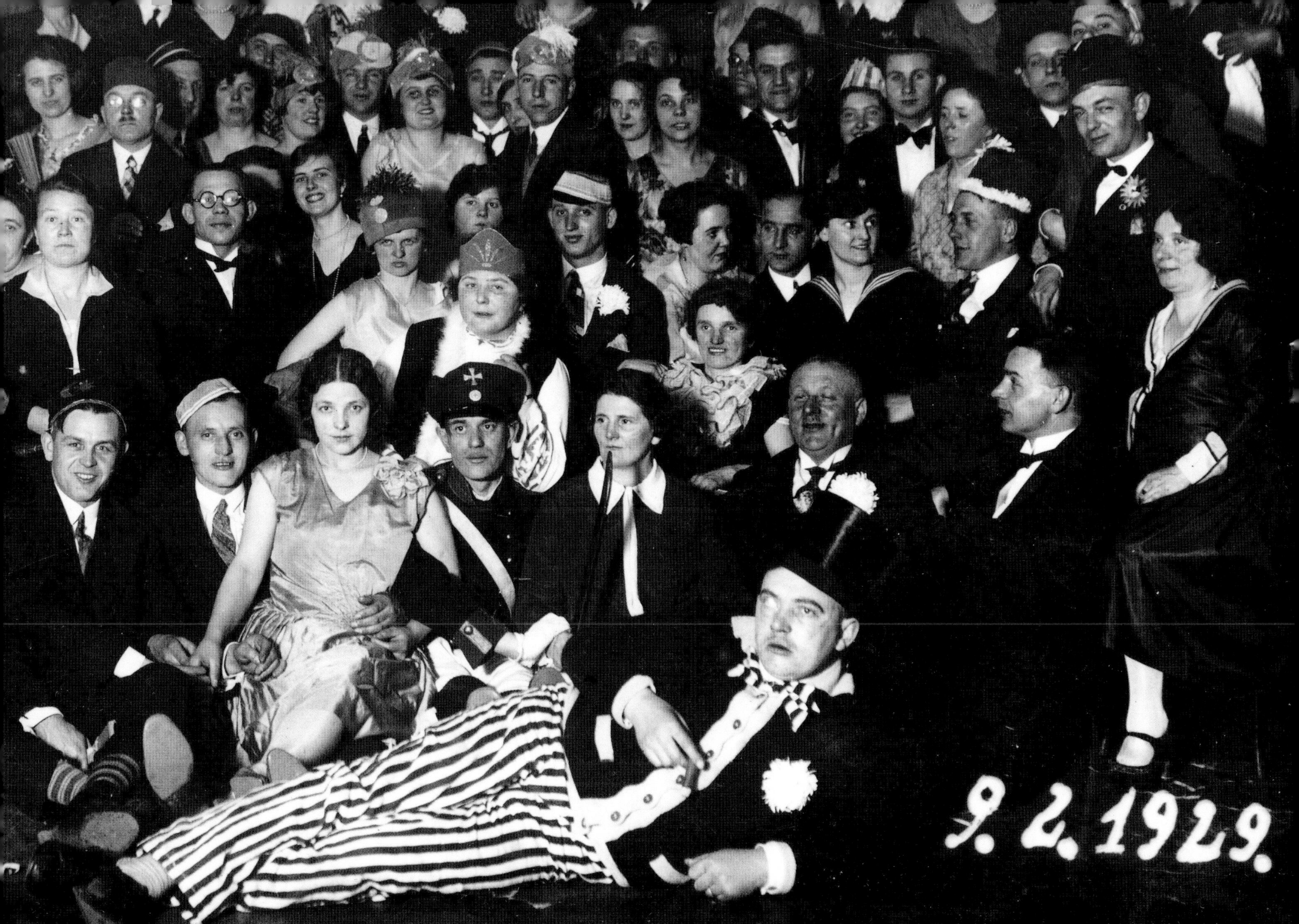
9. 2. 1929.

December 1929

Emil und die Detektive by Erich Kästner, the story of a boy who is caught painting the nose of a public statue red and later turns detective to recover stolen money, is published in Germany. Optimistic in outlook and happy even within its scenario of adversity, it portrays the characters' Berlin slang not as a sign of ignorance or a lack of education but a positive, streetwise asset.

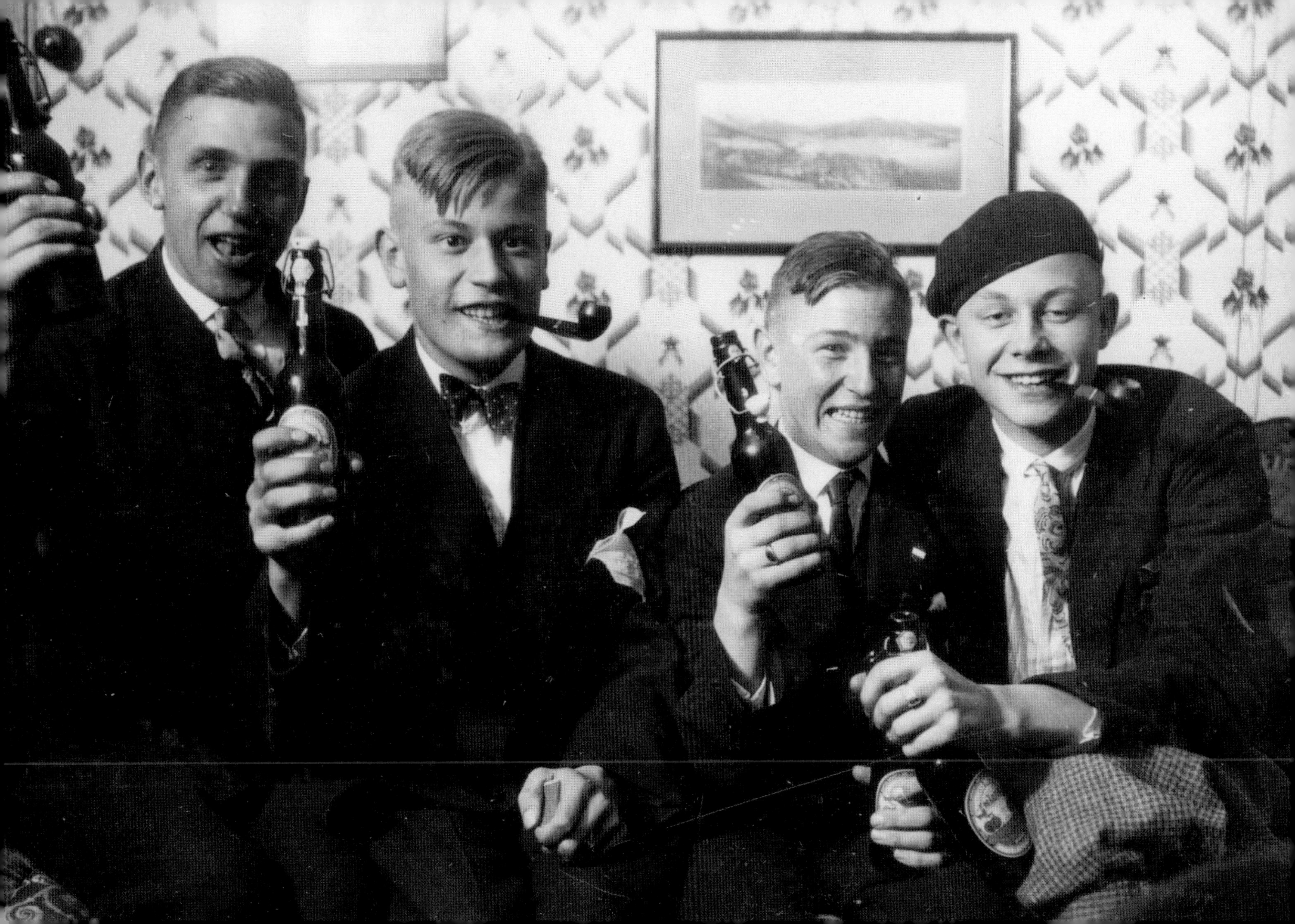

Carl Ludwig Schleich's book *Cocaineism* described the proliferation of cocaine in Berlin as a symptom of the malaise of a modern life continually speeding up.

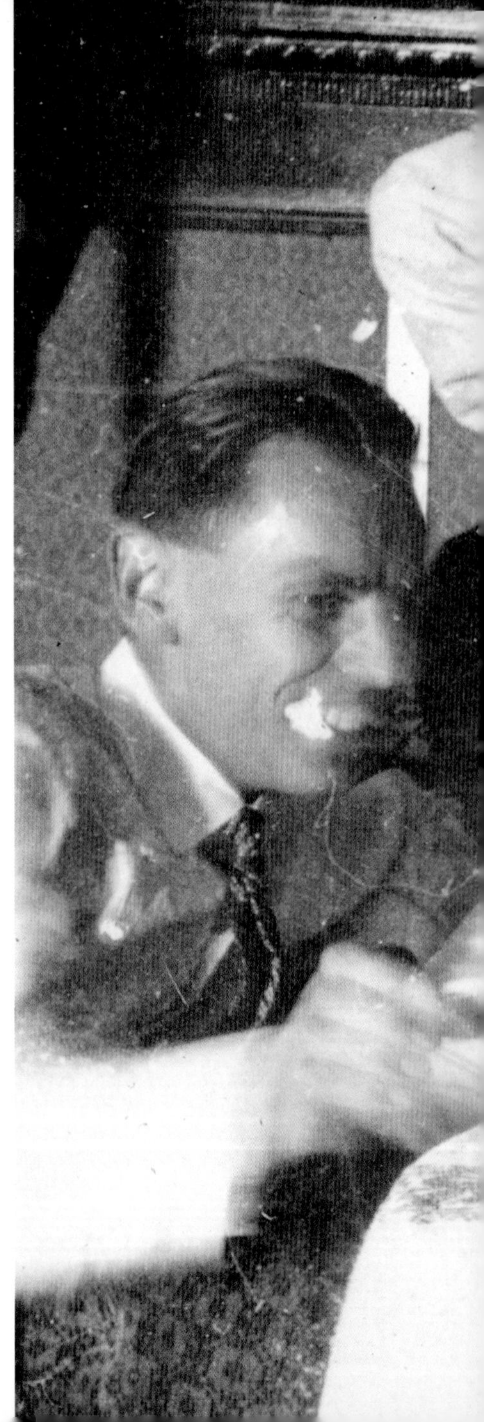

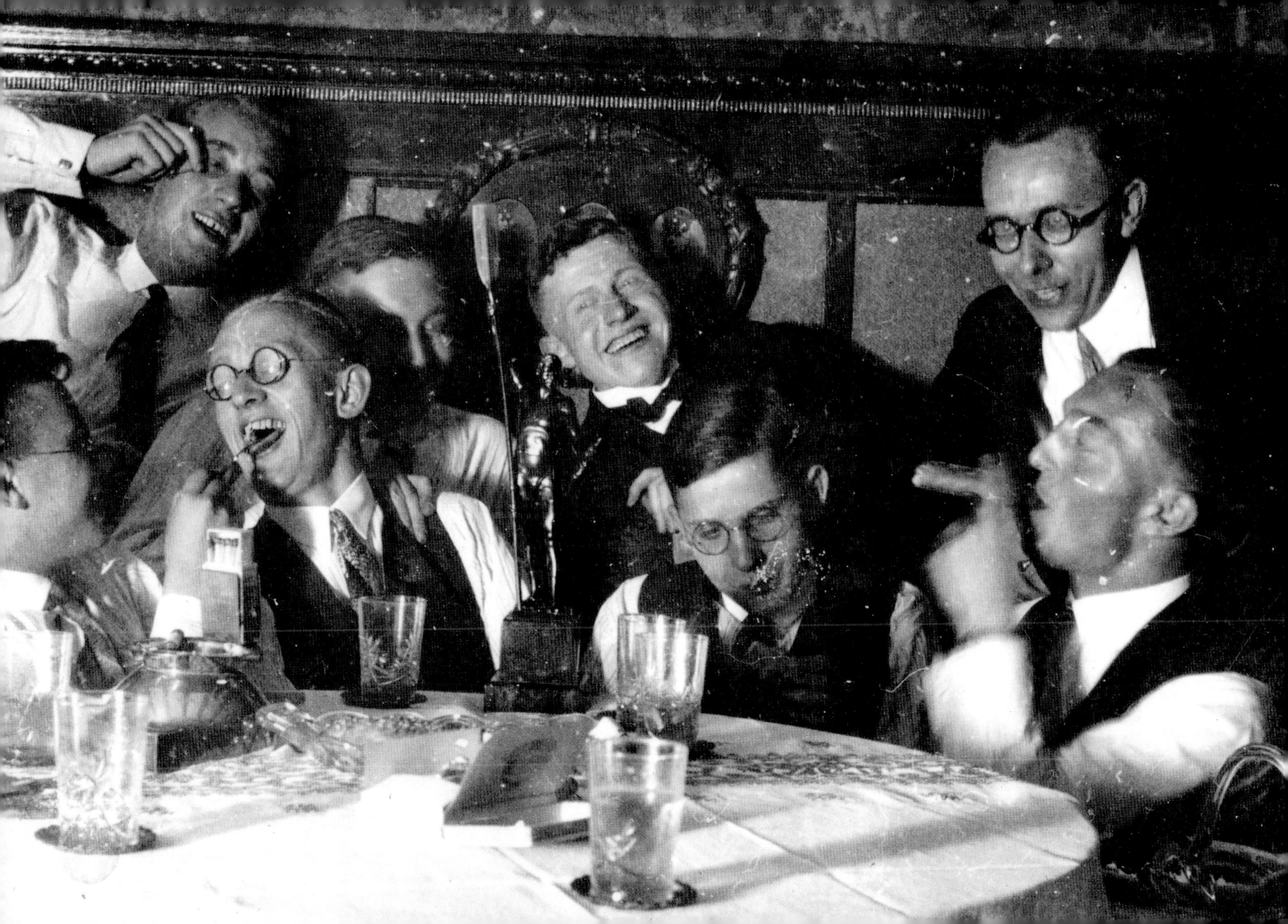

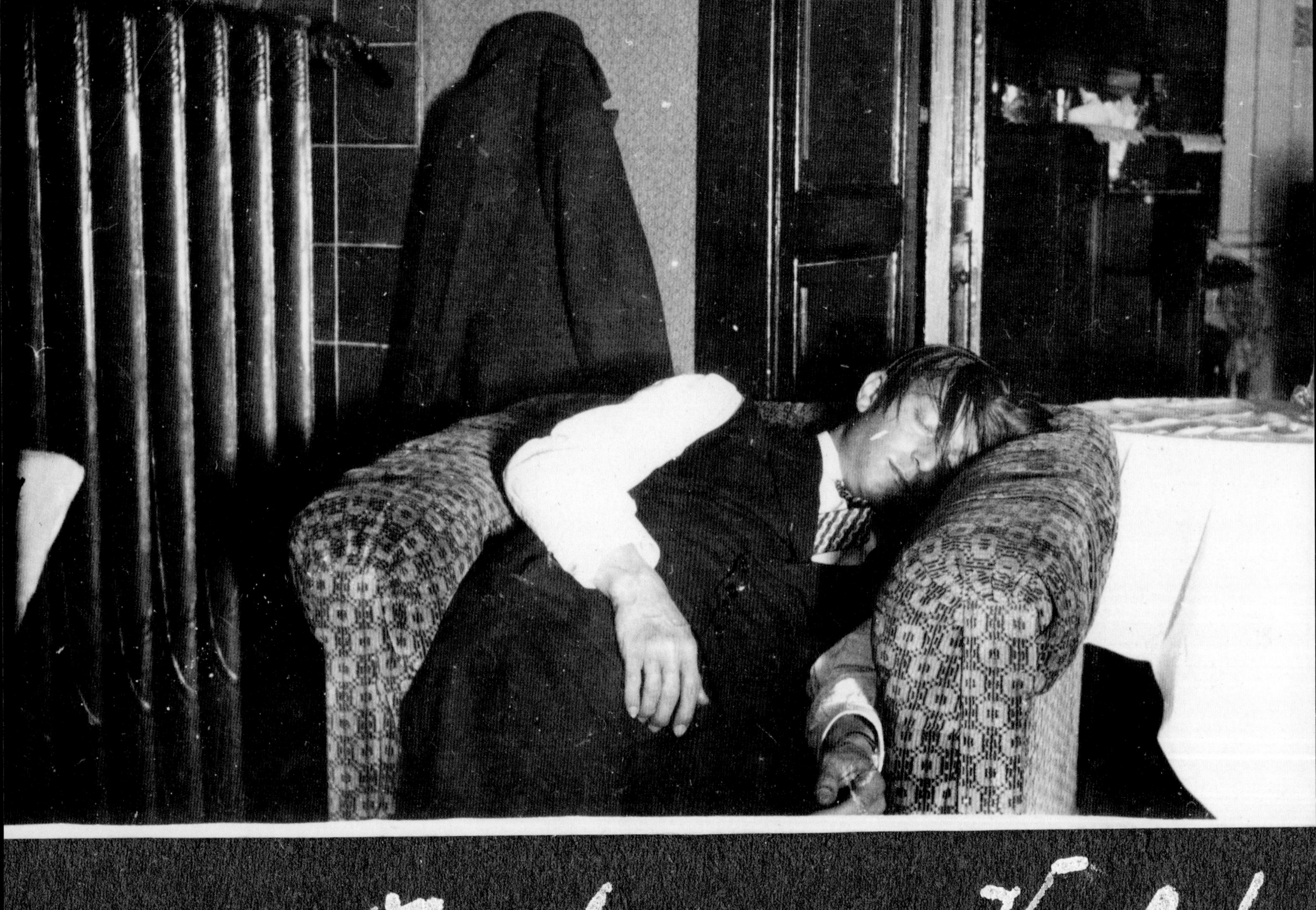

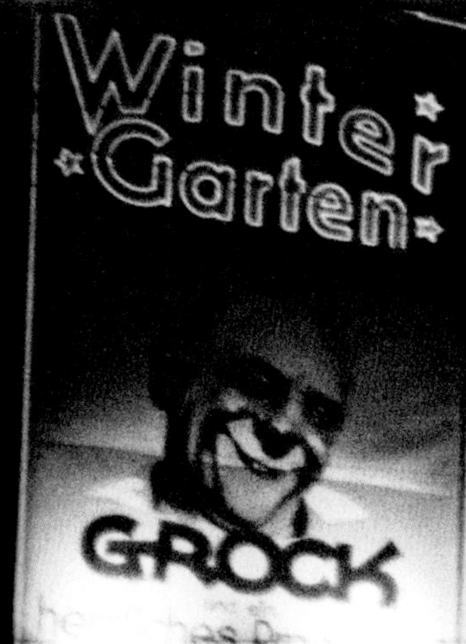
Winter Garten
GROCK
RGARTEN
CAFE WINTERGARTEN
CAFE
WINTERGARTEN

Berlin after dark

1931

In the winter of 1931, a British expatriate with a Leica camera made a personal survey of Berlin's bars and clubs. His night-time perambulations took him all over the city, from opulent modern 'palaces' to underground fringe clubs. The resulting chronicle of Berlin's nightlife indicates his equal fascination with the pneumatic love-letter delivery systems, the glitzy showgirls, and the icy elegance of the *Garçonnes*.

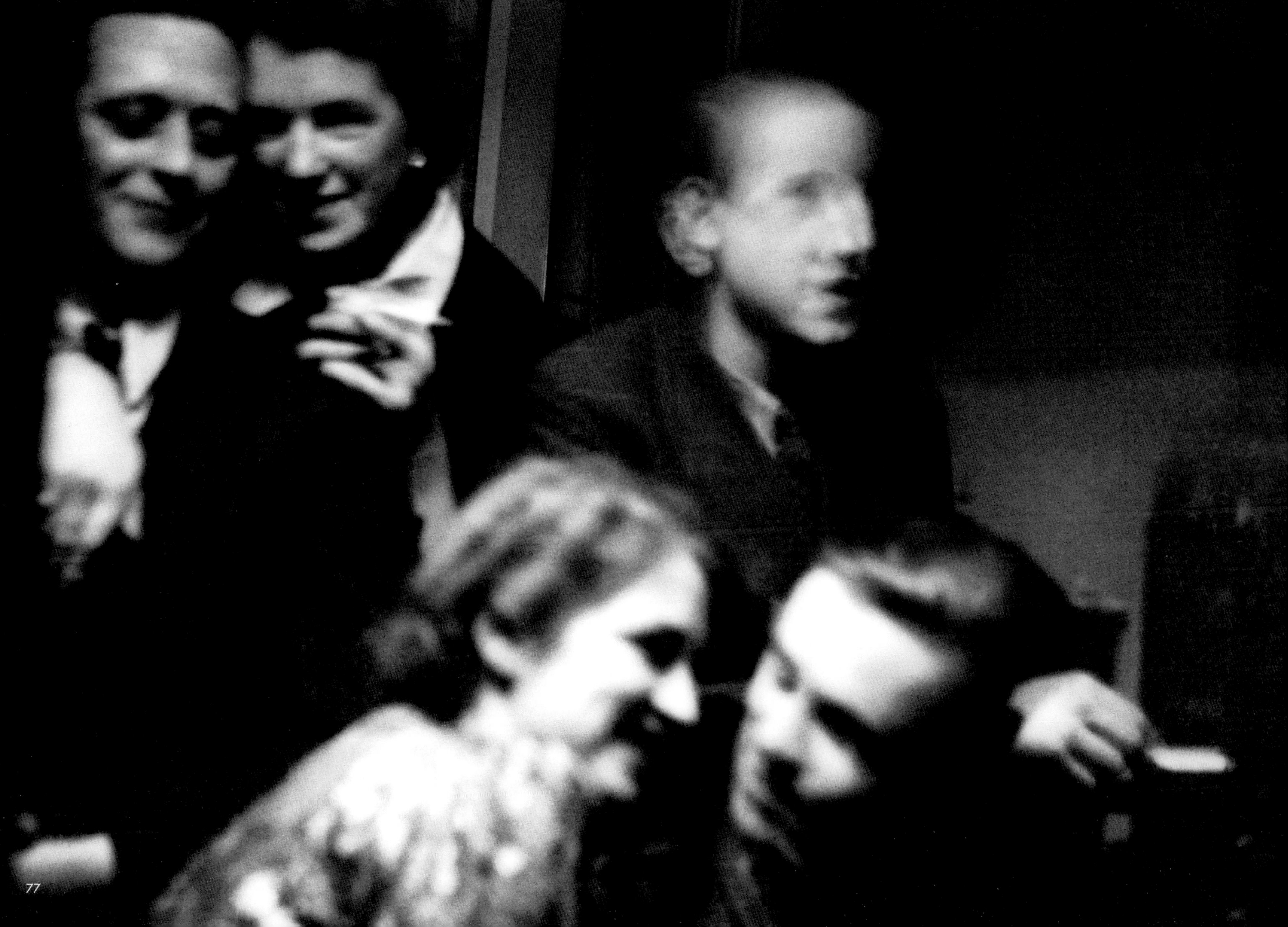

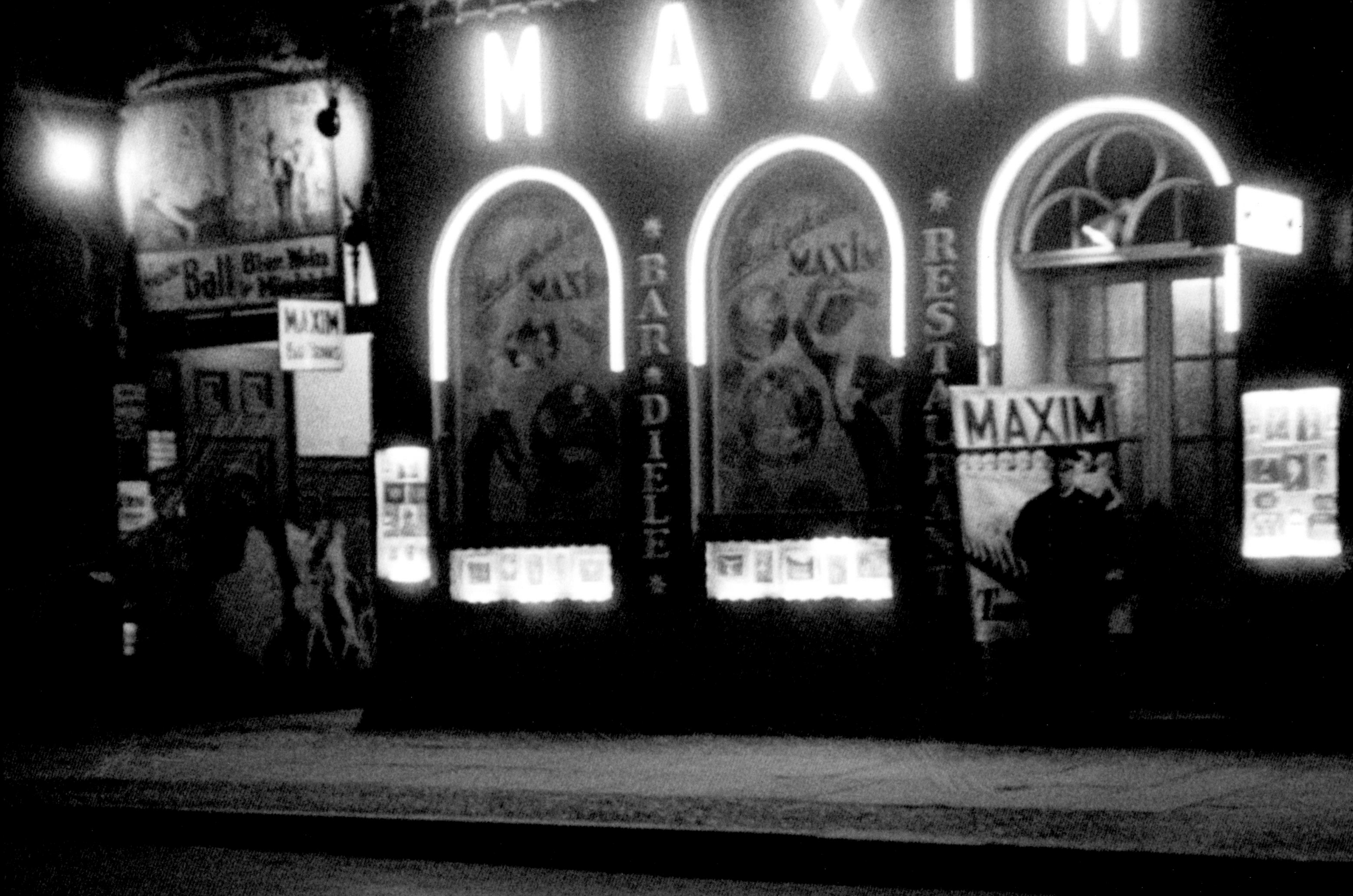

Maxim's, Mitte

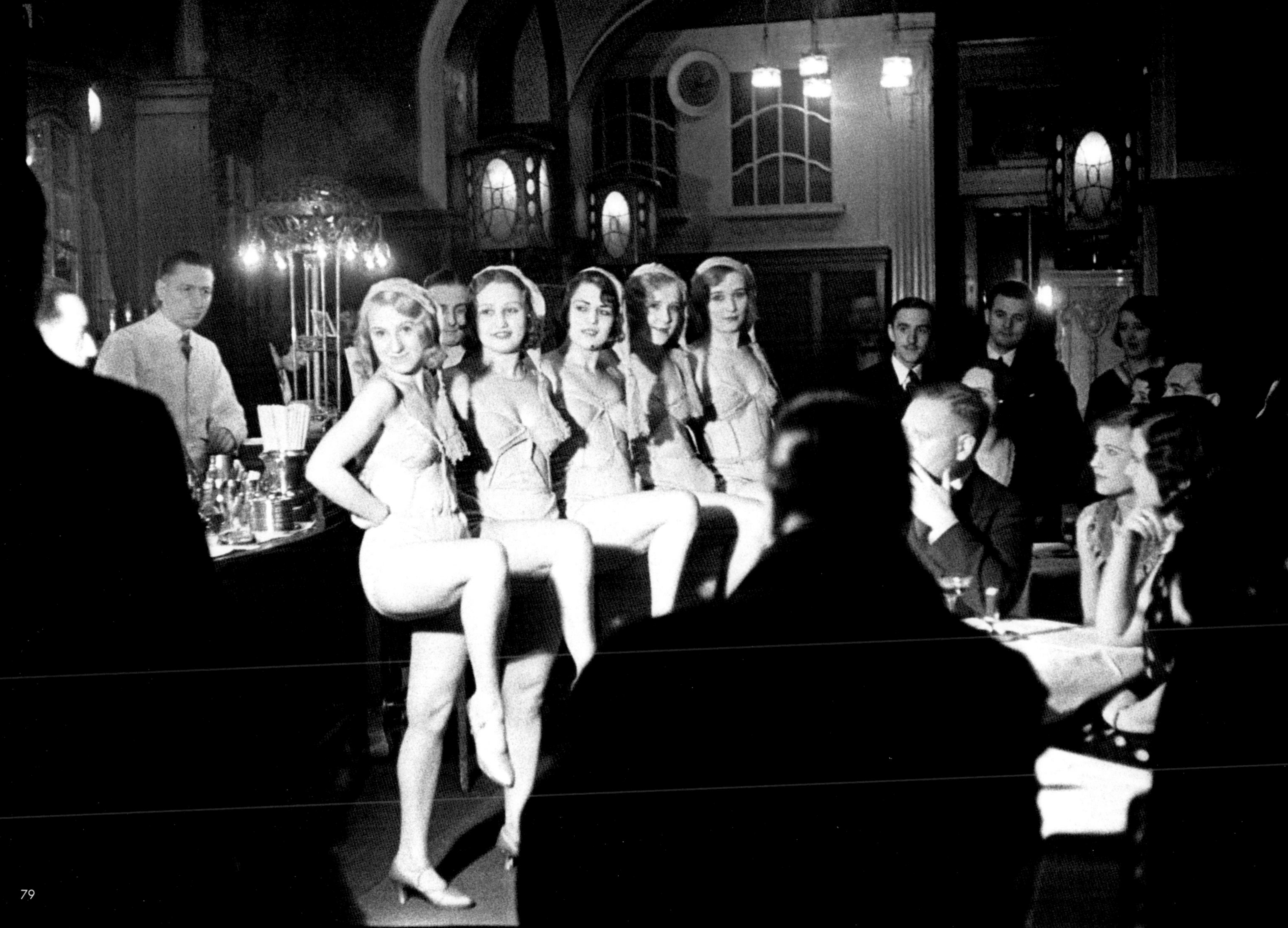

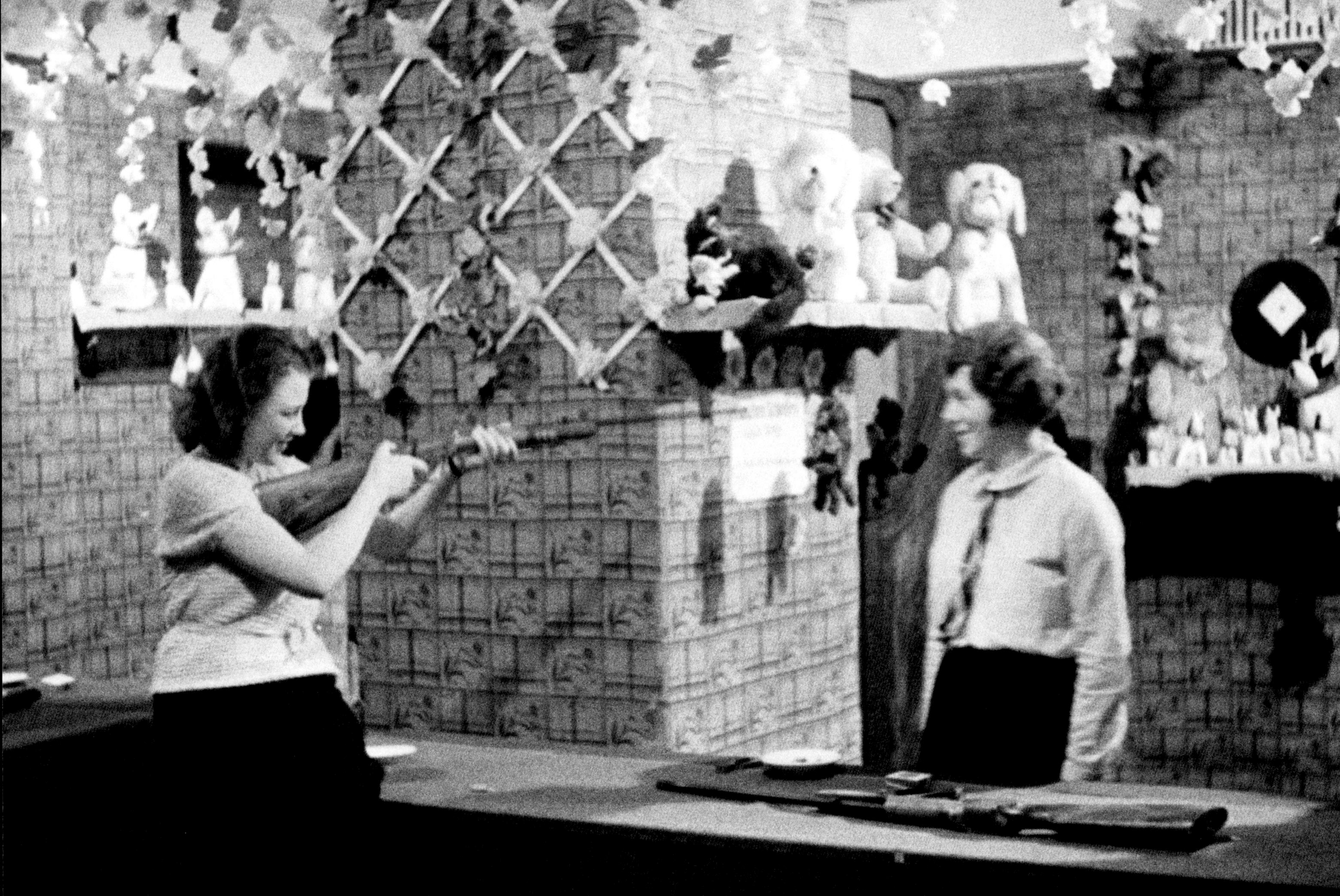

The Alexander-Palast, Alexanderplatz

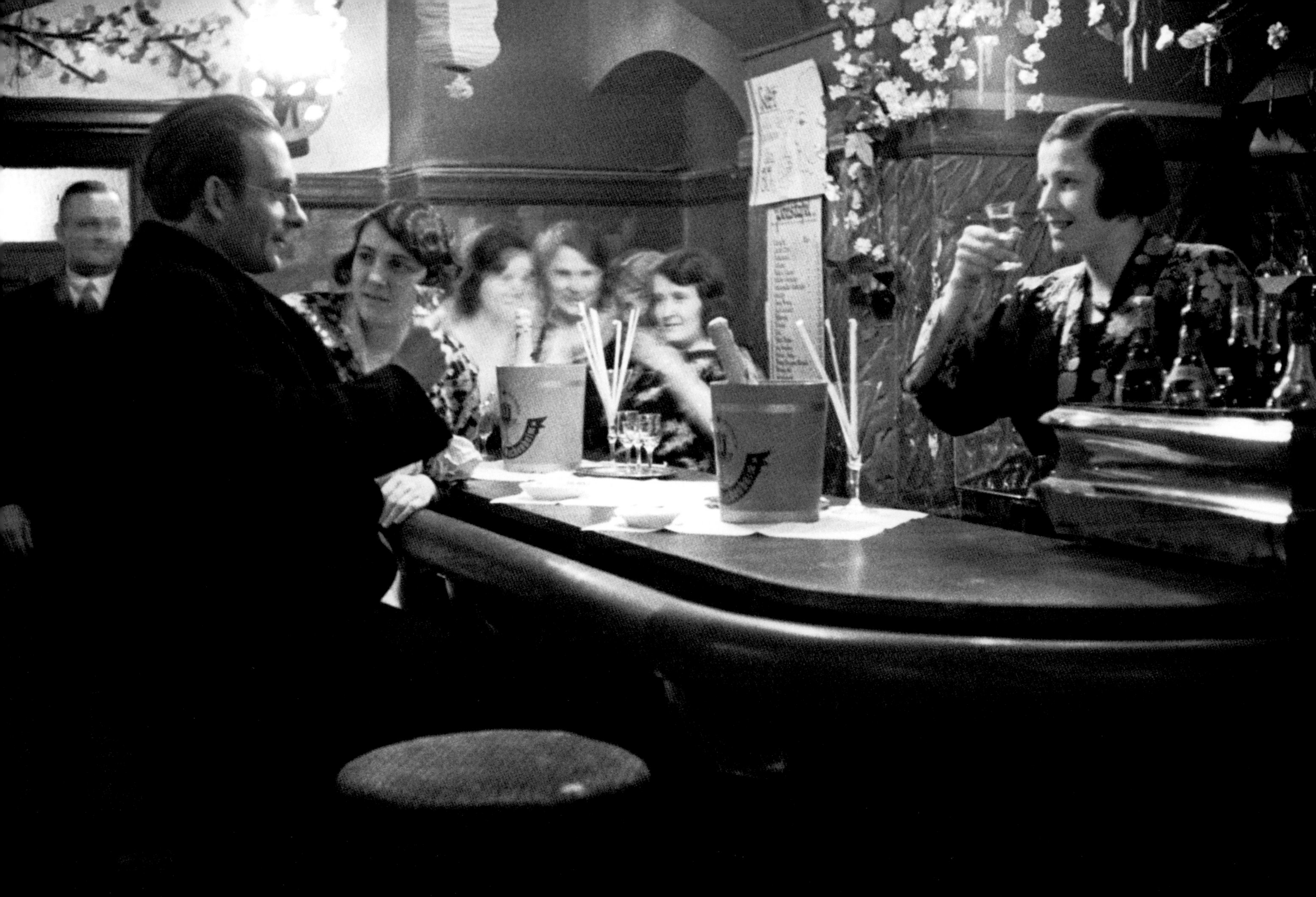

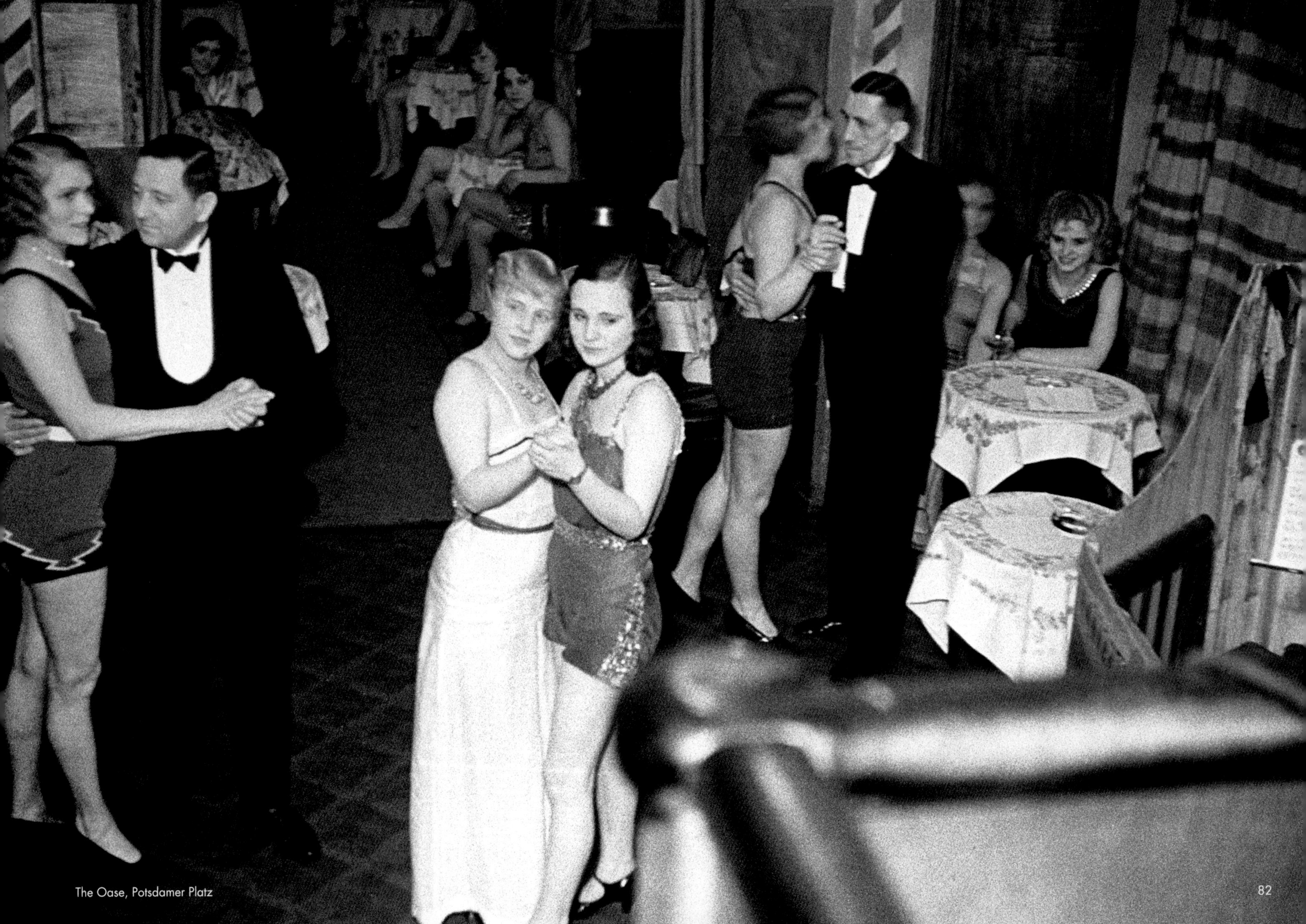
The Oase, Potsdamer Platz

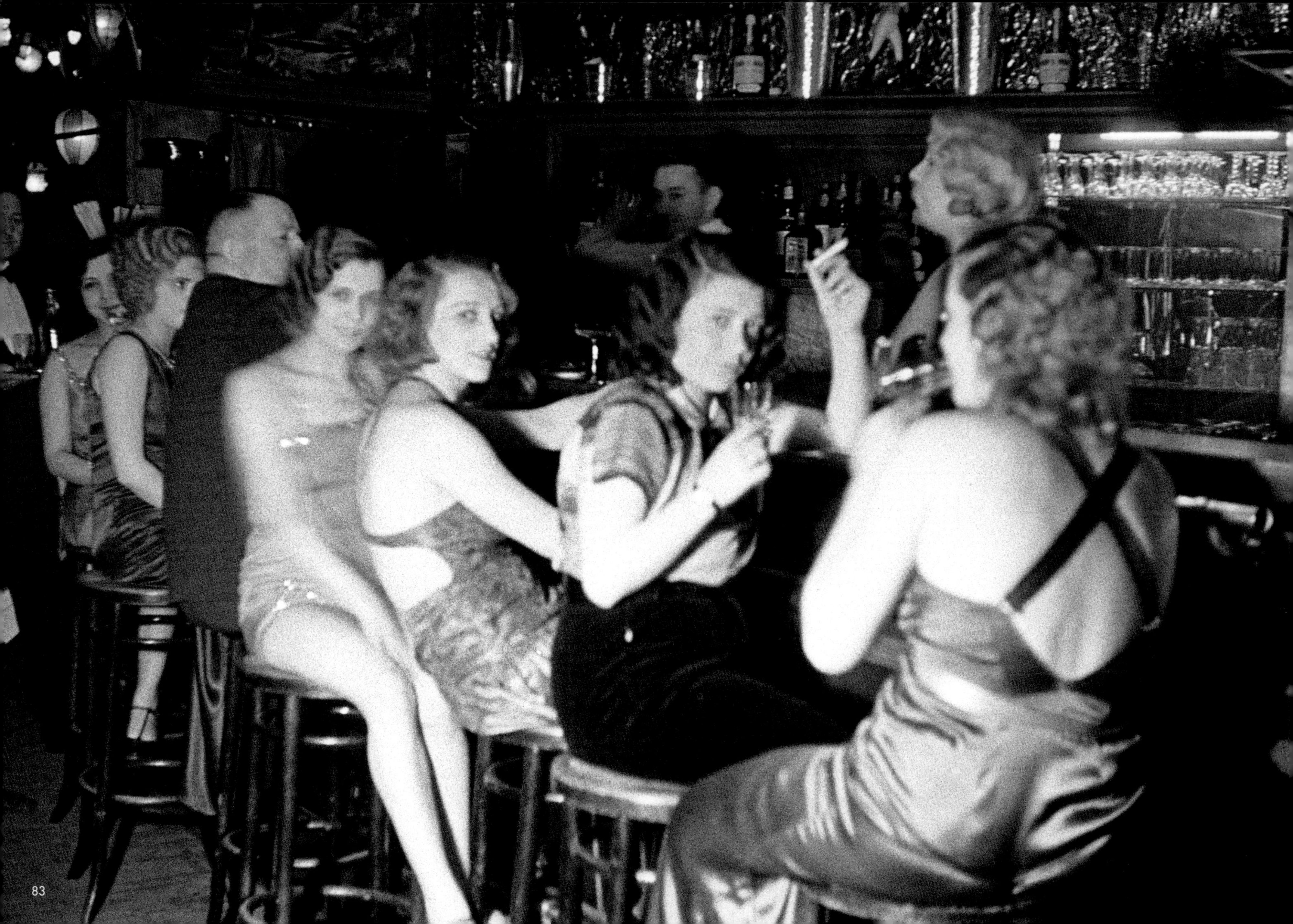

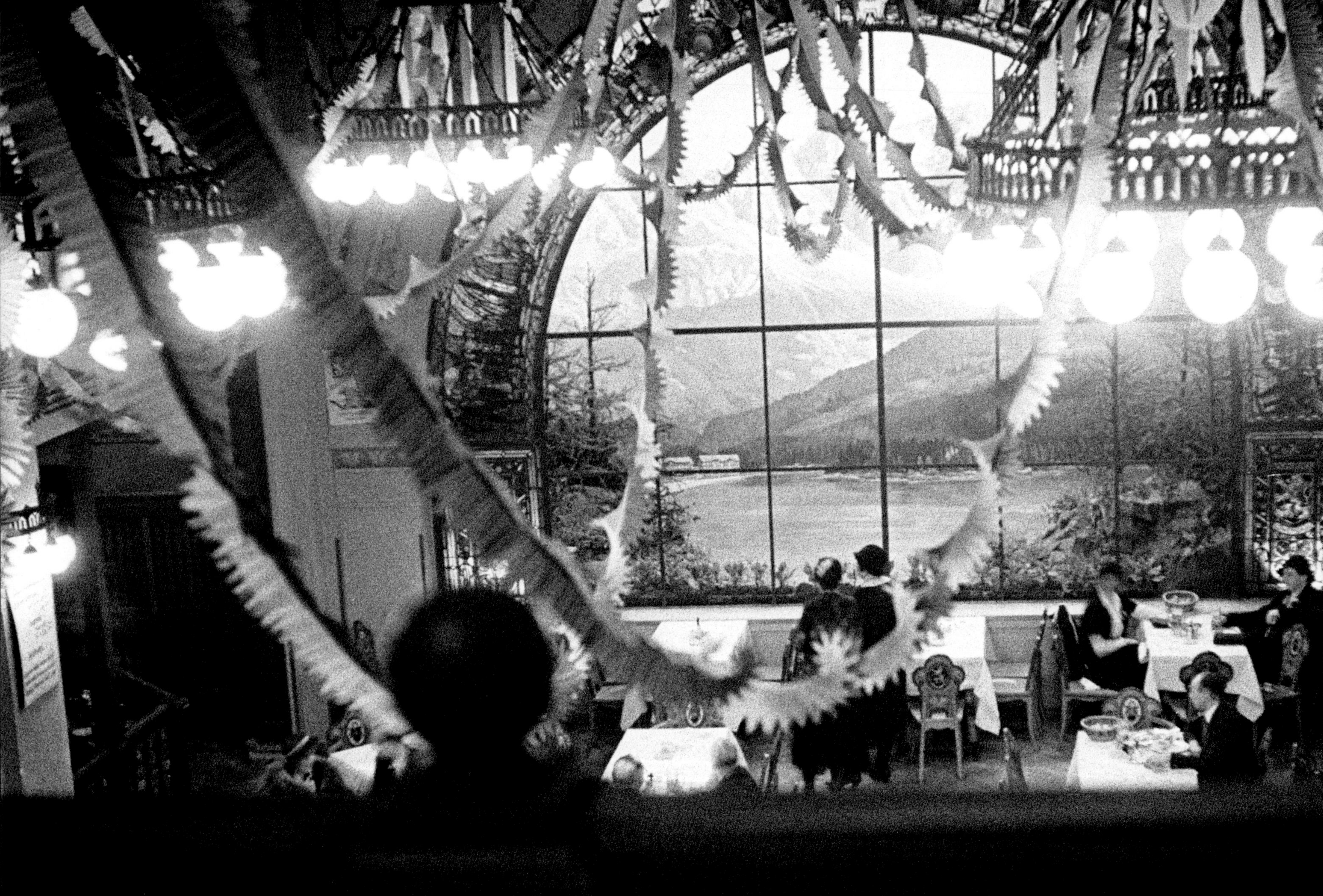

Haus Vaterland, Potzdamer Platz

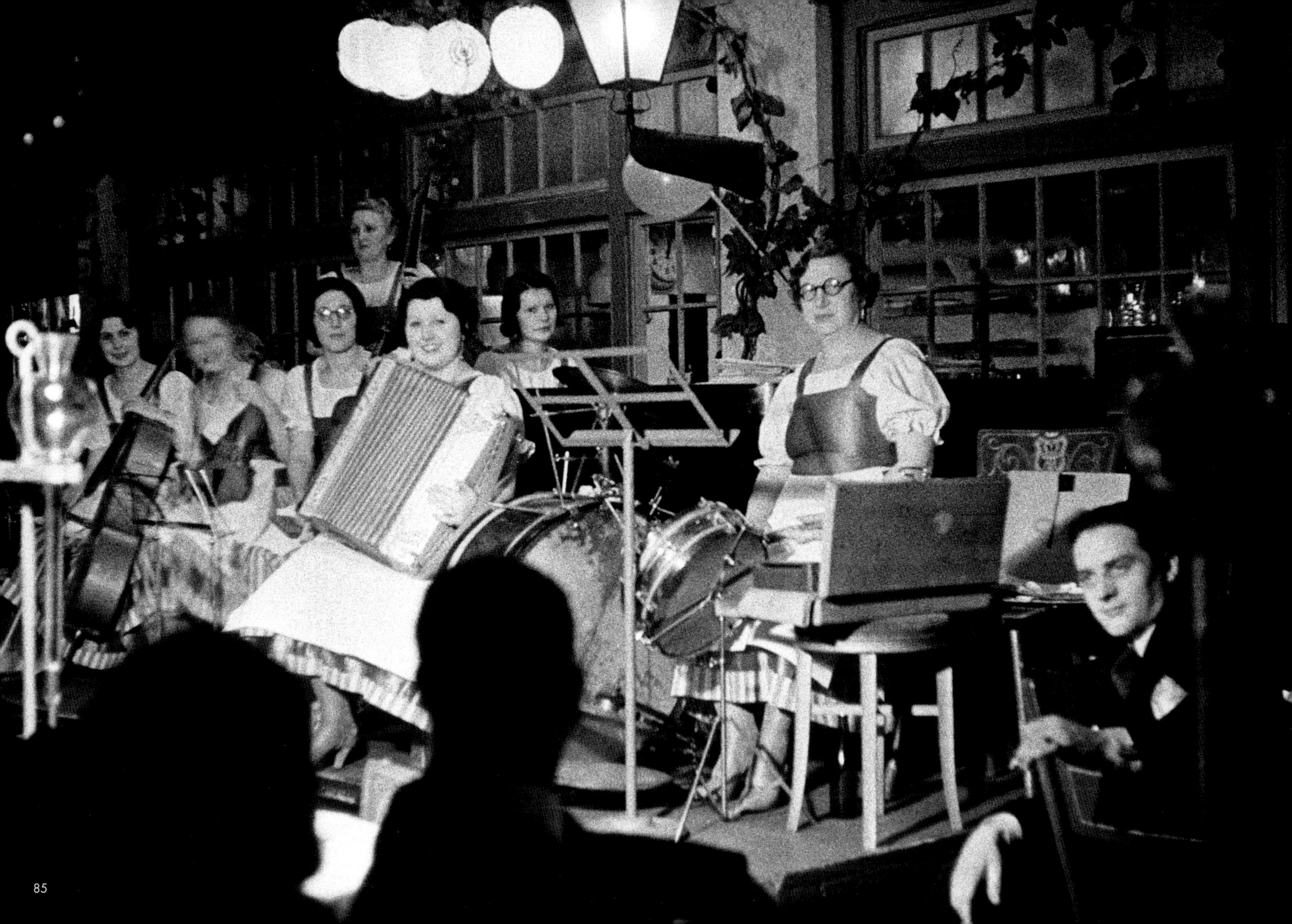

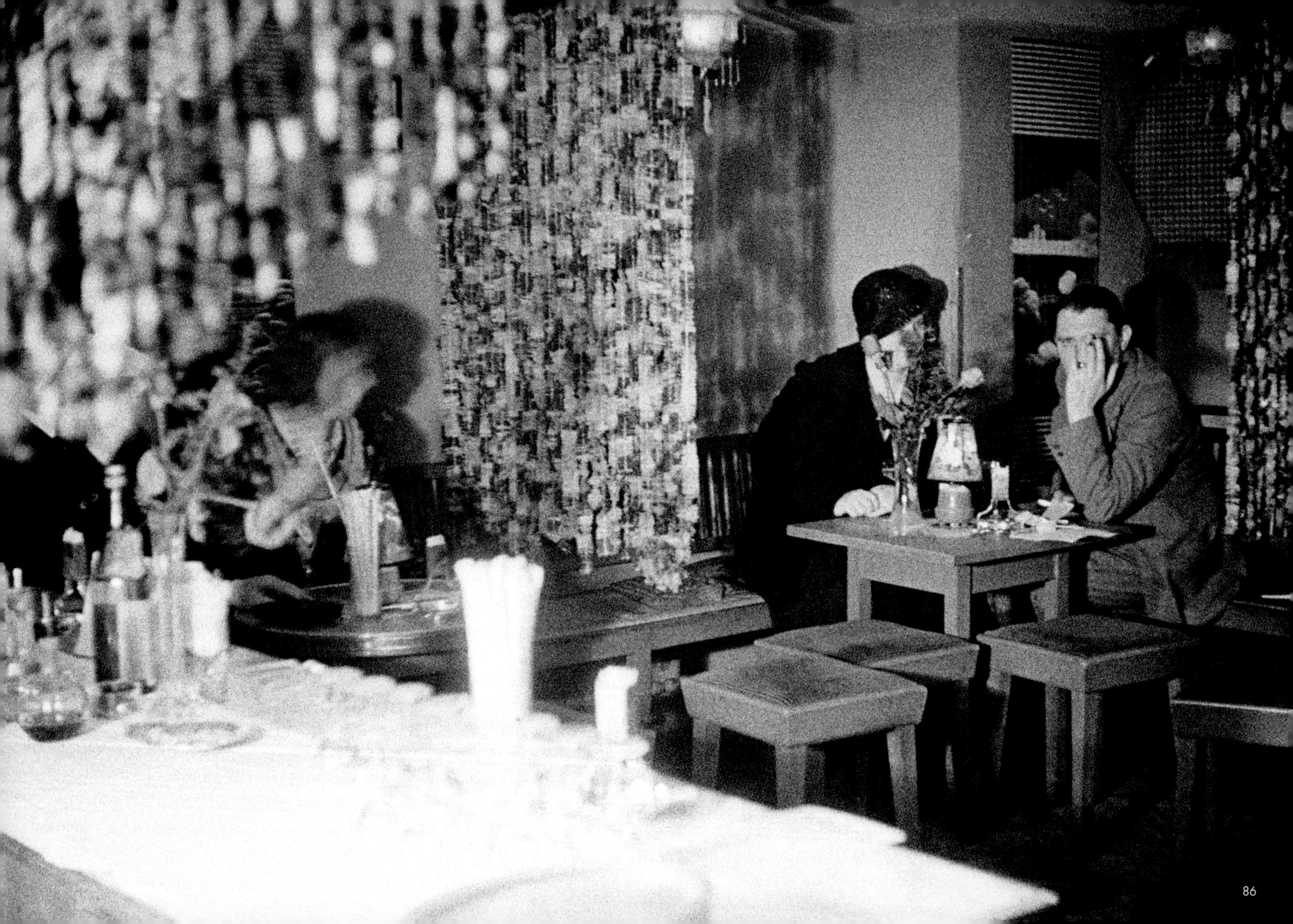

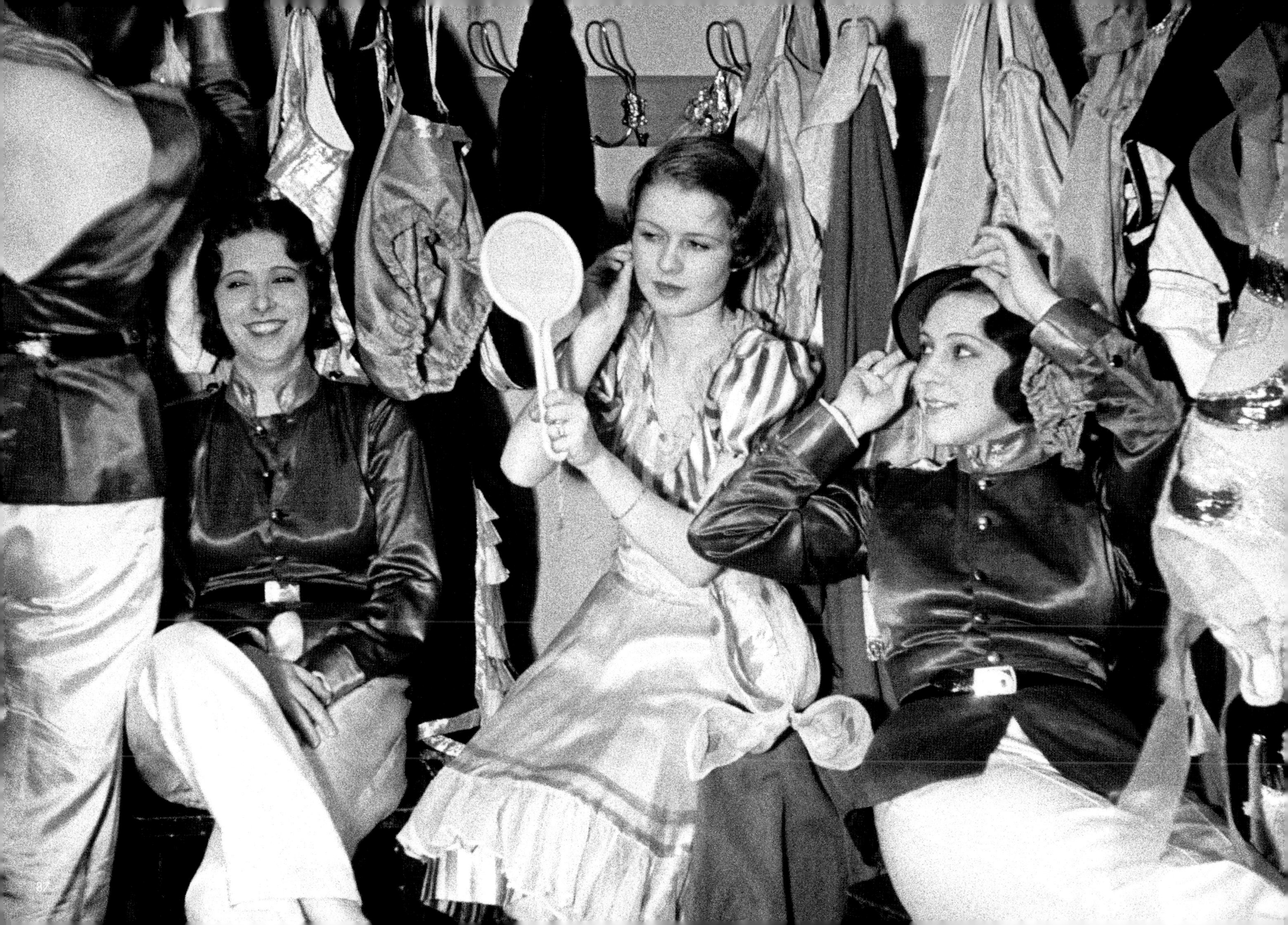

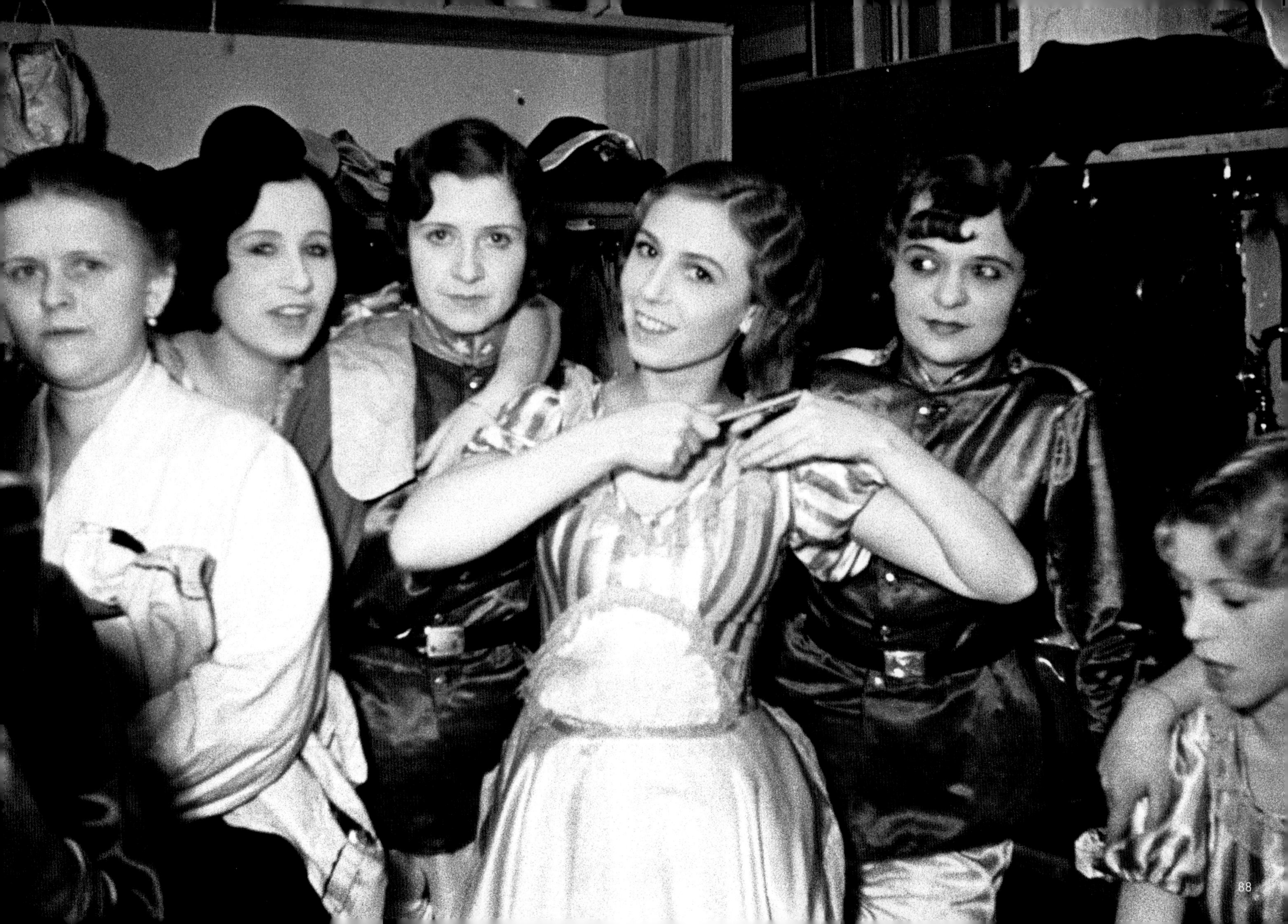

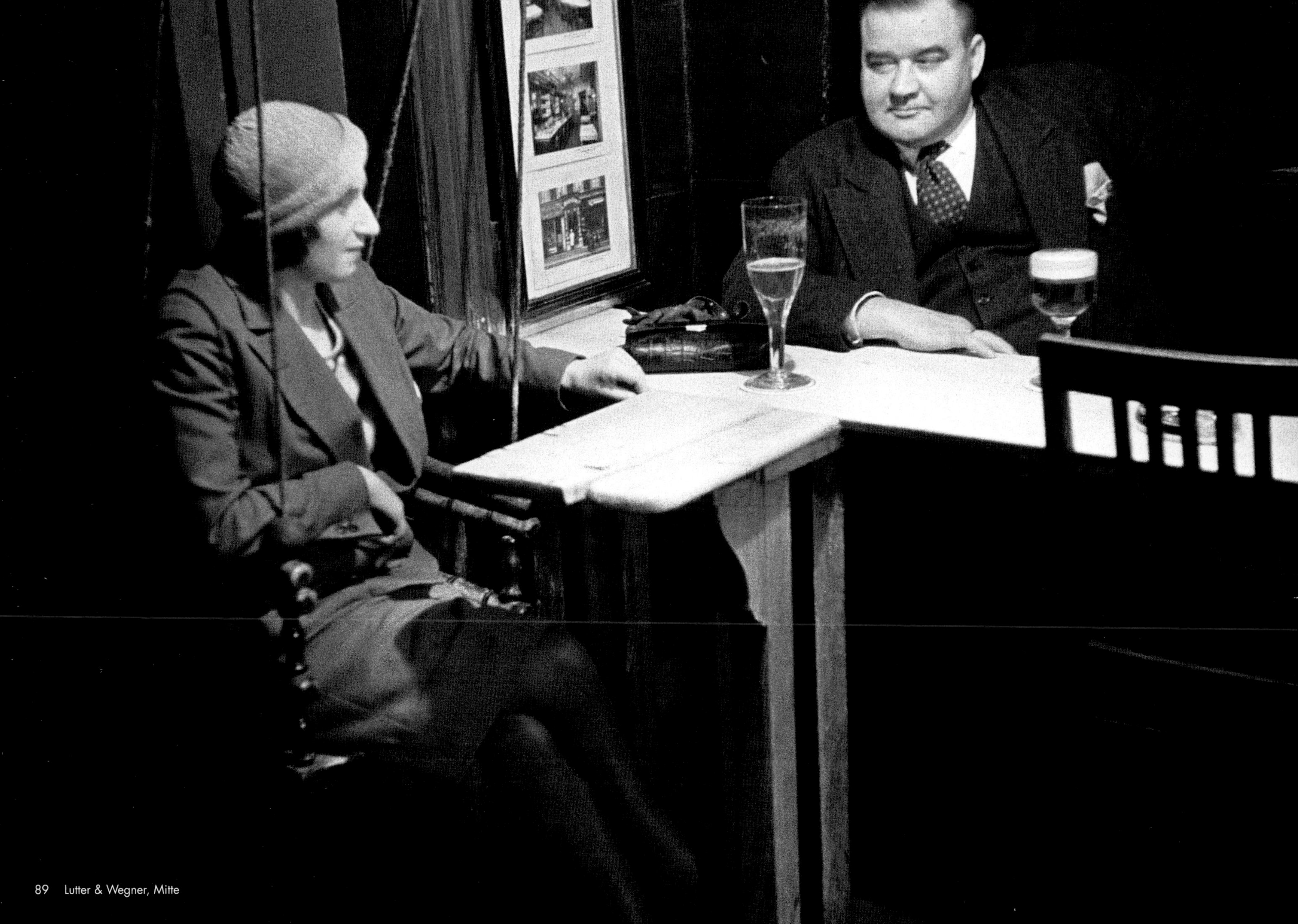

89 Lutter & Wegner, Mitte

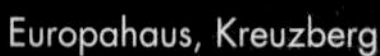

Europahaus, Kreuzberg

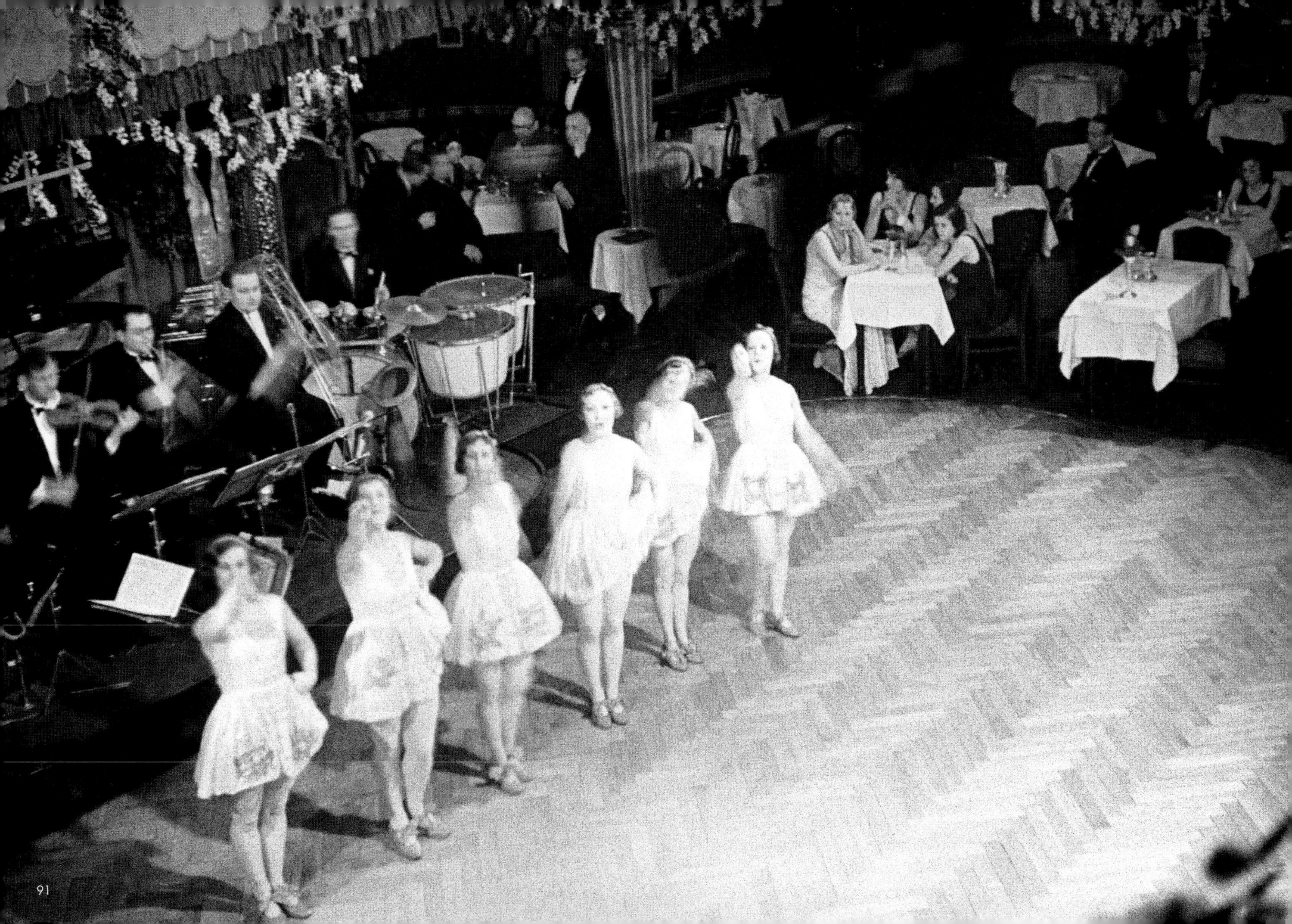

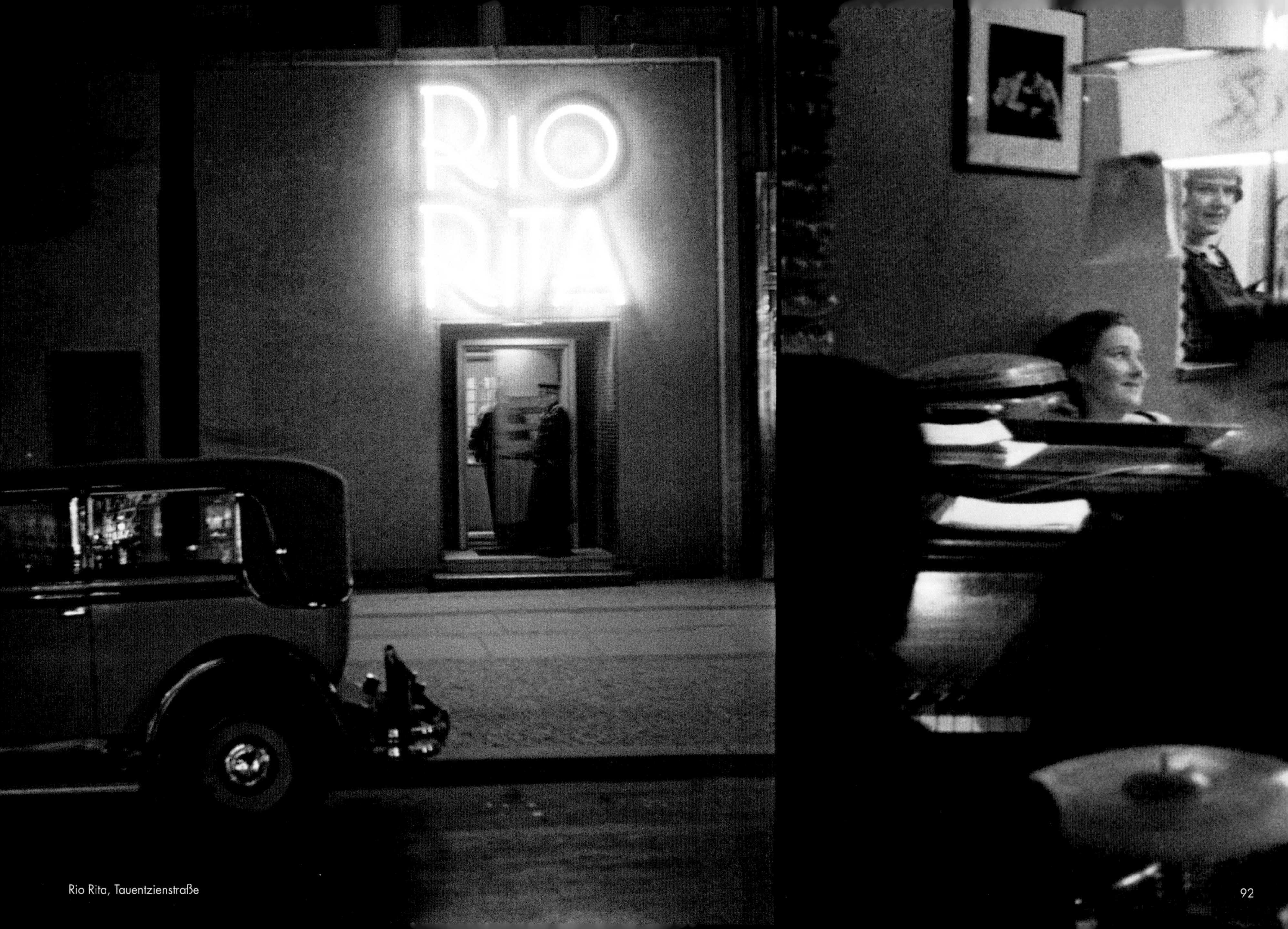

Rio Rita, Tauentzienstraße

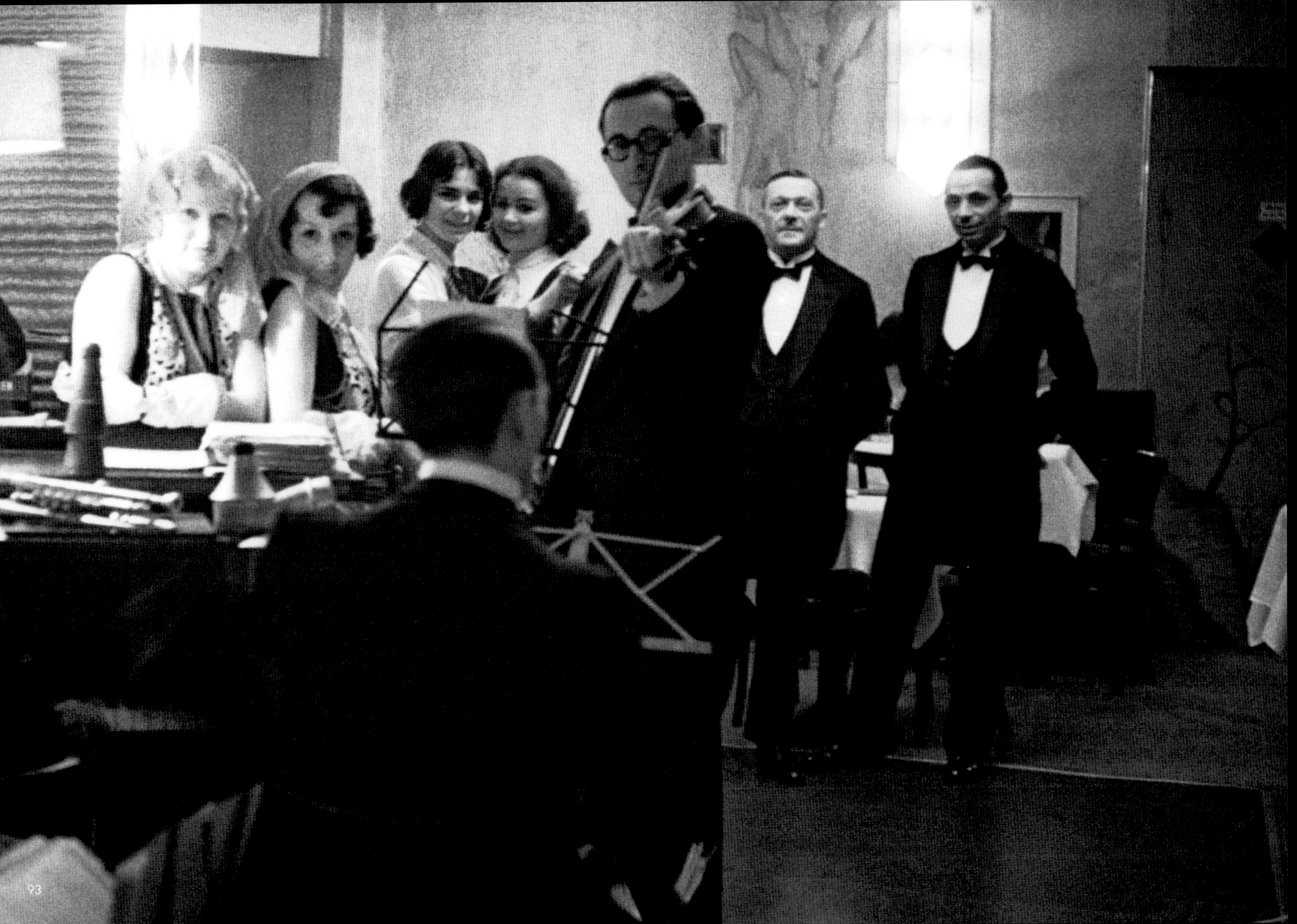

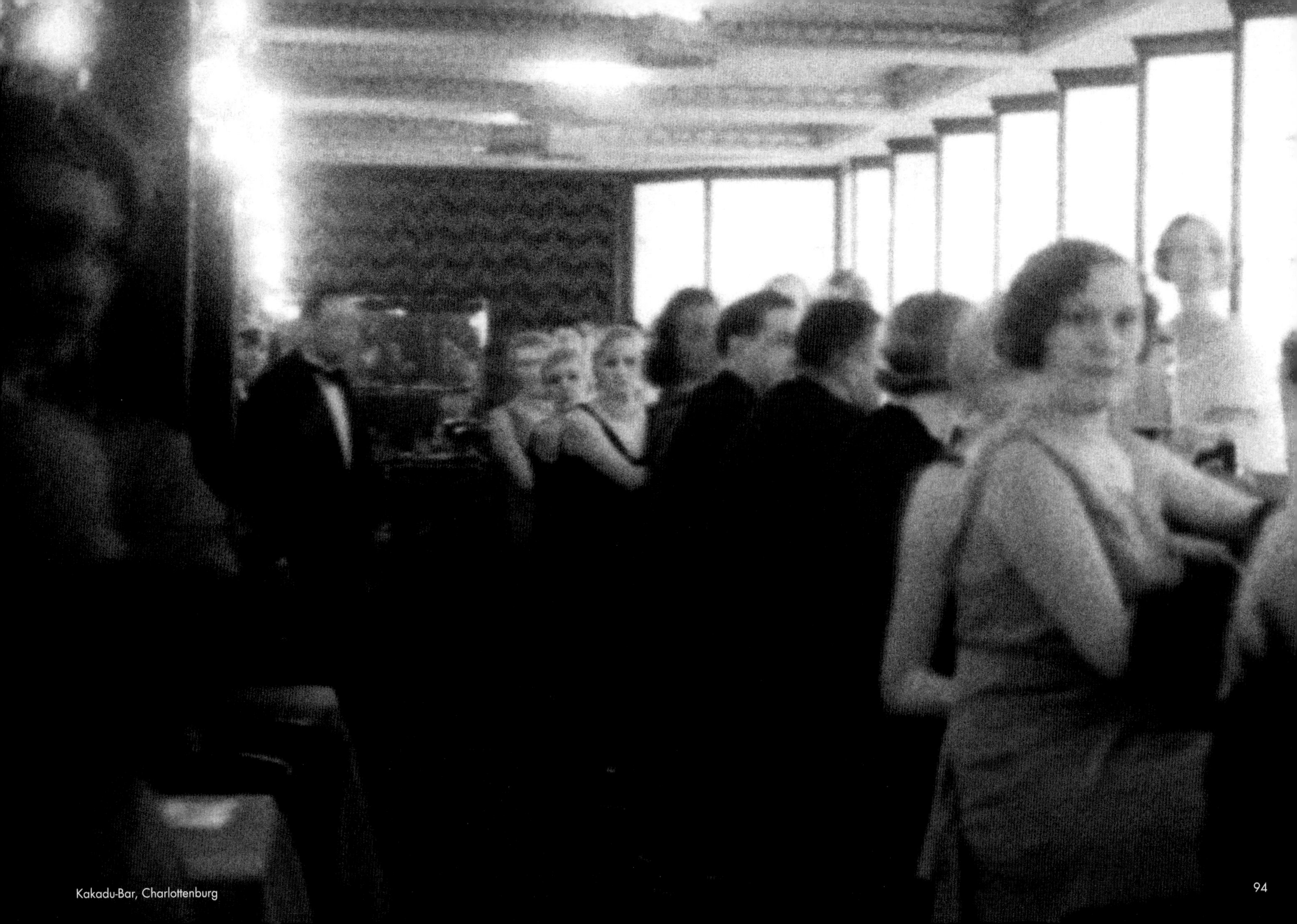

Kakadu-Bar, Charlottenburg

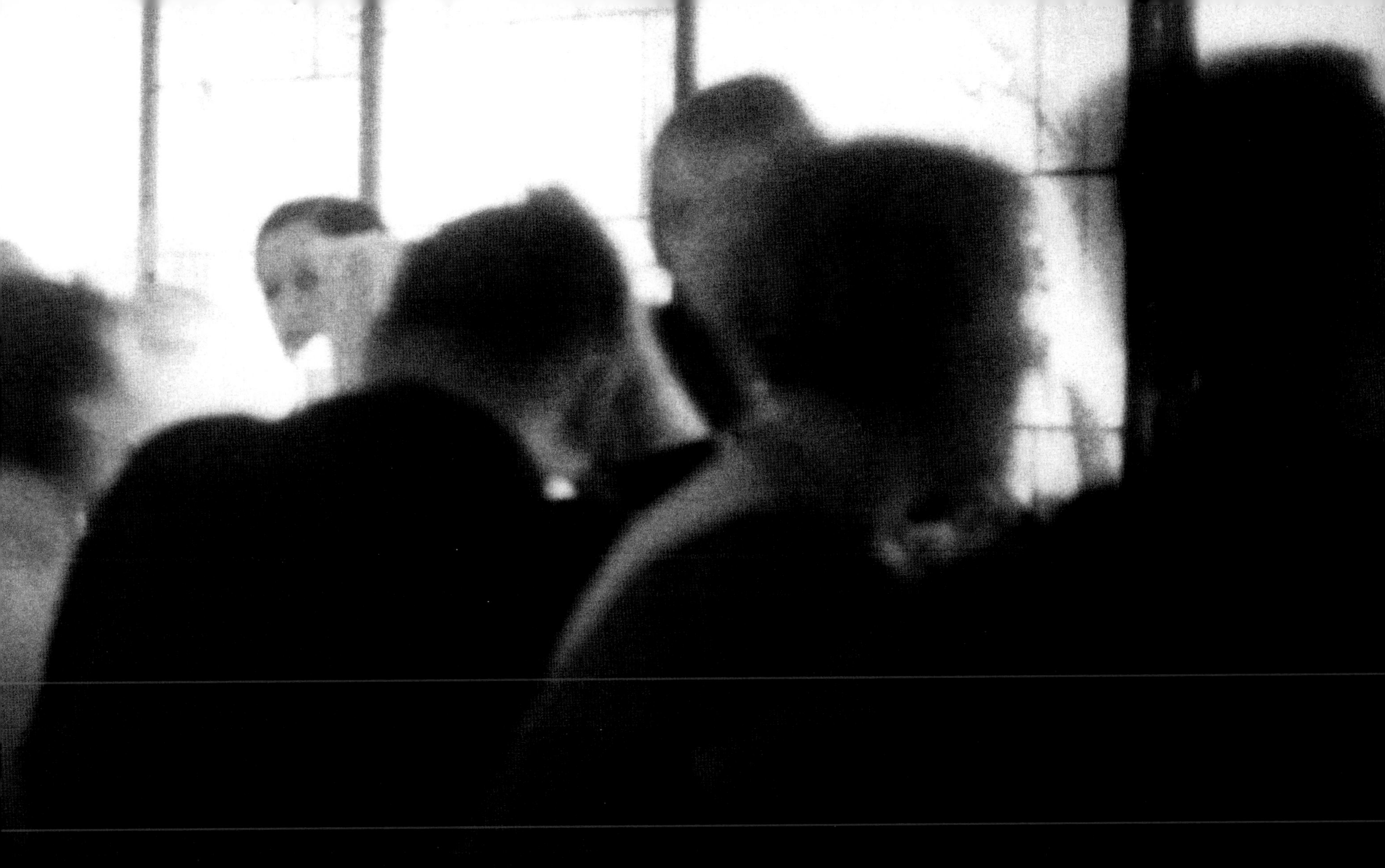

The Femina-Palast, Charlottenburg

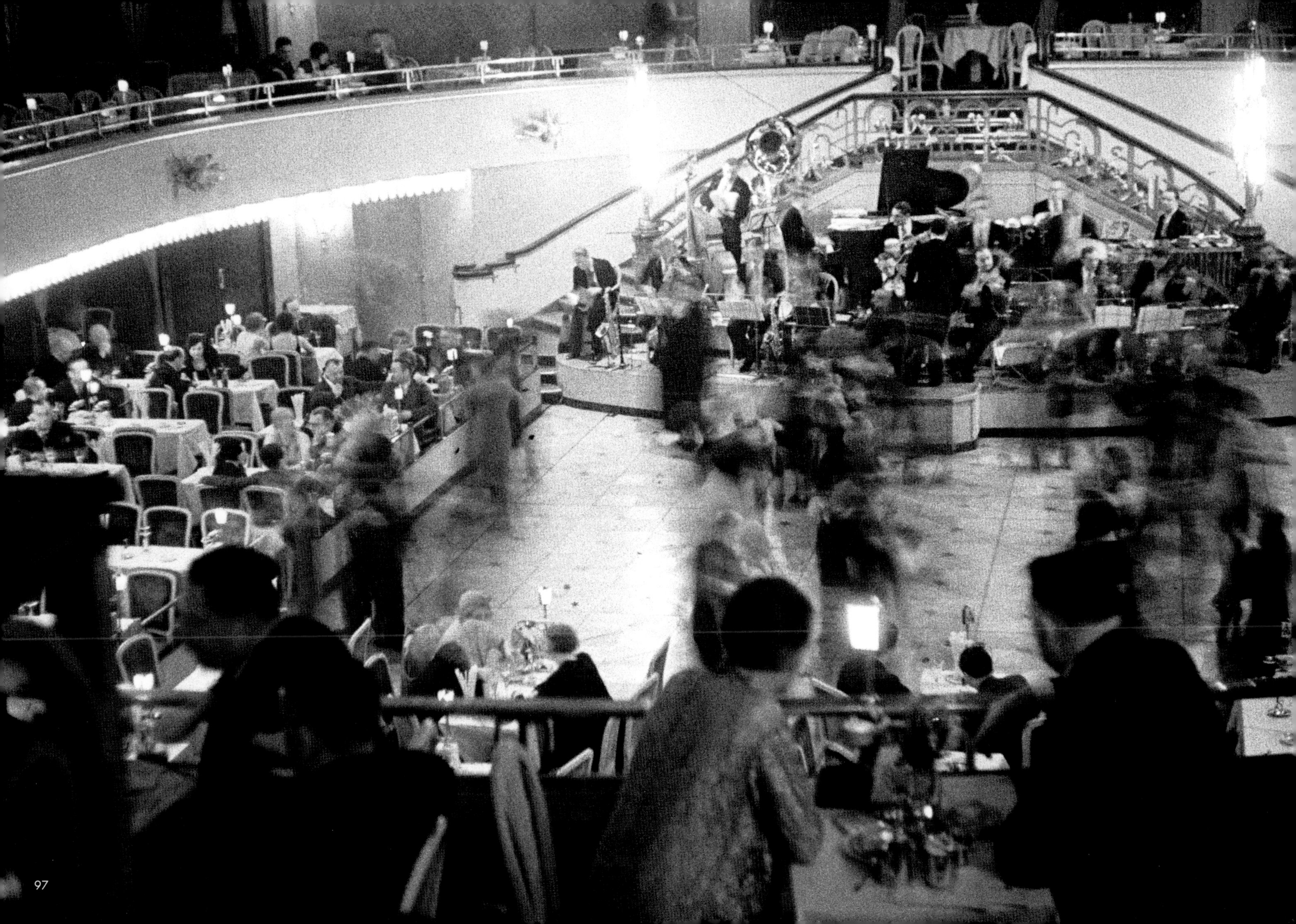

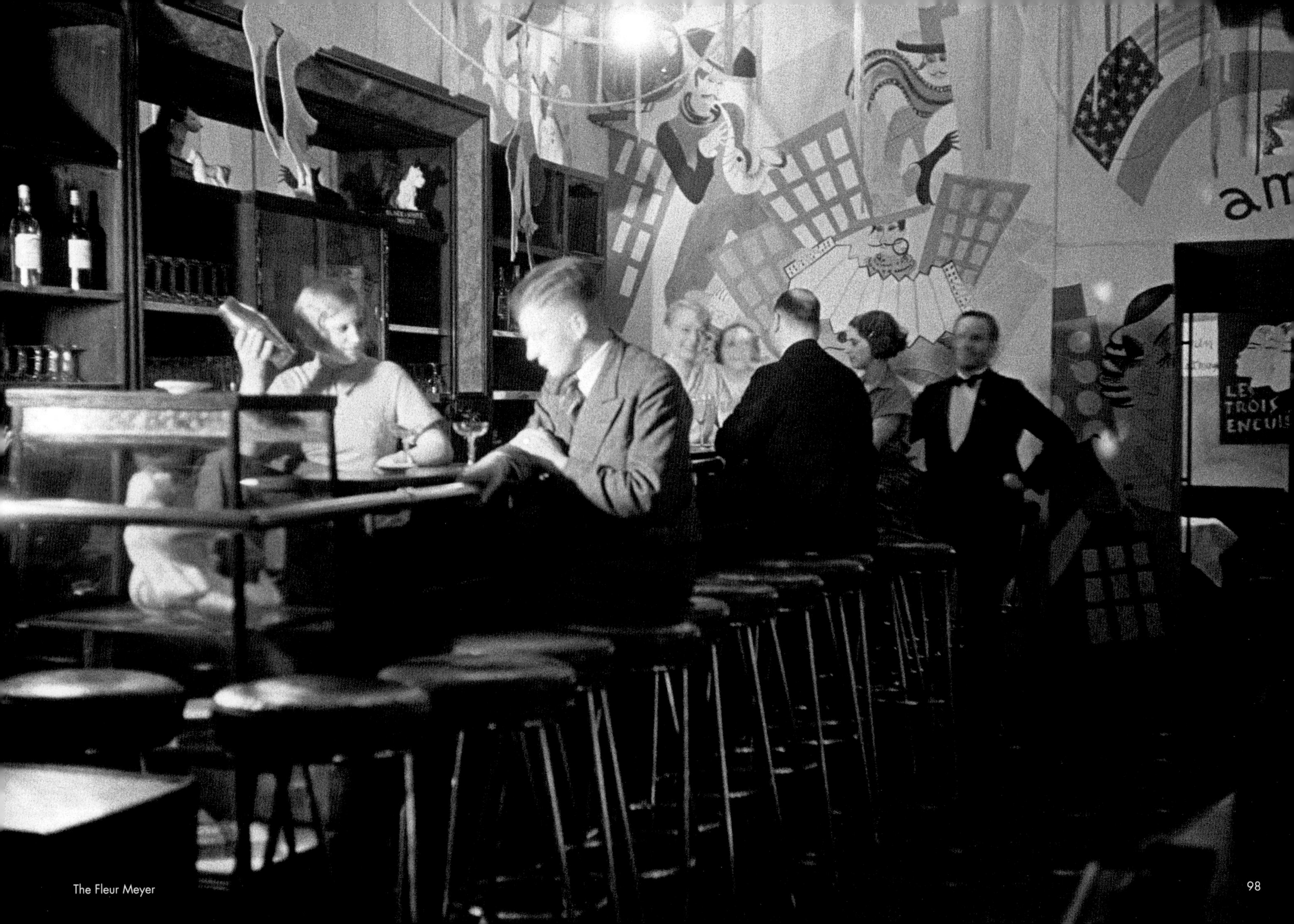
LES
TROIS

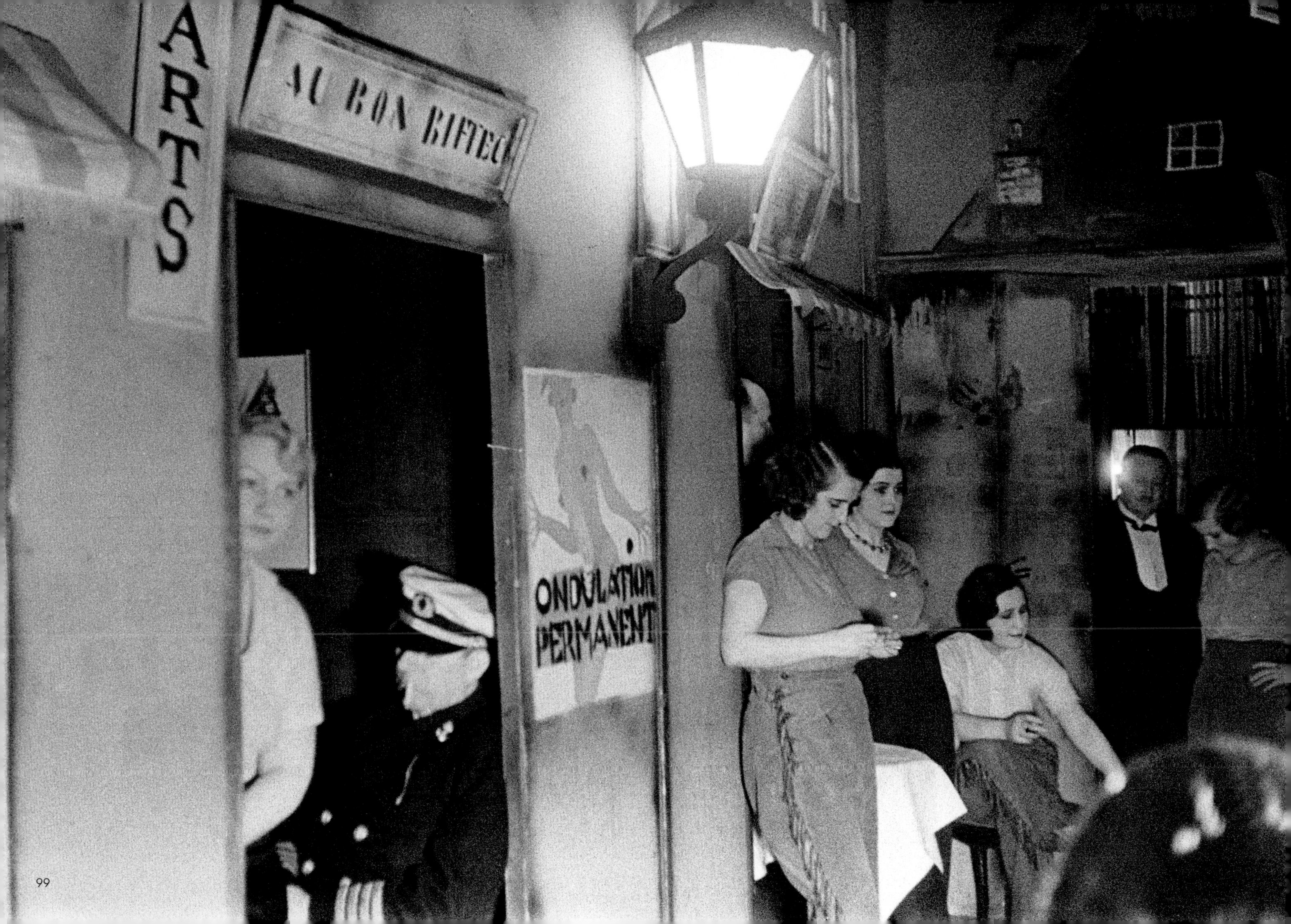
ARTS
AU BON BIFTEC
ONDULATION
PERMANENT

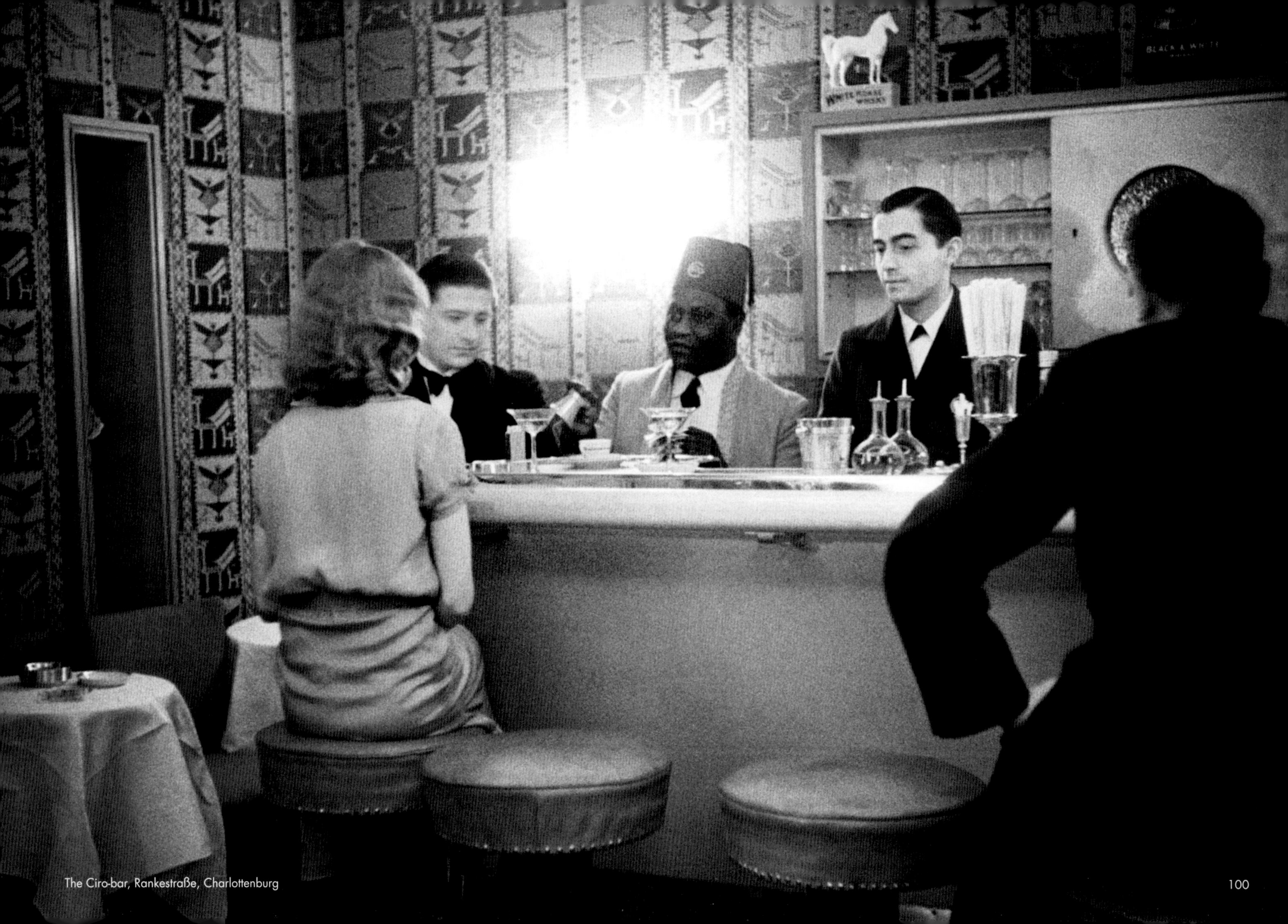

The Ciro-bar, Rankestraße, Charlottenburg

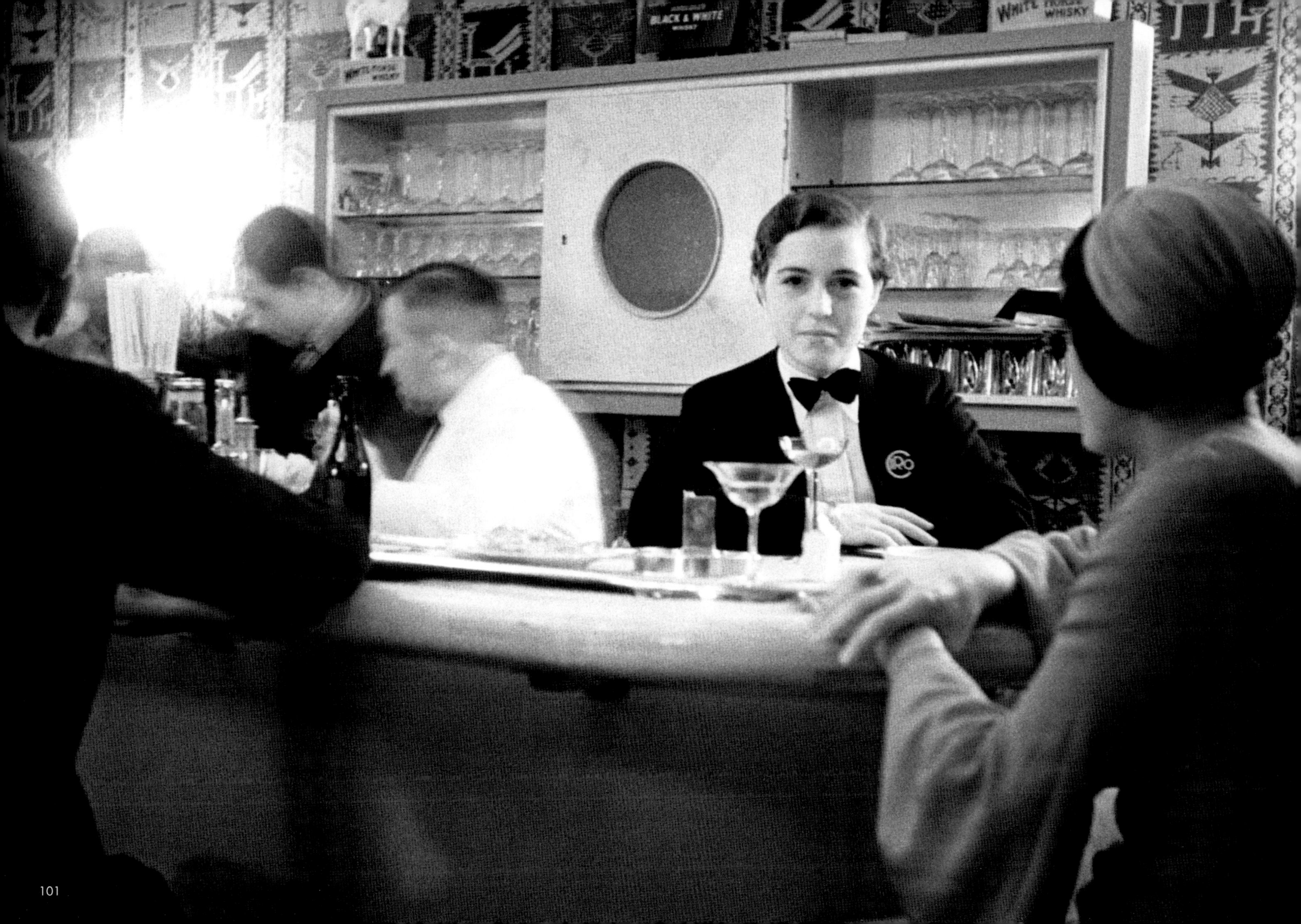
BLACK & WHITE
WHITE
WHISKY

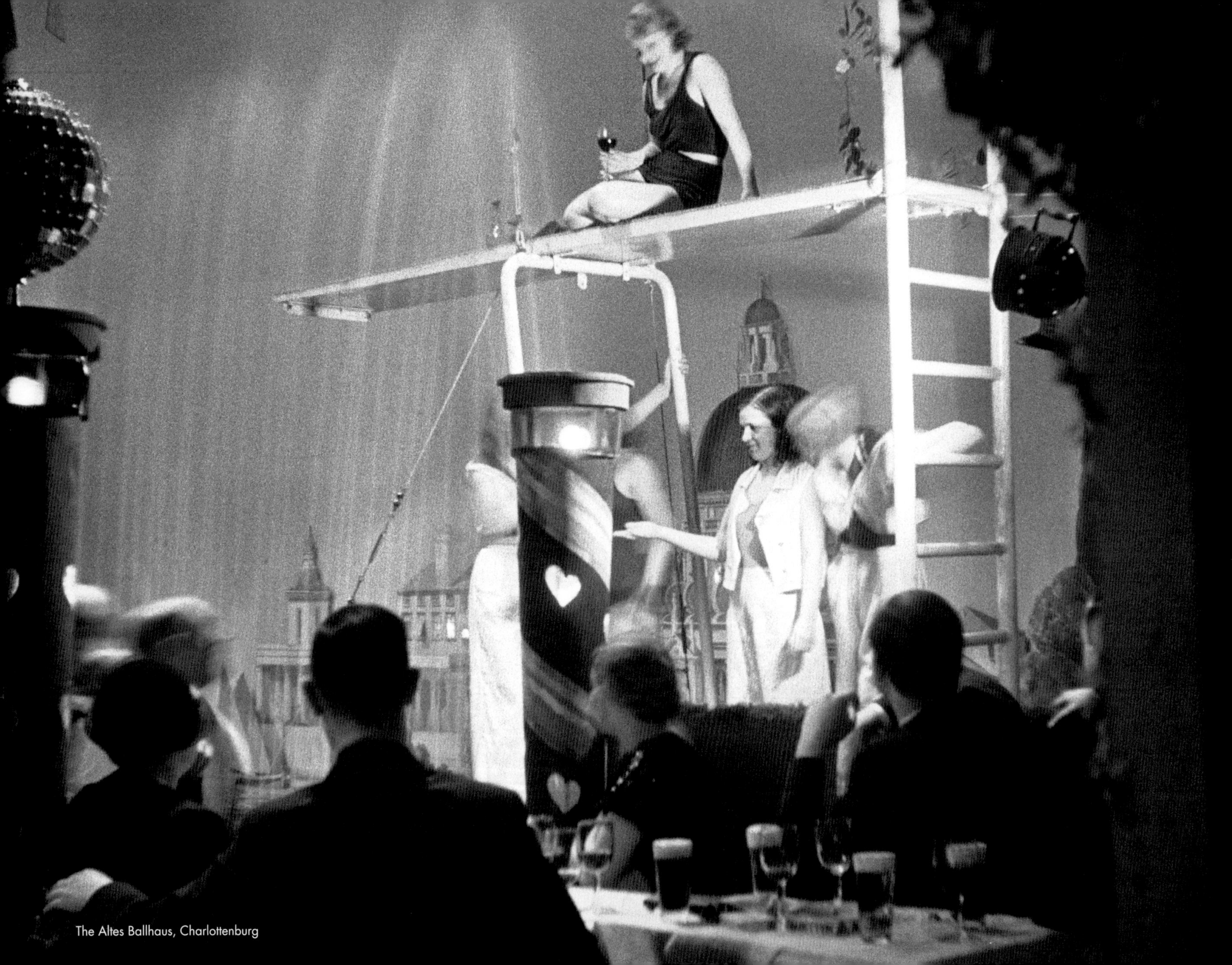

The Altes Ballhaus, Charlottenburg

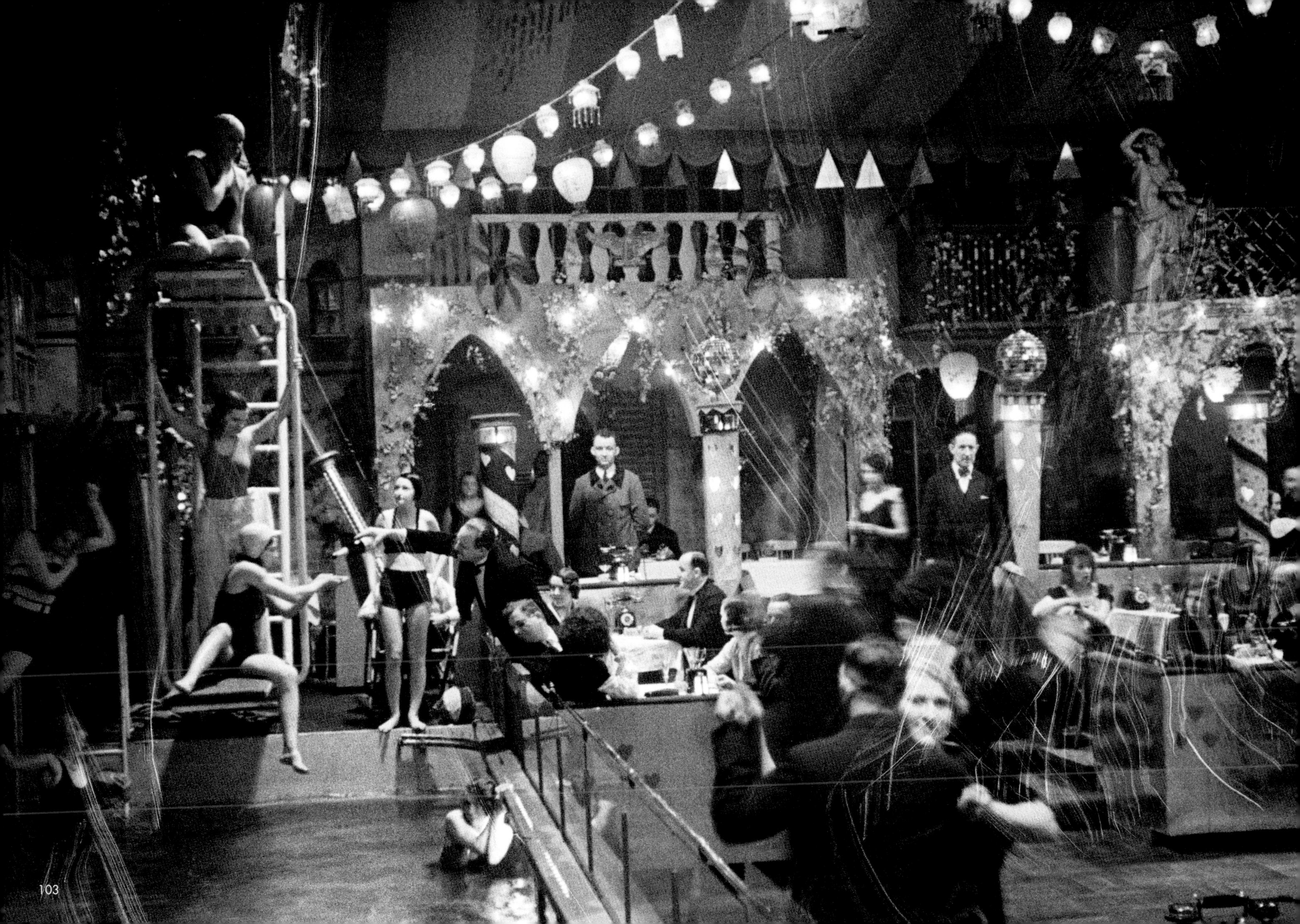

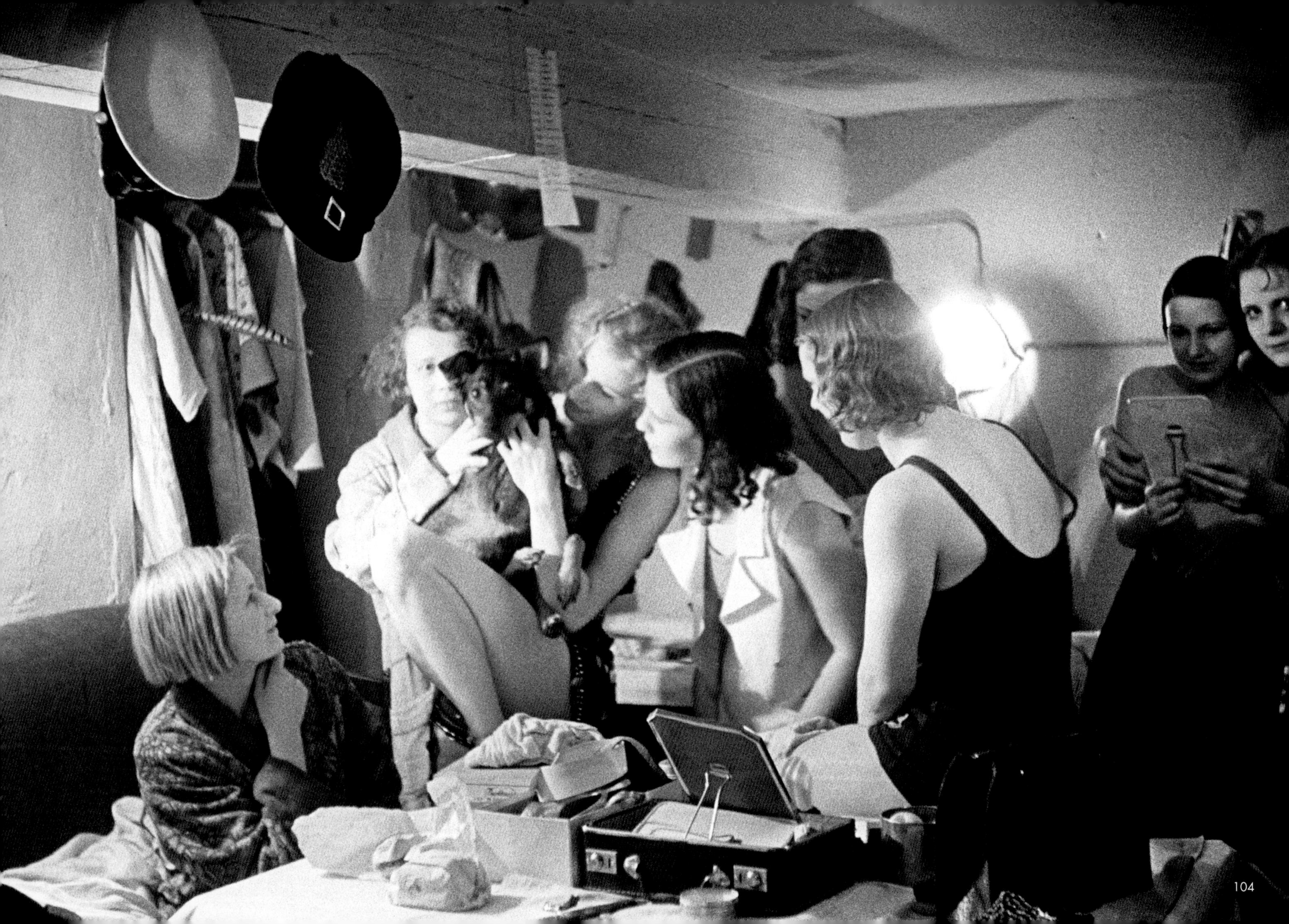

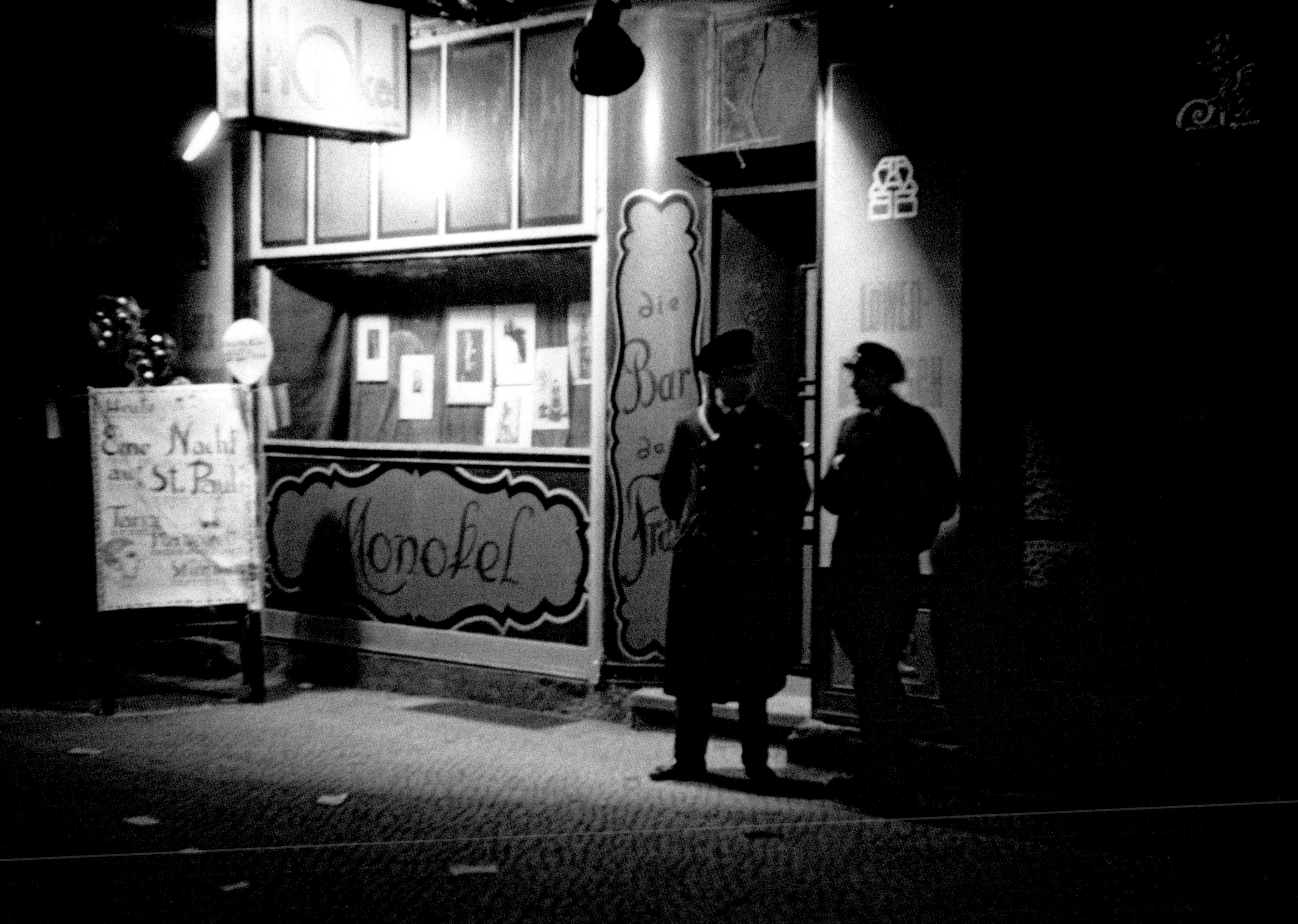

 The Monokel

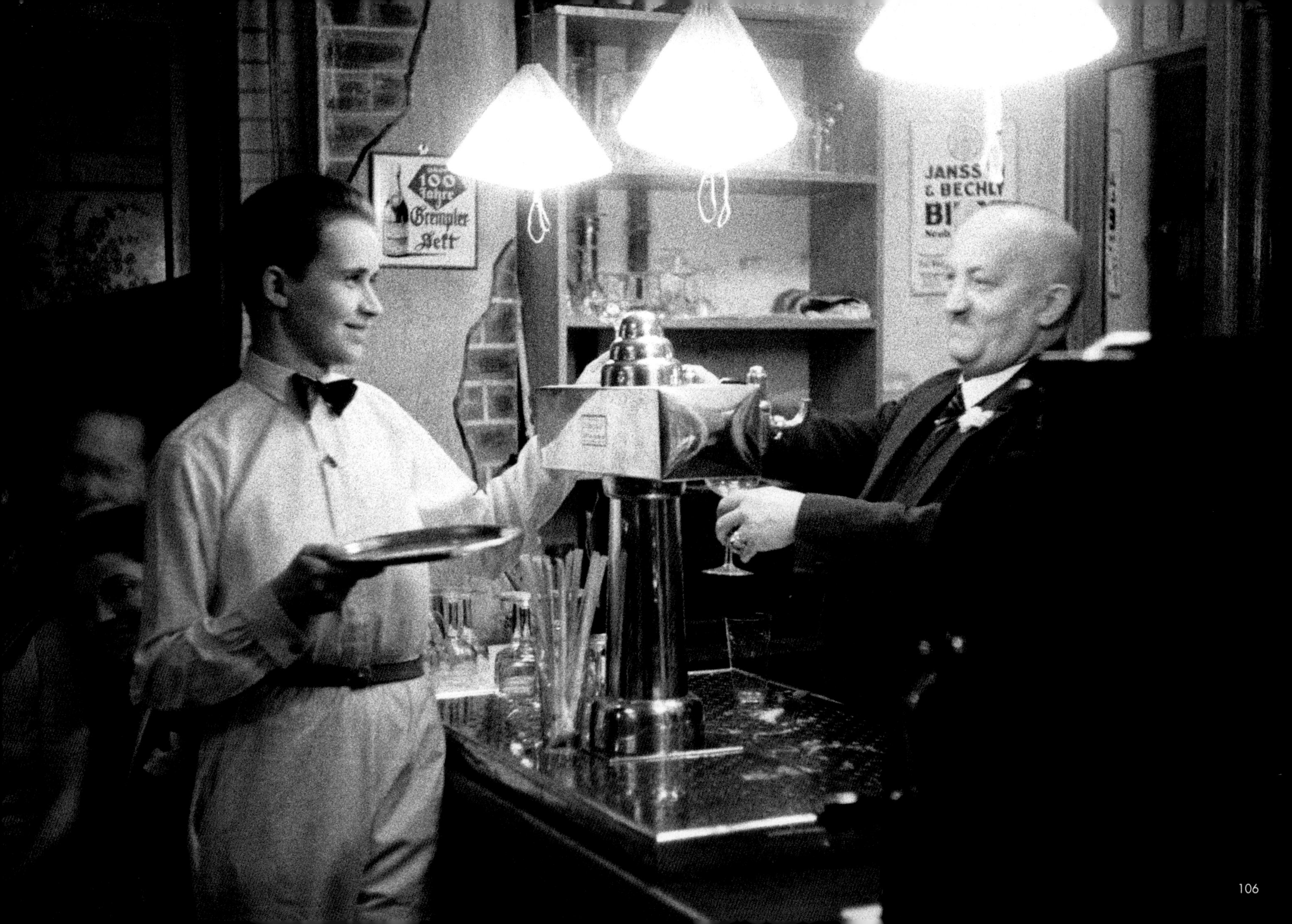
100 Jahre
Grempler Sekt
& BECHLY

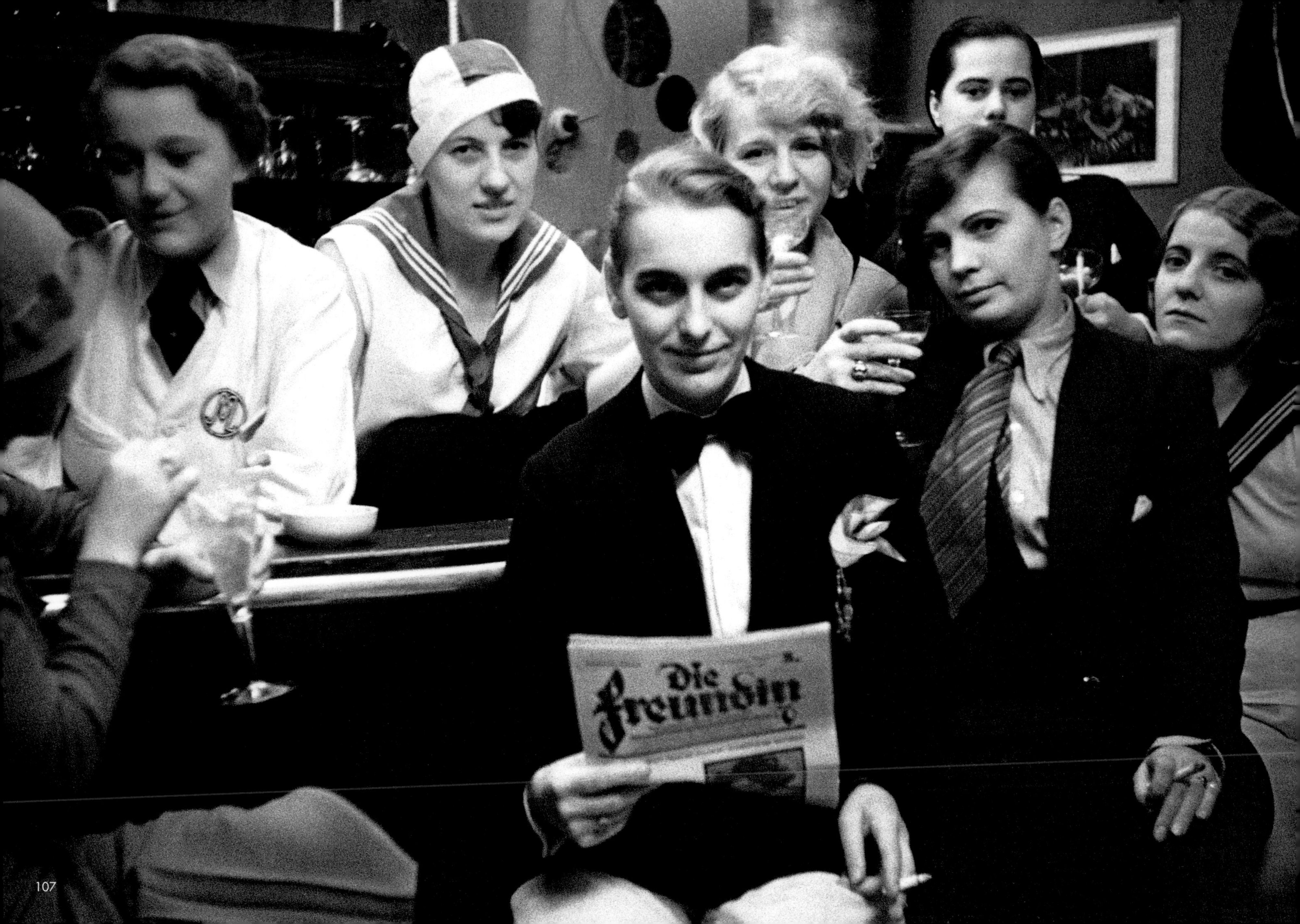
Die Freundin

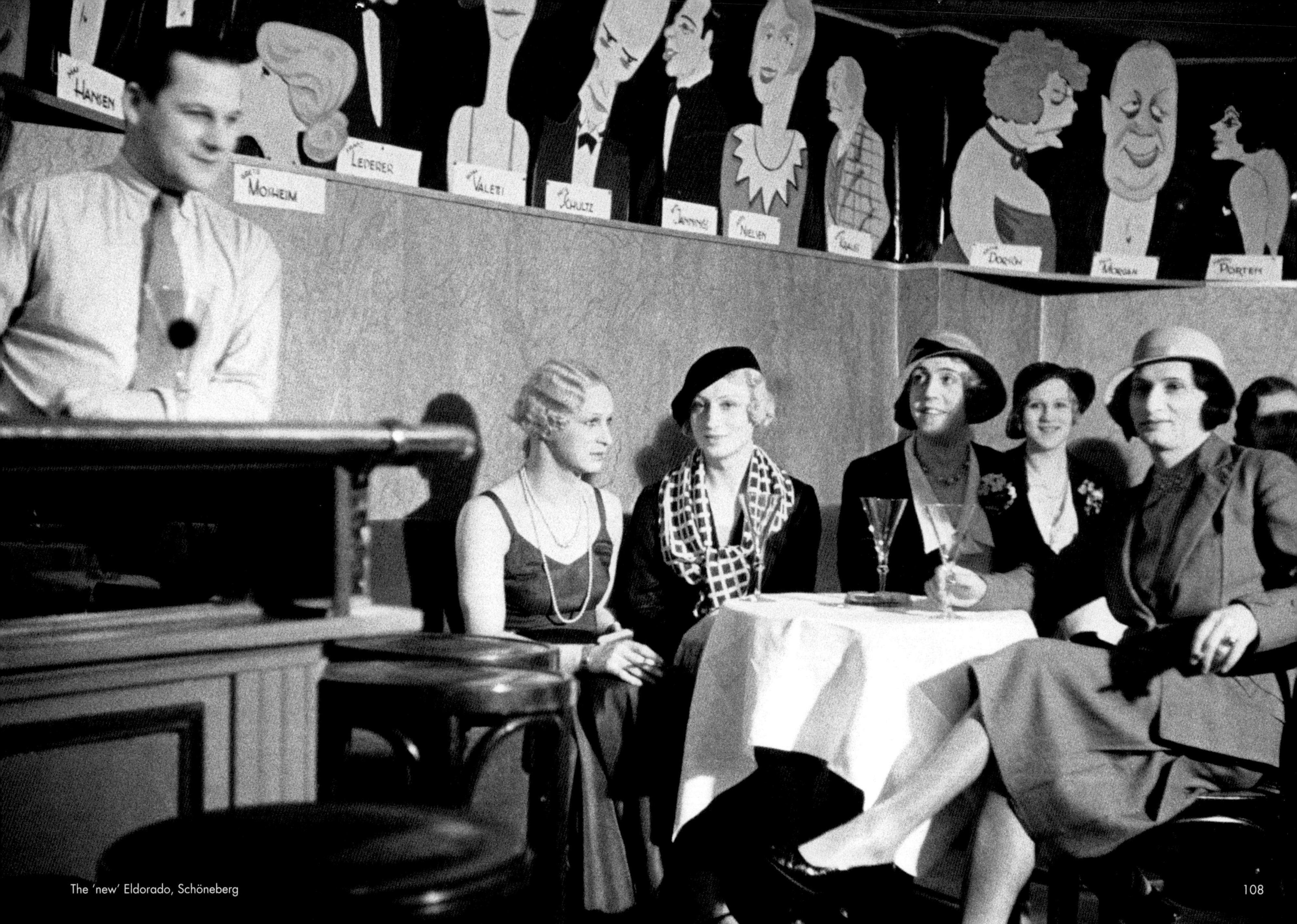

The 'new' Eldorado, Schöneberg

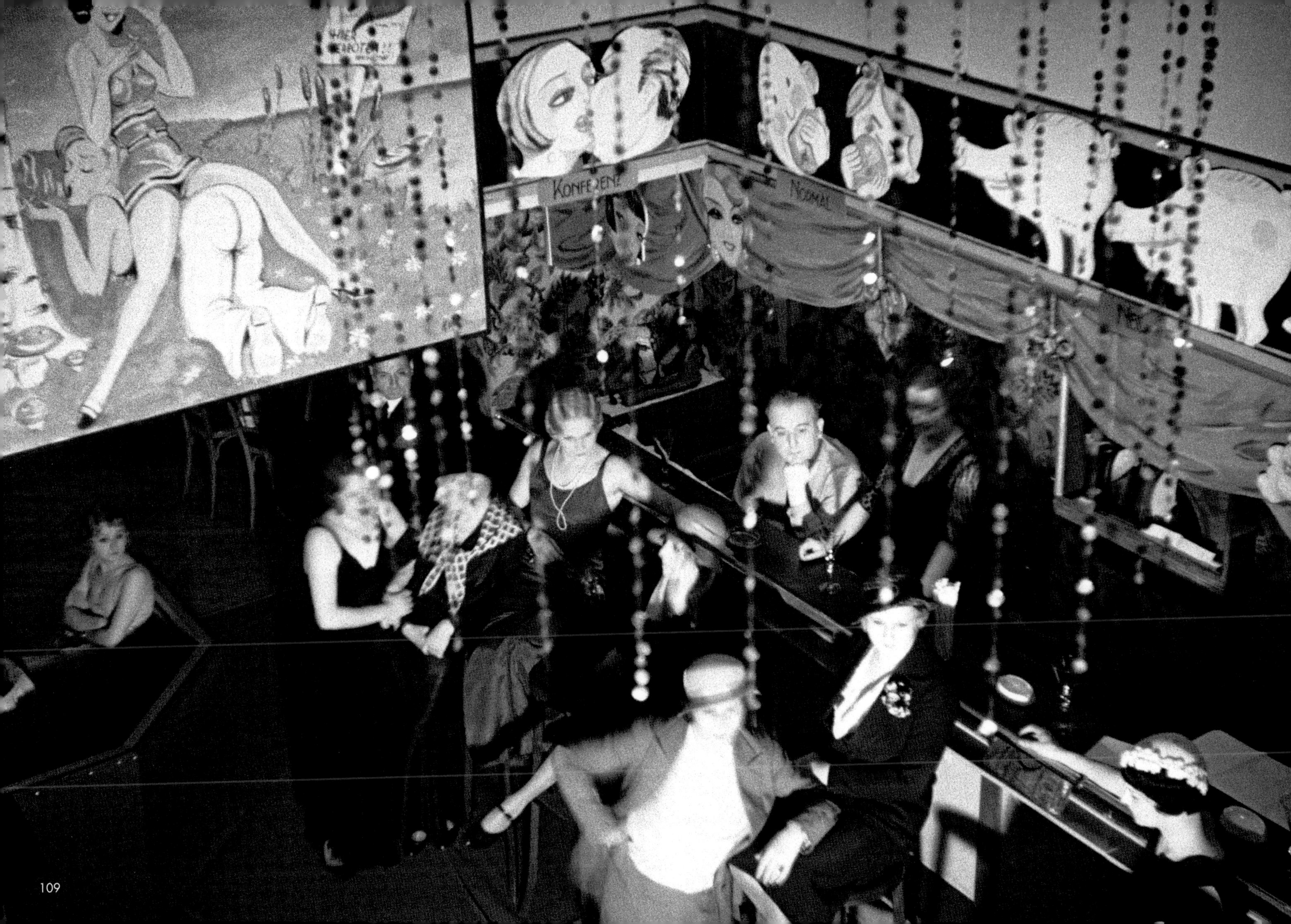

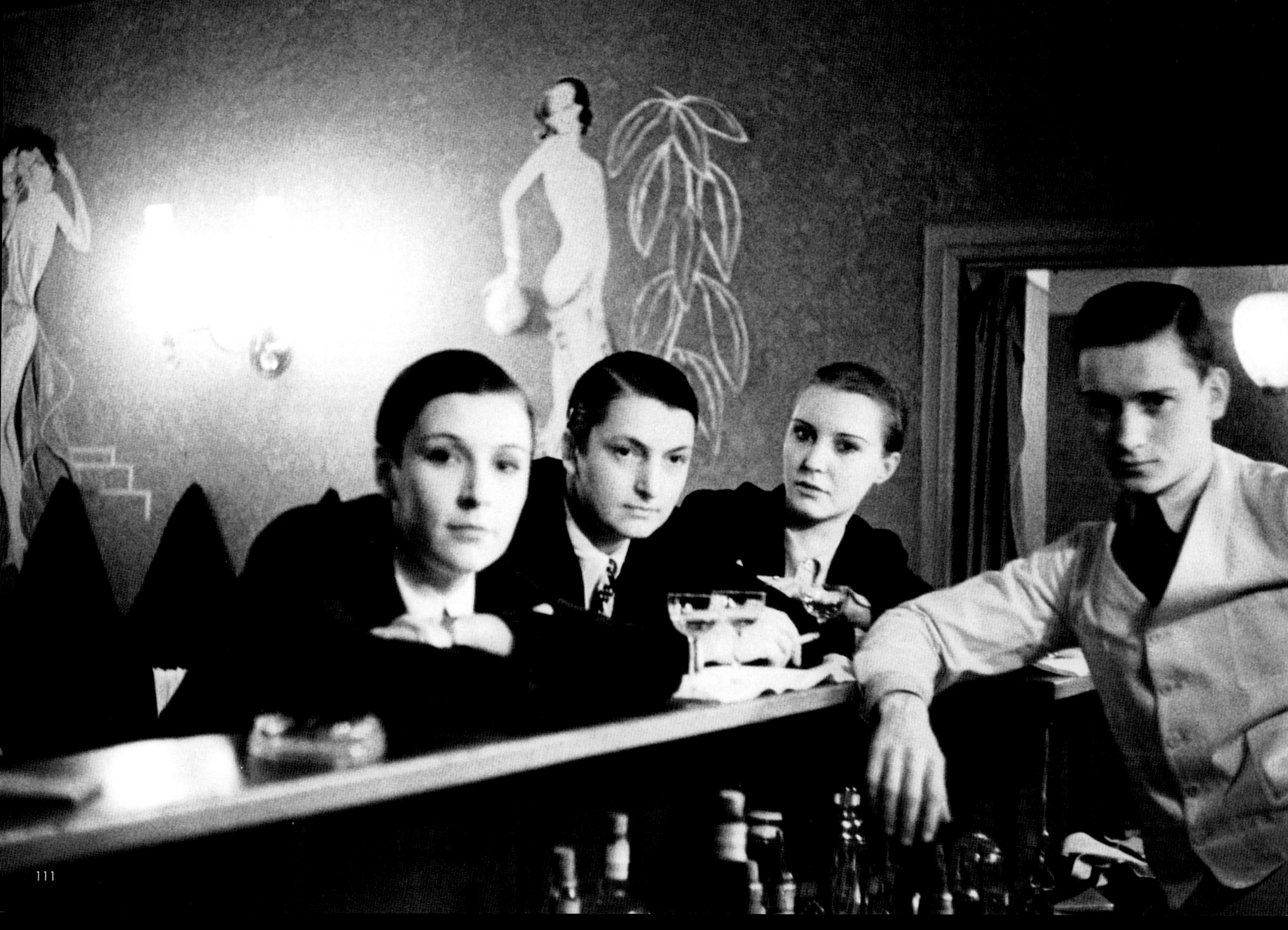

Berlin after dark captions

Pages 78–79
"Heut' geh'n wir ins Maxim" ("Today we're going to Maxim's") was the motto of a small but elegant bar in Berlin's Mitte district that capitalised on the Paris establishment of the same name.

Pages 80–81
The shooting gallery and bar at Alexander-Palast, a sprawling dance palace where big-band jazz dances were held between 9.00 pm and 1.00 am. It was known for attracting a homosexual and transvestite clientele.

Pages 82–83
On slow nights at the short-lived Oase nightclub, taxi dancers demonstrated their moves with waiters and each other to encourage paying customers to hire them.

Pages 84–88
Haus Vaterland was a vast complex near Potzdamer Platz whose bars and restaurants could accommodate six thousand revellers.

Page 84
The Löwenbräu room was a huge Bavarian Biergarten with a lake vista. Guests were treated to yodelling and nightly burlesques of southern German dance.

Page 85
The all-girl Vaterland Band.

Page 86
The Tanz-Tee, a Japanese tea garden inside Haus Vaterland.

Pages 87–88
The Vaterland Girls performed nightly in the Palm Tree Room.

Page 89
Lutter & Wegner operated several cafes and restaurants that were popular with intellectuals, artists, and actors.

Pages 90–91
The Europahaus was one of Berlin's first high-rise buildings and a relatively gaudy example of *Neue Sachlichkeit* architecture – a modernist style characterised by geometric but simple exteriors wrapped in steel, glazed concrete, or glass. The nightly variety show at the Europa Tanz Pavillion was a major attraction.

Pages 92–93
Rio Rita, located between Schöneberg and Charlottenburg, had cream and gold panelling and a cosy dance floor. Its small jazz ensemble began at 9.00 pm, and the hostesses – who received commission on the drinks they ordered for customers – were notoriously flirtatious and knowledgeable about local gossip.

Pages 94–95
The Kakadu boasted the longest bar in the world, a vegetarian restaurant, a jazz orchestra, and a cabaret. Its open fireplaces encouraged revealing attire.

Pages 96–97
The Femina-Palast was an enormous modernist complex that opened in 1929 amid great fanfare. Modern conveniences included lifts that could comfortably fit 16 people and communication between distant guests was possible via vacuum tube-delivered mail and telephones on every table. The dance floor could be elevated and the glass roof opened on warm nights to welcome in the moonlight and view of the stars.

Pages 98–99
French-themed Fleur Meyer featured a Bar Américain, artificial trees, and romantic alleyways lit by streetlights, all of which were indoors.

Pages 100–101
Egyptian Ahmed Mustafa's Ciro-bar was a jazz and swing club managed by his nephew and one of a number of new establishments owned by 'foreigners'. Some visitors were unnerved by the *kavass*, or Turkish guard.

Pages 102–104
The Altes Ballhaus featured a shooting gallery, Egyptian-themed lounges, and an indoor swimming pool accented by ten-foot fountains and populated by bathing beauties.

Page 104
Backstage at the Altes Ballhaus.

Pages 105–107
Lesbian activist Lotte Hahn served drinks at her bar Monokel in Charlottenburg. Like the nightclub of the same name in Paris, the Monokel catered to women dressed as men.

Page 107
For many, the monthly magazine *Die Freundin* was a symbol of identity. It featured consistently eye-opening covers, lesbian-themed short stories, historical investigations into homosexuality, letters, poems, and event listings. Its pages hosted a long-running dispute about whether bisexuality is damaging to the social advances made by lesbians and homosexuals.

Pages 108–109
"Hier ist's richtig" ("It's fine here") read the sign that welcomed guests to the 'new' Eldorado in Schöneberg which coexisted with the smaller 'old' Eldorado in Charlottenburg. Both catered to men dressed as women, women dressed as men, and everything in between. It was sufficiently famous for American *Vogue* to write about it.

Page 111
Despite Victor Margueritte's 1922 novel *La Garçonne* being an unabashed attack on the modern, liberated woman, its title was adopted by women who preferred wearing men's clothing, and became the name of a magazine catering to lesbians and transvestites.

part III

1930
1931

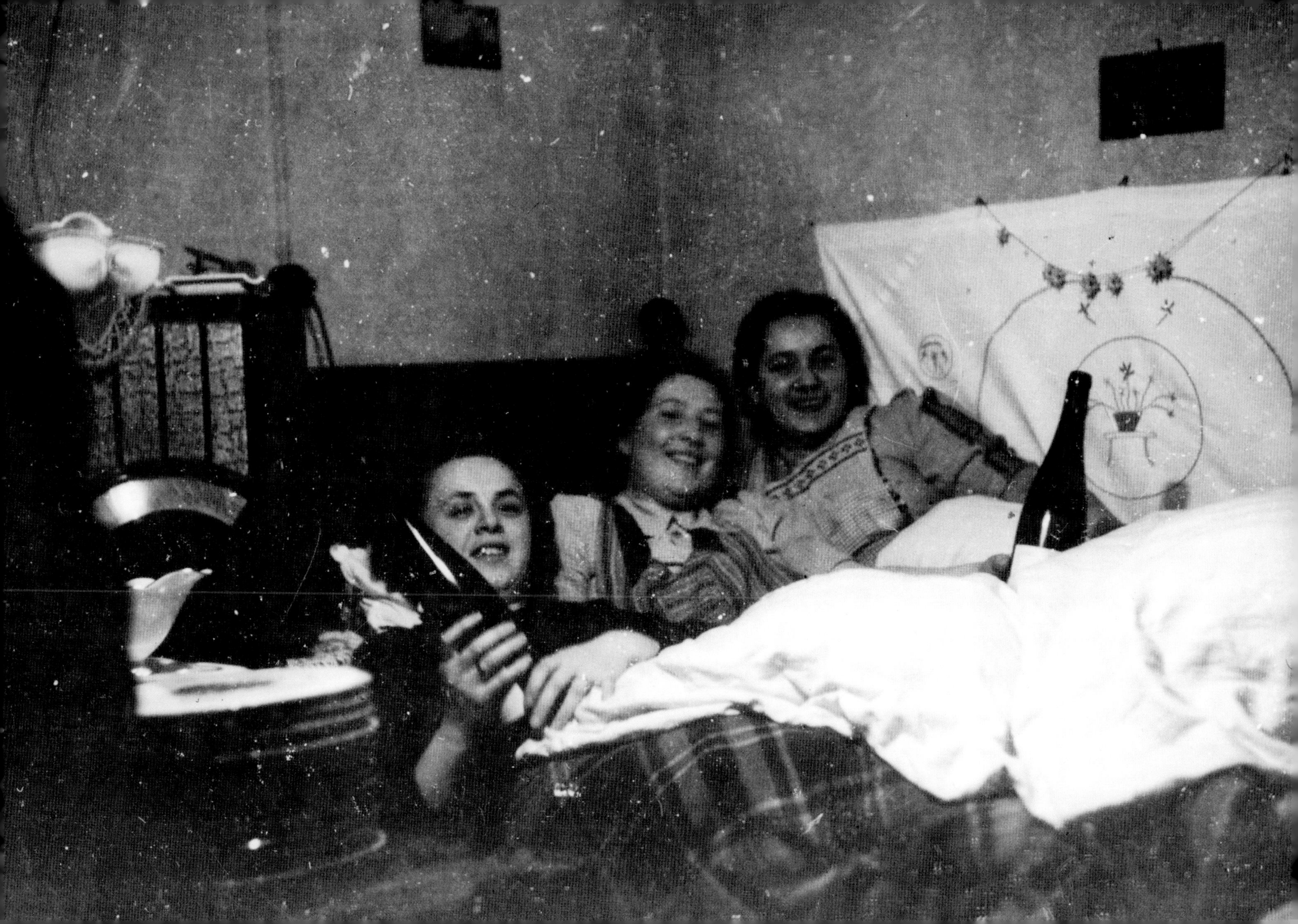

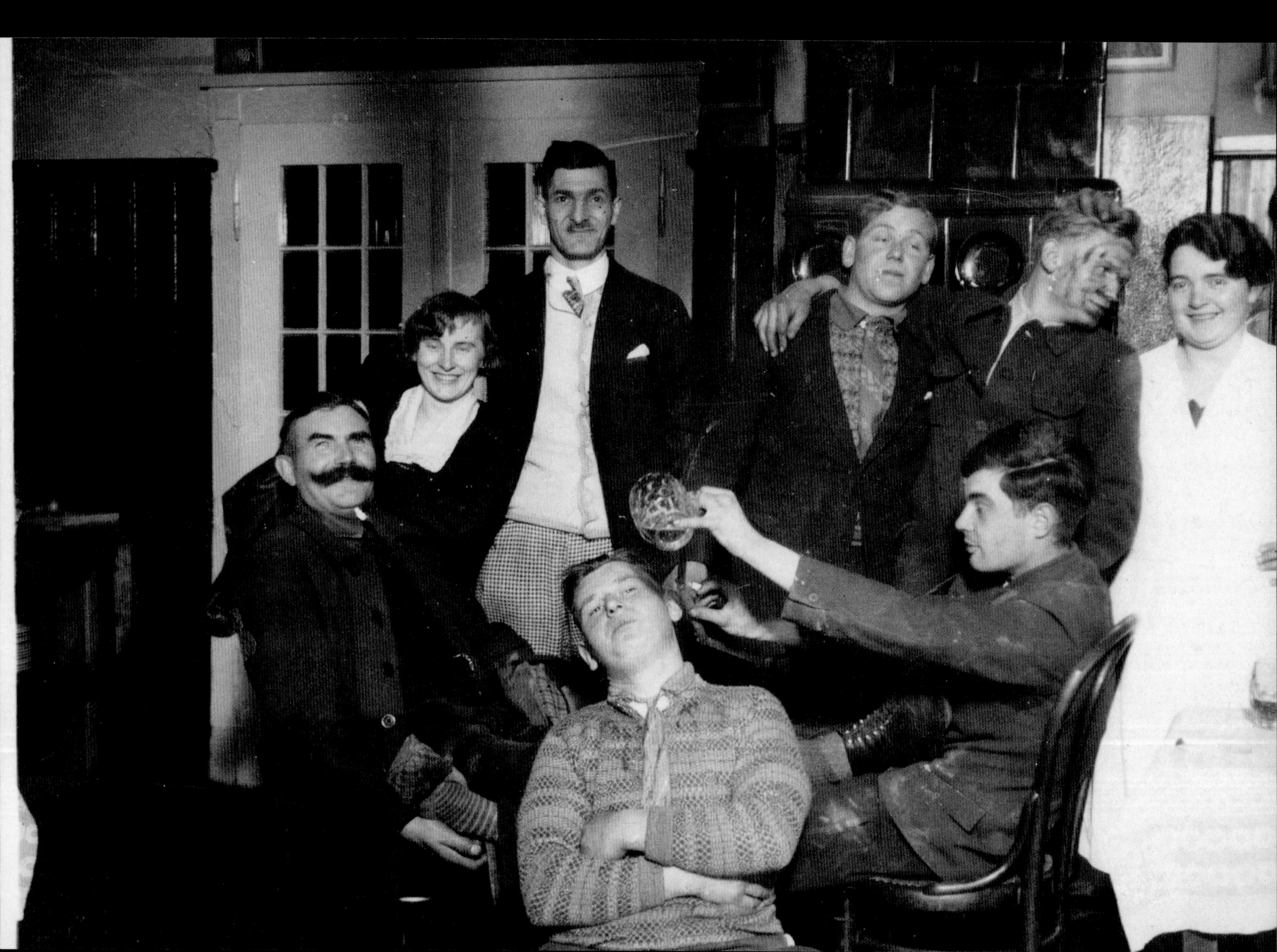

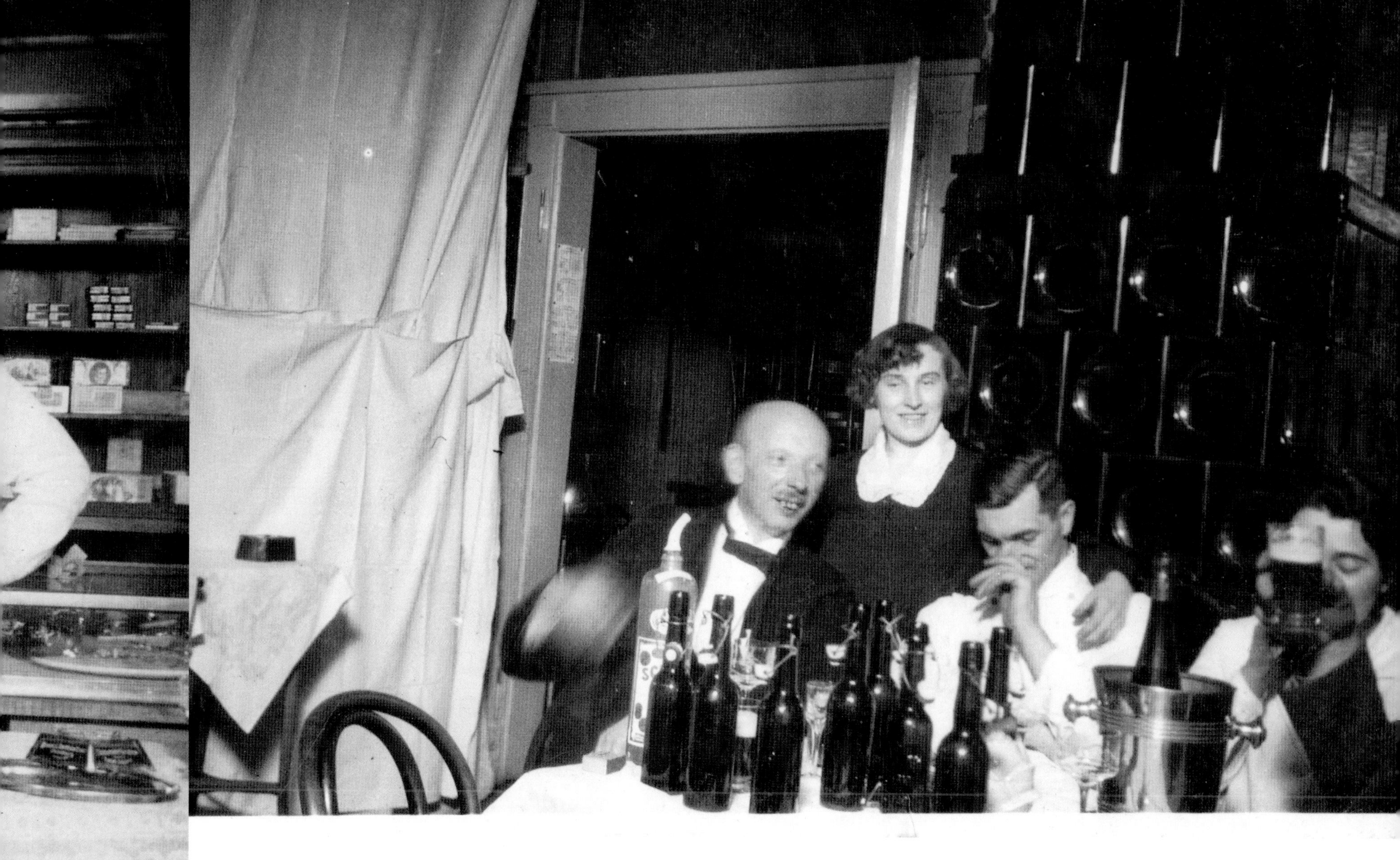

At Wulfert's Hotel in Torfhaus, a village in central Germany's Harz mountains. In the 1930s parts of the Harz mountain range were assigned to become Germany's first national parks, but the plan was aborted in favour of building armaments factories.

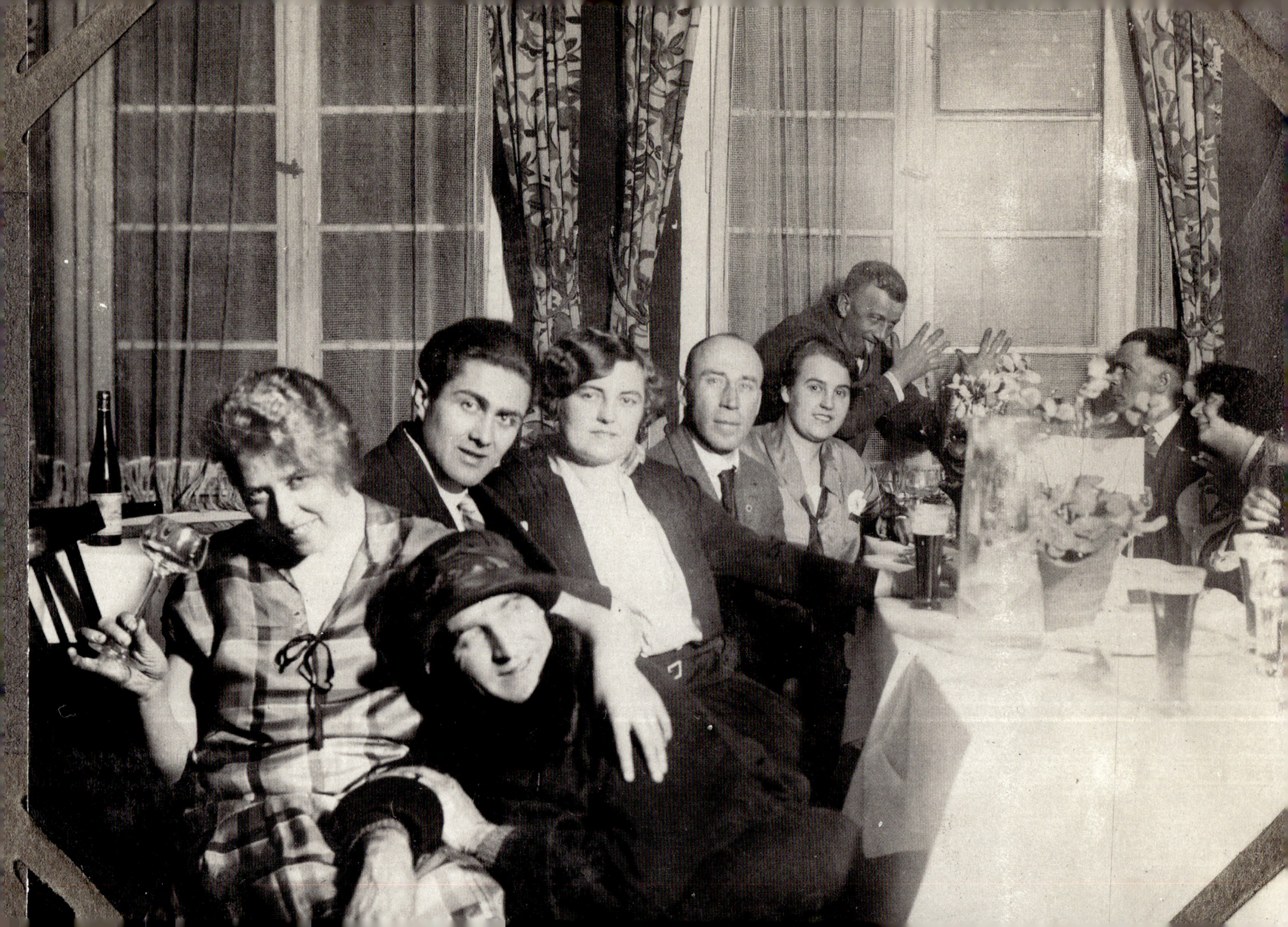

October 1930

In Britain, Harry Craddock publishes *The Savoy Cocktail Book*, bringing together highlights from earlier drinking tomes and recipes perfected during his training in the United States and subsequent tenure at the bar of the Savoy Hotel in London. It includes a section for prohibition-stricken Americans, and immediately becomes the *de facto* bible for bartenders all over the world.

Bavarian friends maintain the party spirit en route to Trient during a holiday in Switzerland

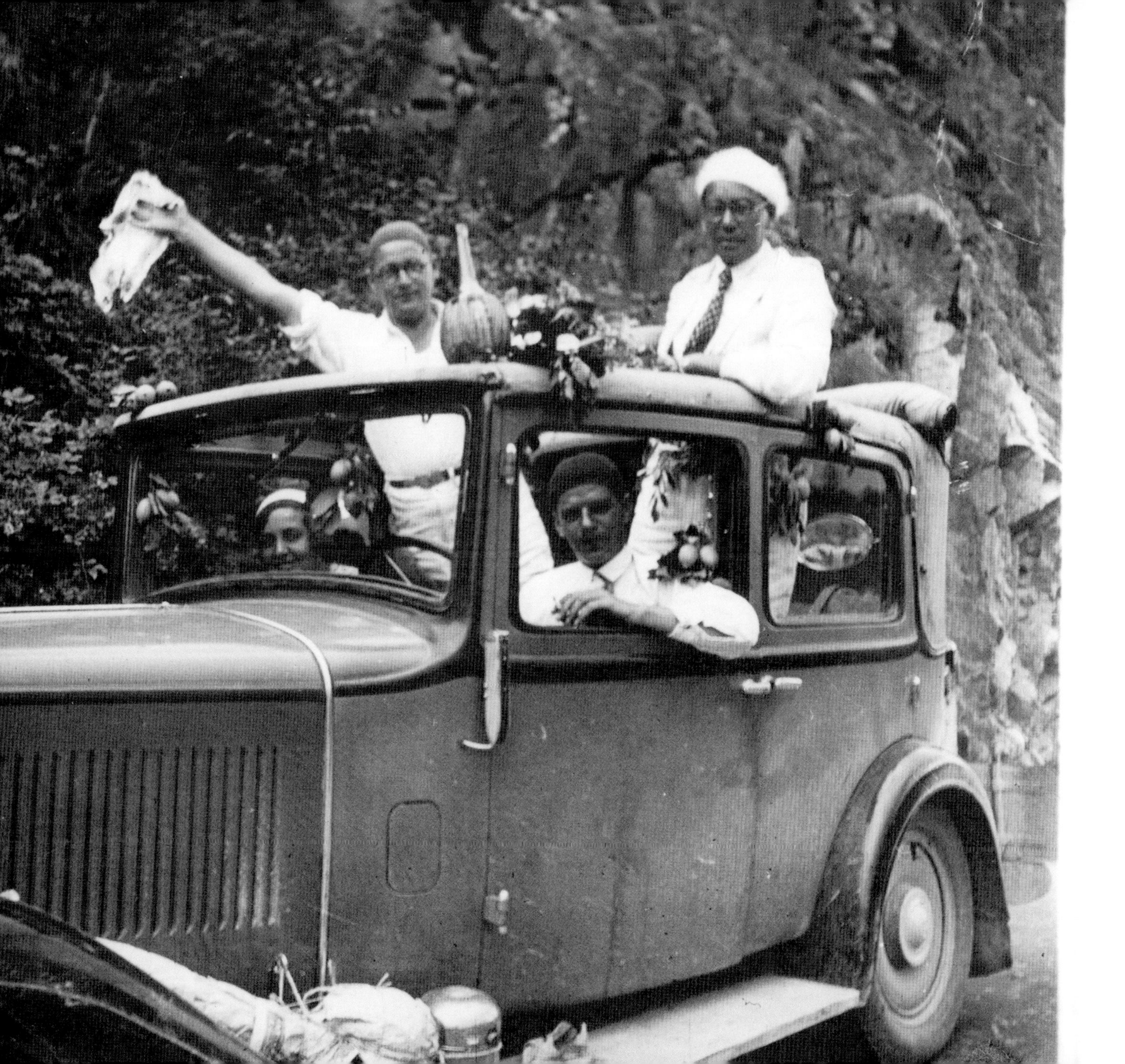

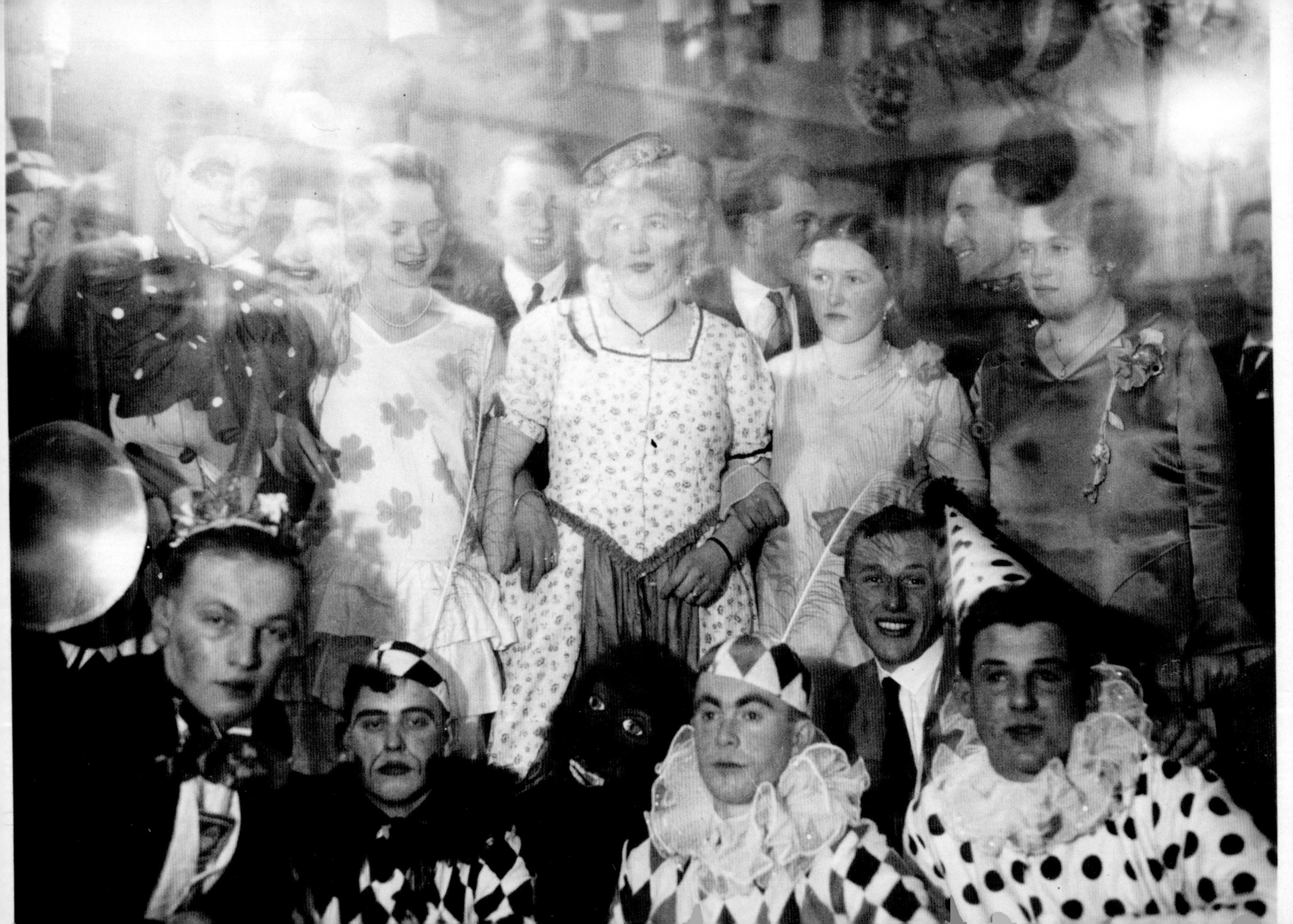

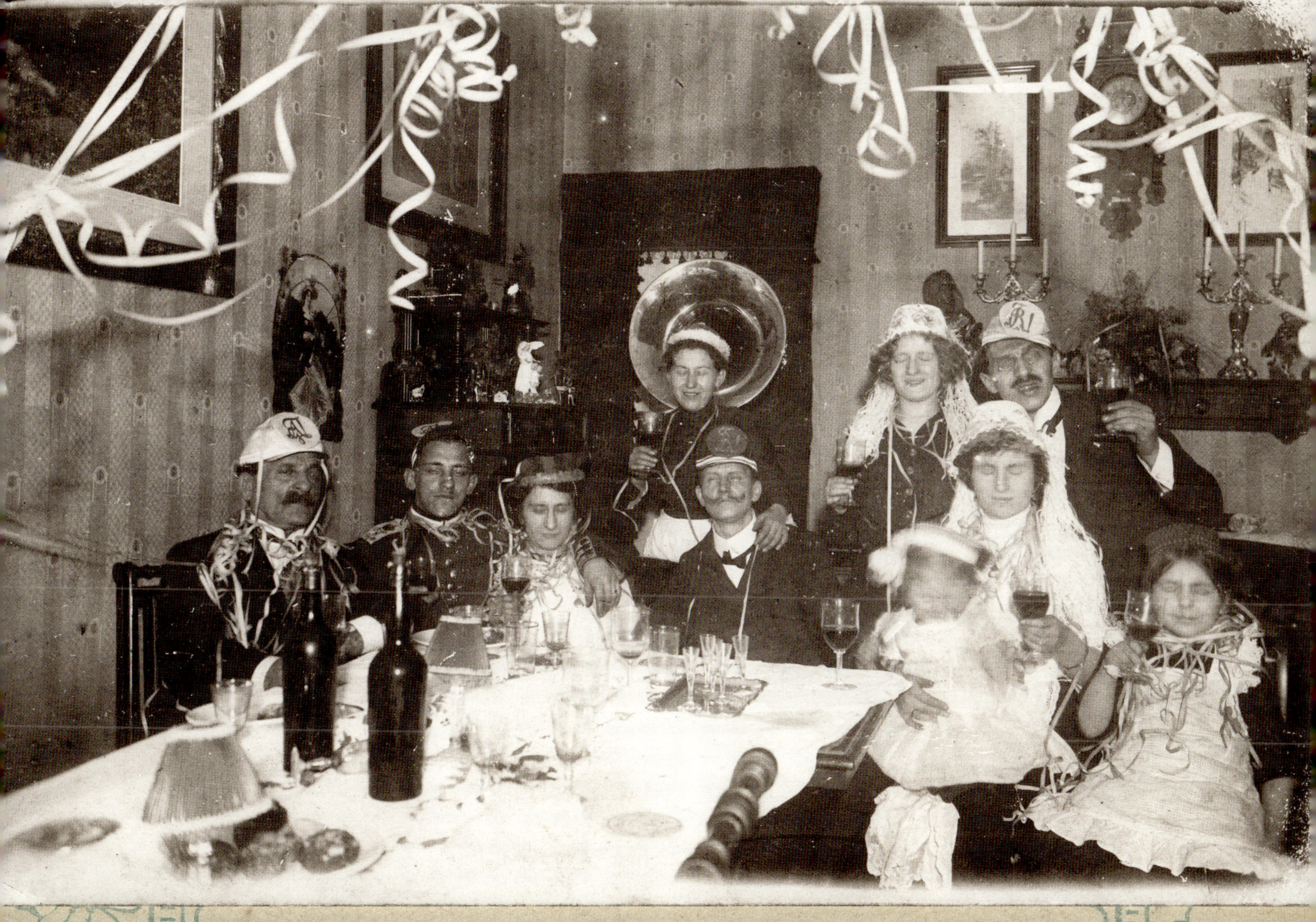

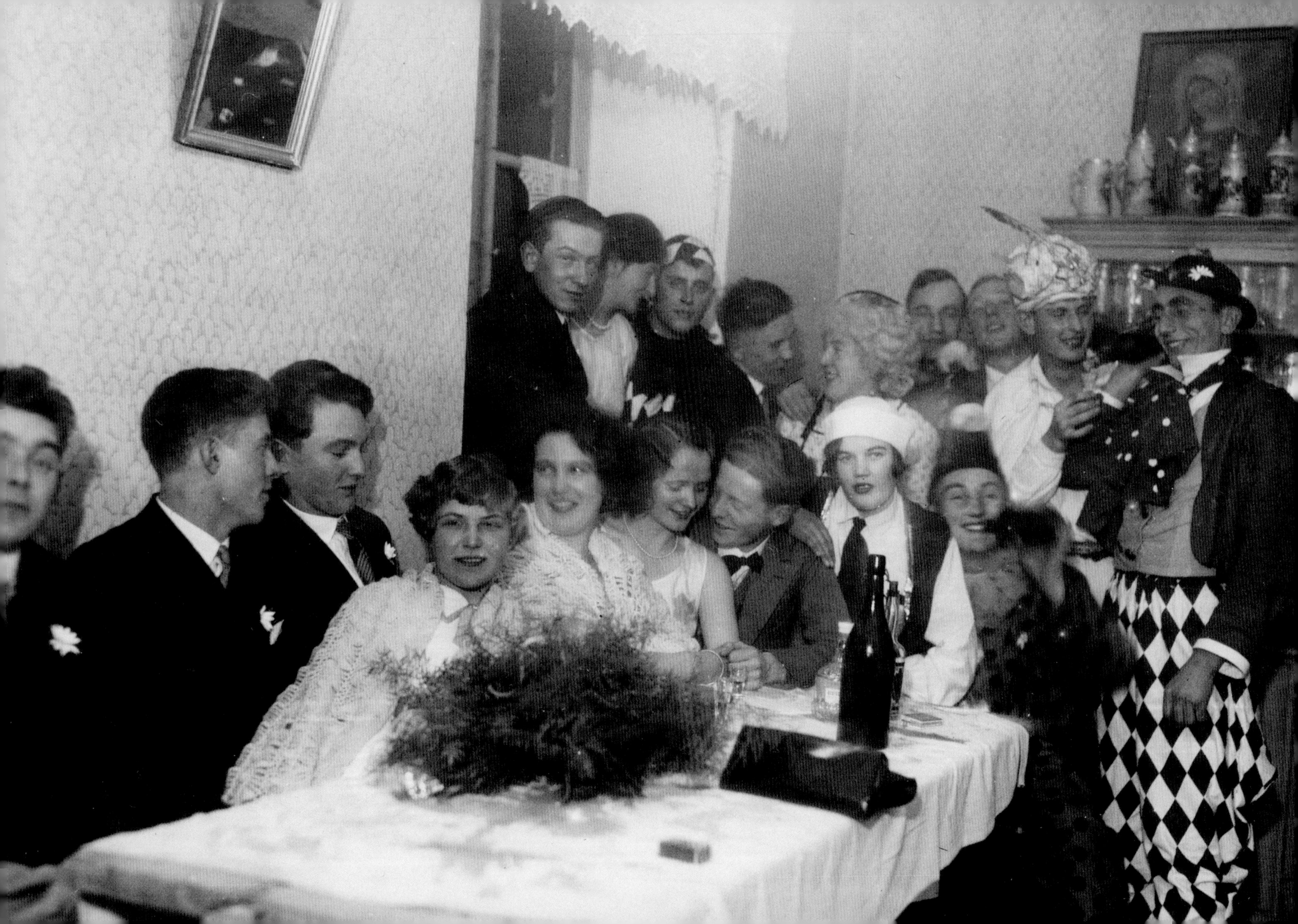

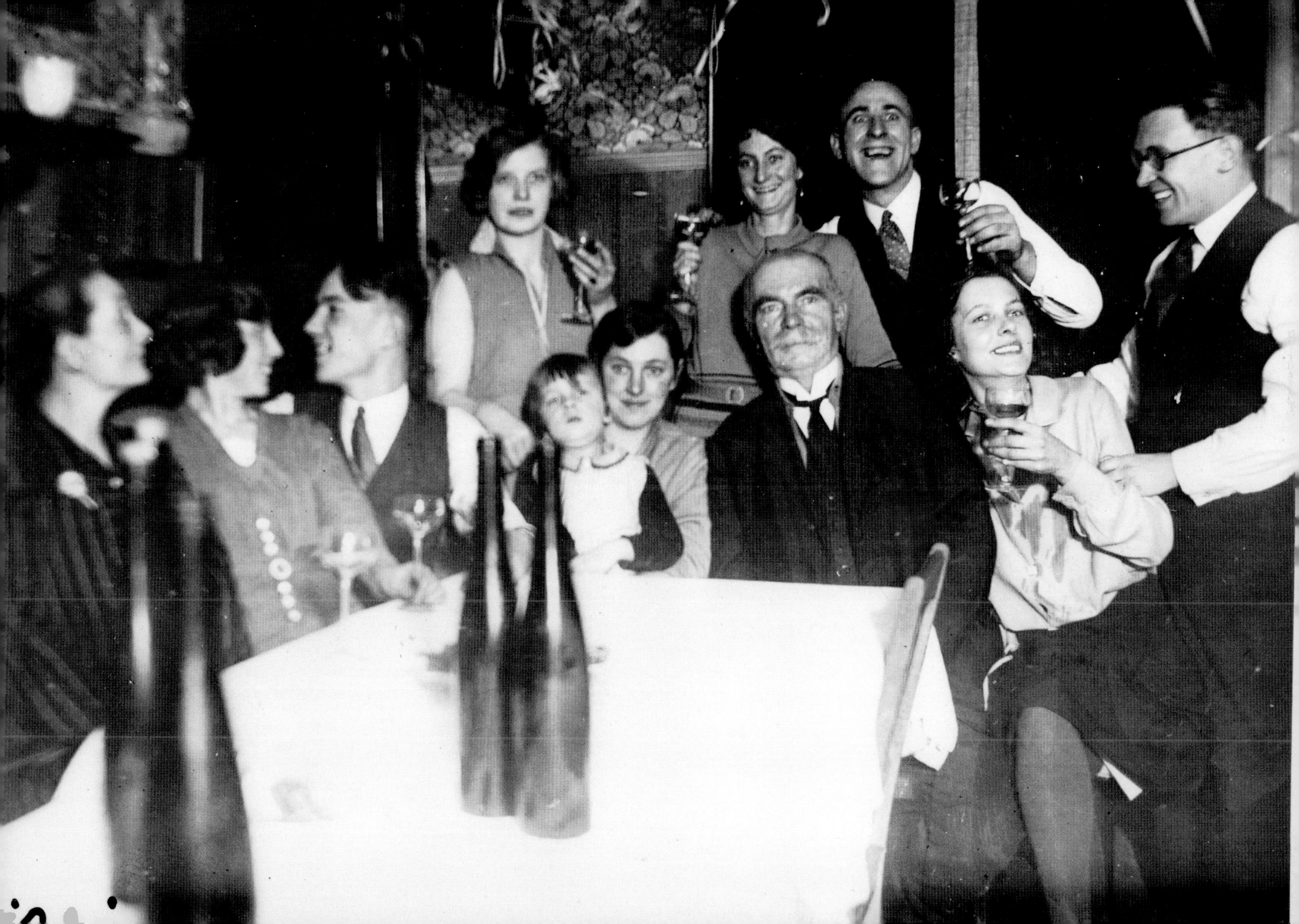

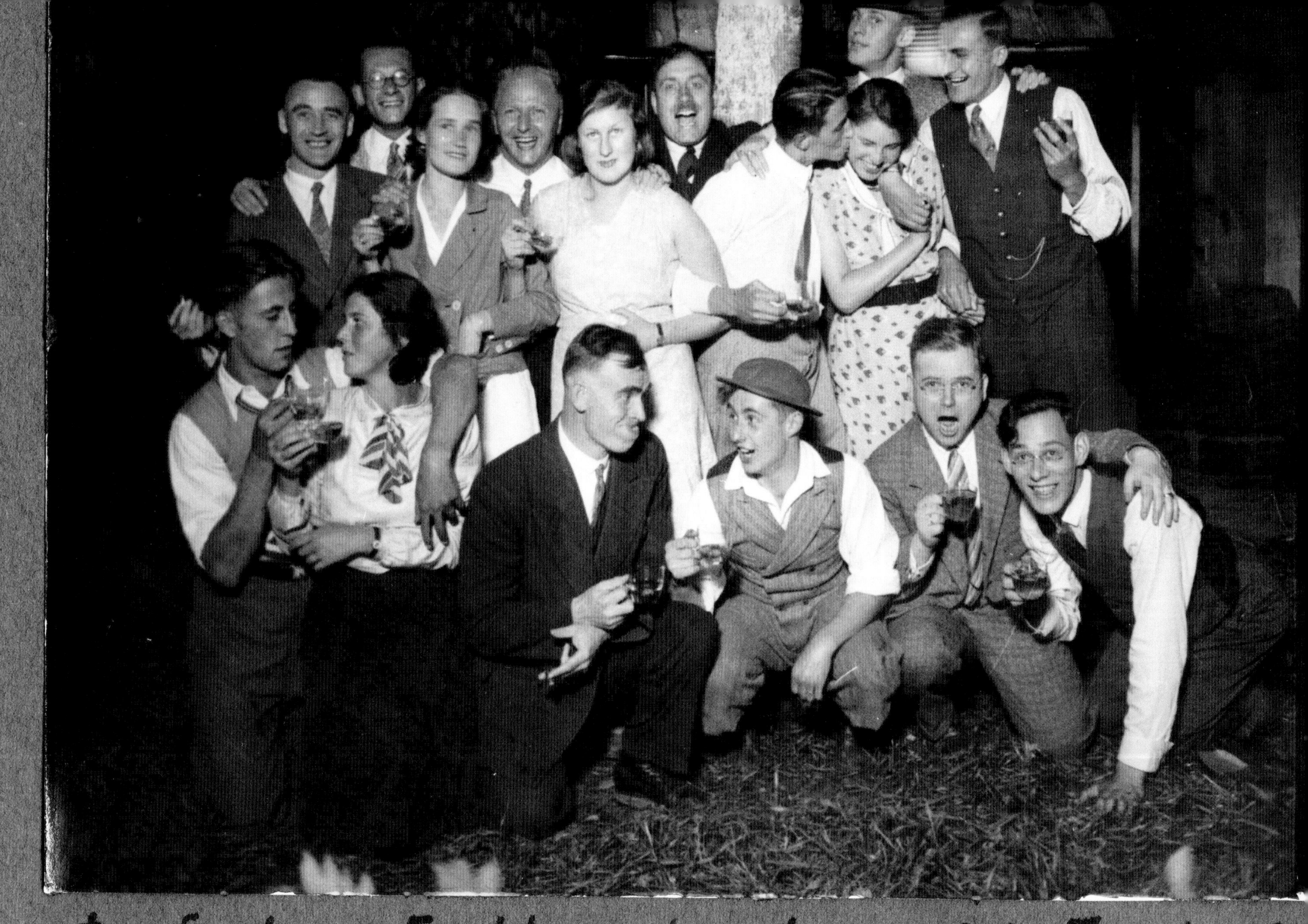

Gartenfest m Erdbeerbowle 20 Juni 19

ERDBEERBOWLE (STRAWBERRY PUNCH)

1 pound of wild strawberries
1.5 cups of sugar
4 bottles Mosel wine
Ice

Dice a pound of wild strawberries into a large bowl. Mix in 1.5 cups of sugar and two bottles of Mosel wine. Leave to sit for an hour, then add two more bottles of Mosel. Put the mixture on ice. When ladling, add an inch of German champagne to each punch glass.
Makes 30 glasses.

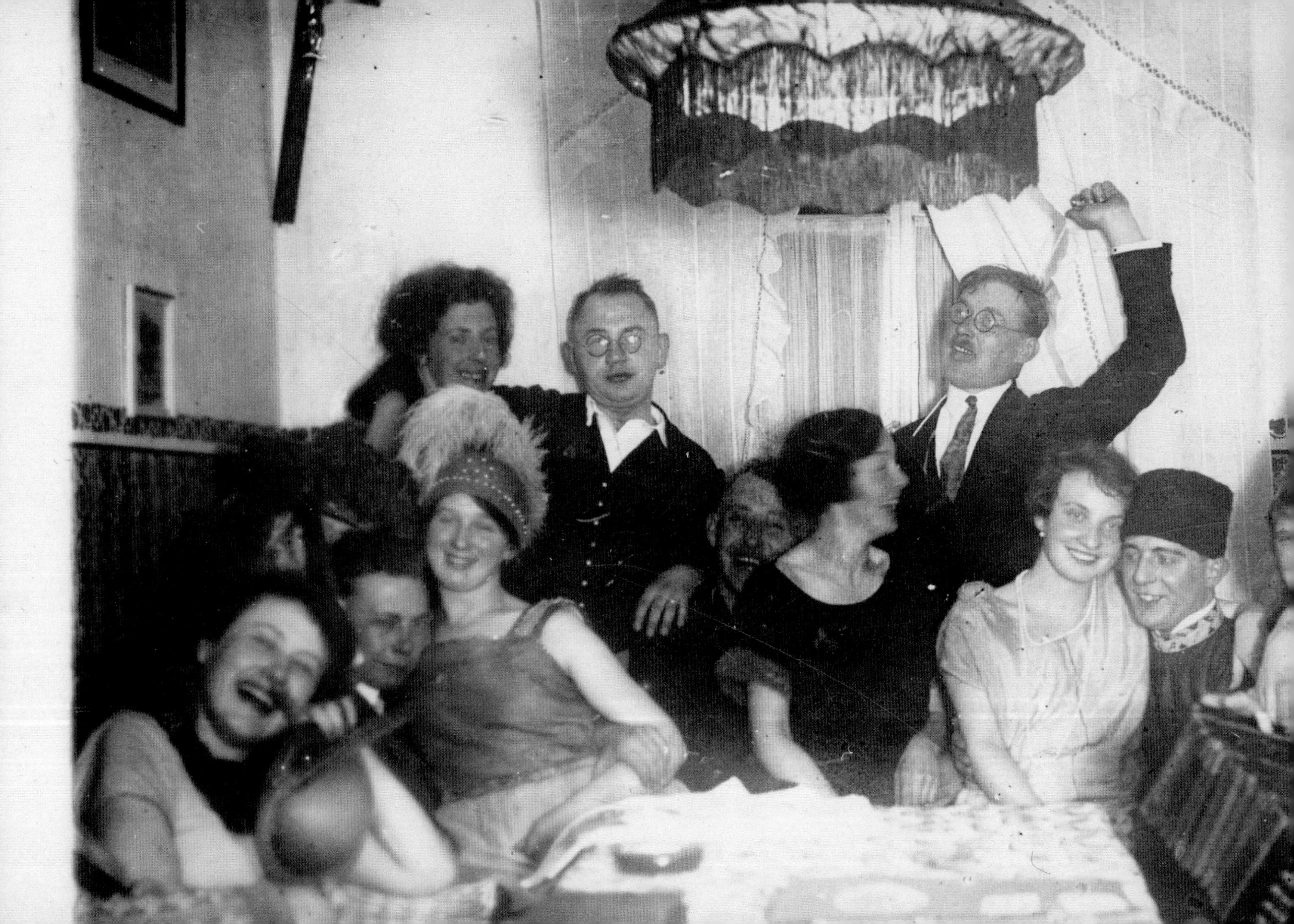

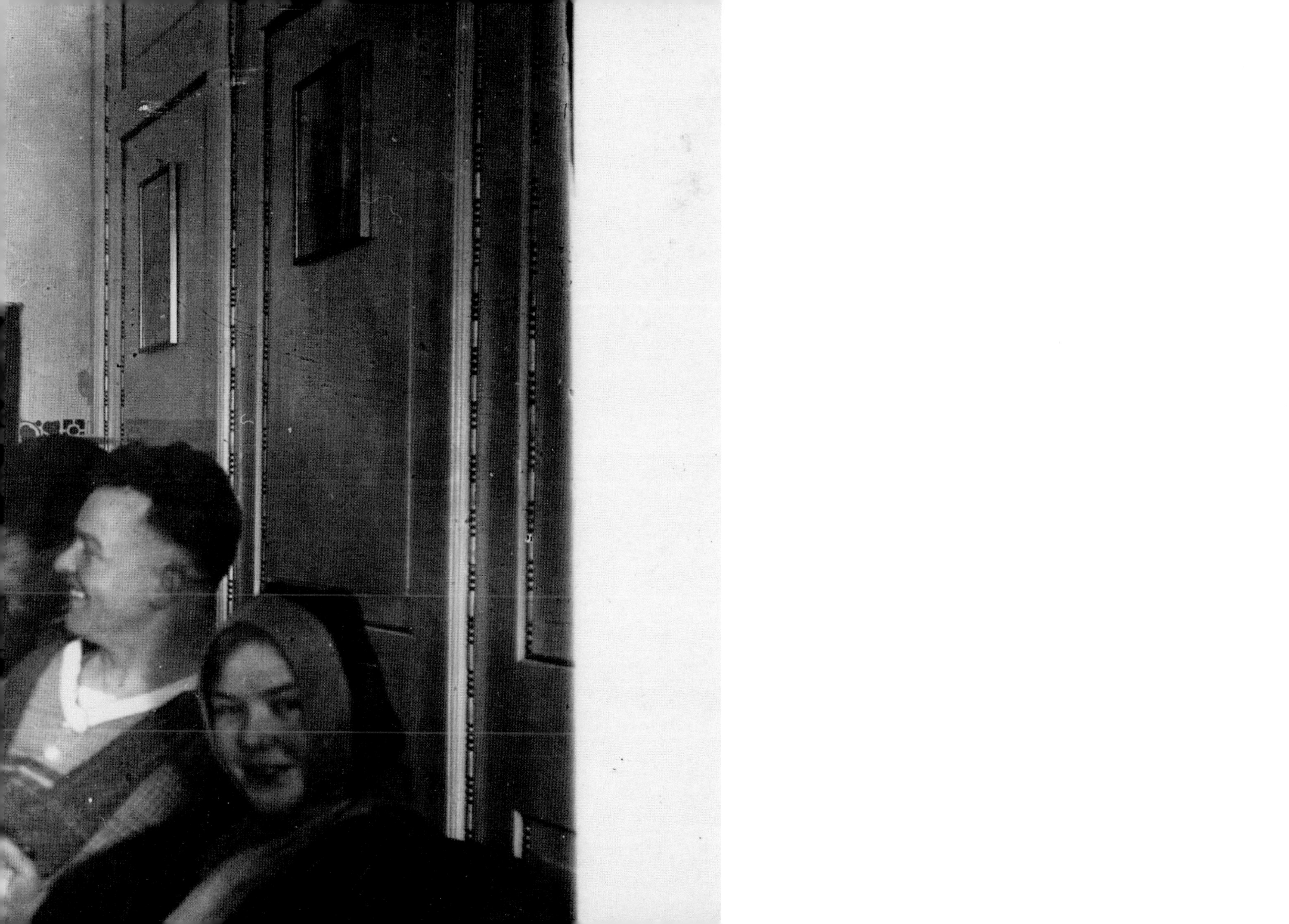

International interlude

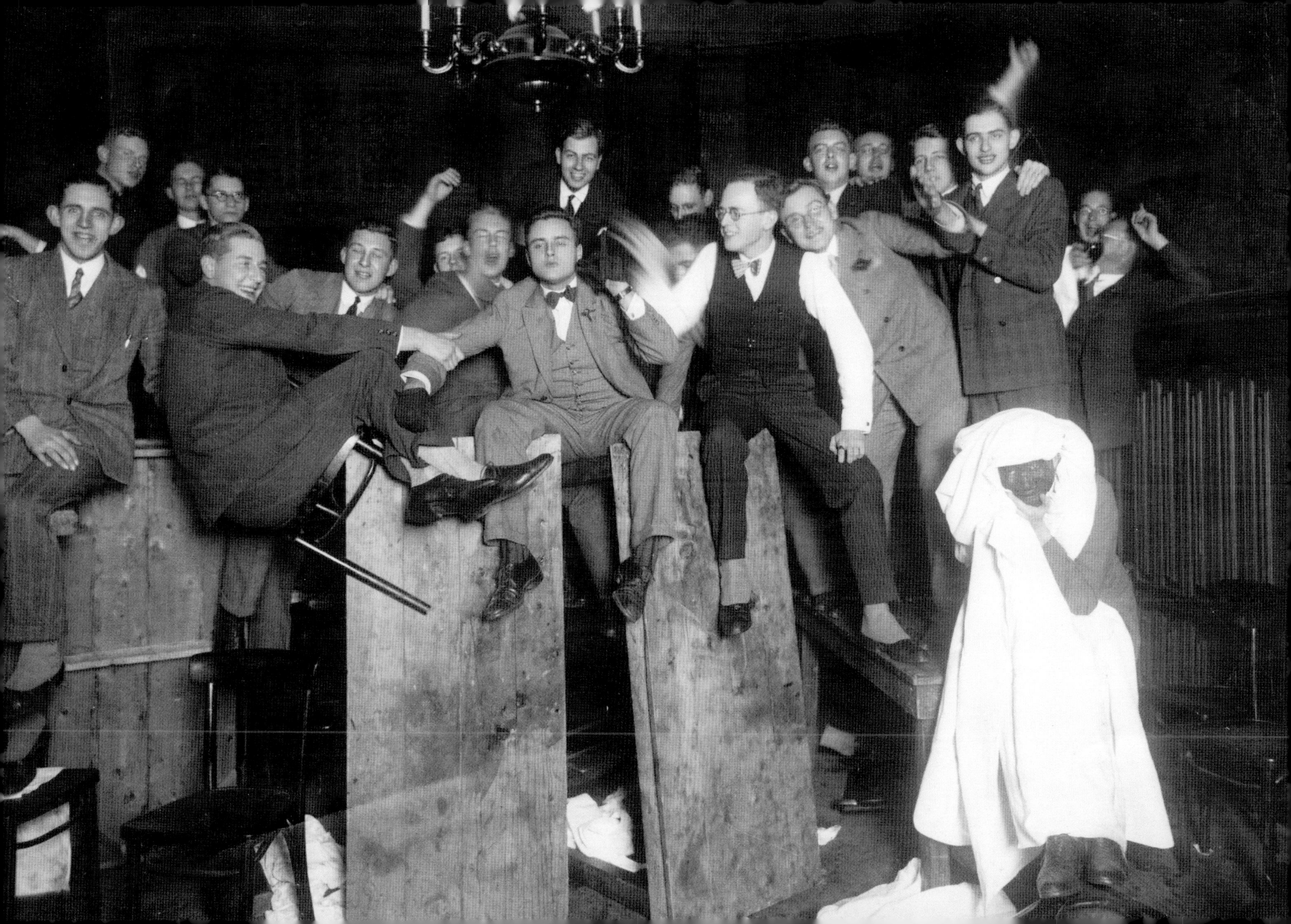

It is universally acknowledged that the British love to dress up, and London between the wars was a haze of furs, moustaches, and pyjamas unsuitable for sleep. The West End hosted a labyrinth of legitimate nightclubs and unlicensed 'bottle parties'. The Georgian streets of Soho – the setting for Kurt Weill and Bertolt Brecht's *The Threepenny Opera*, a jazz opera about betrayal in the underworld, corruption, and Weimar capitalism – struggled to accommodate an artistic milieu alongside grassroots fascists.

Previous page: Amsterdam, Holland

Right: London, England

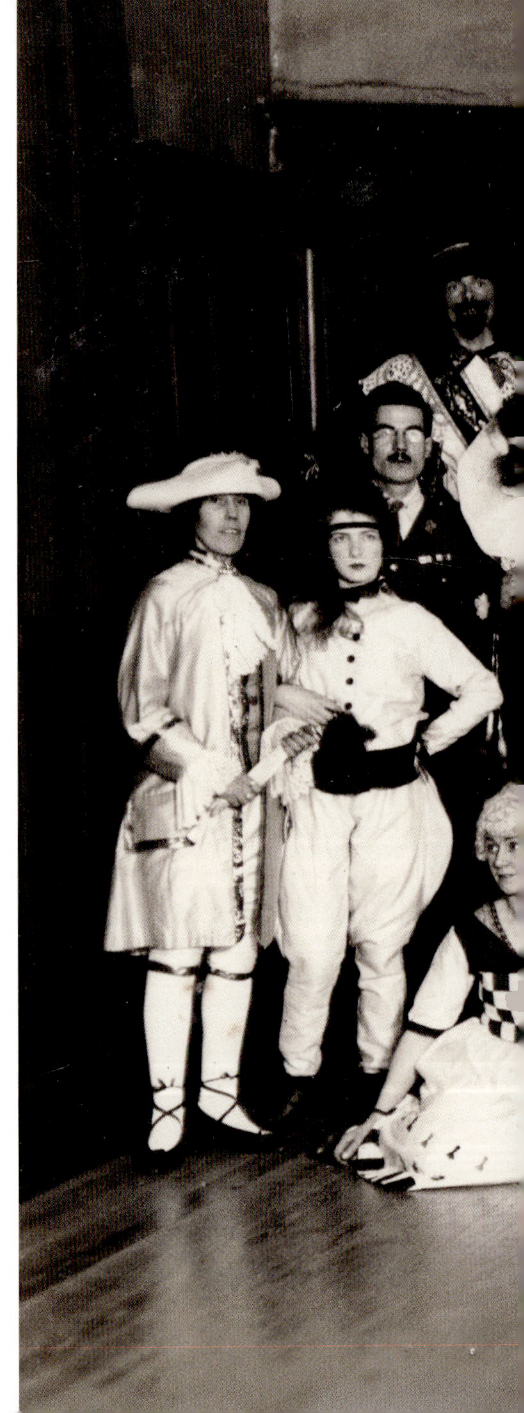

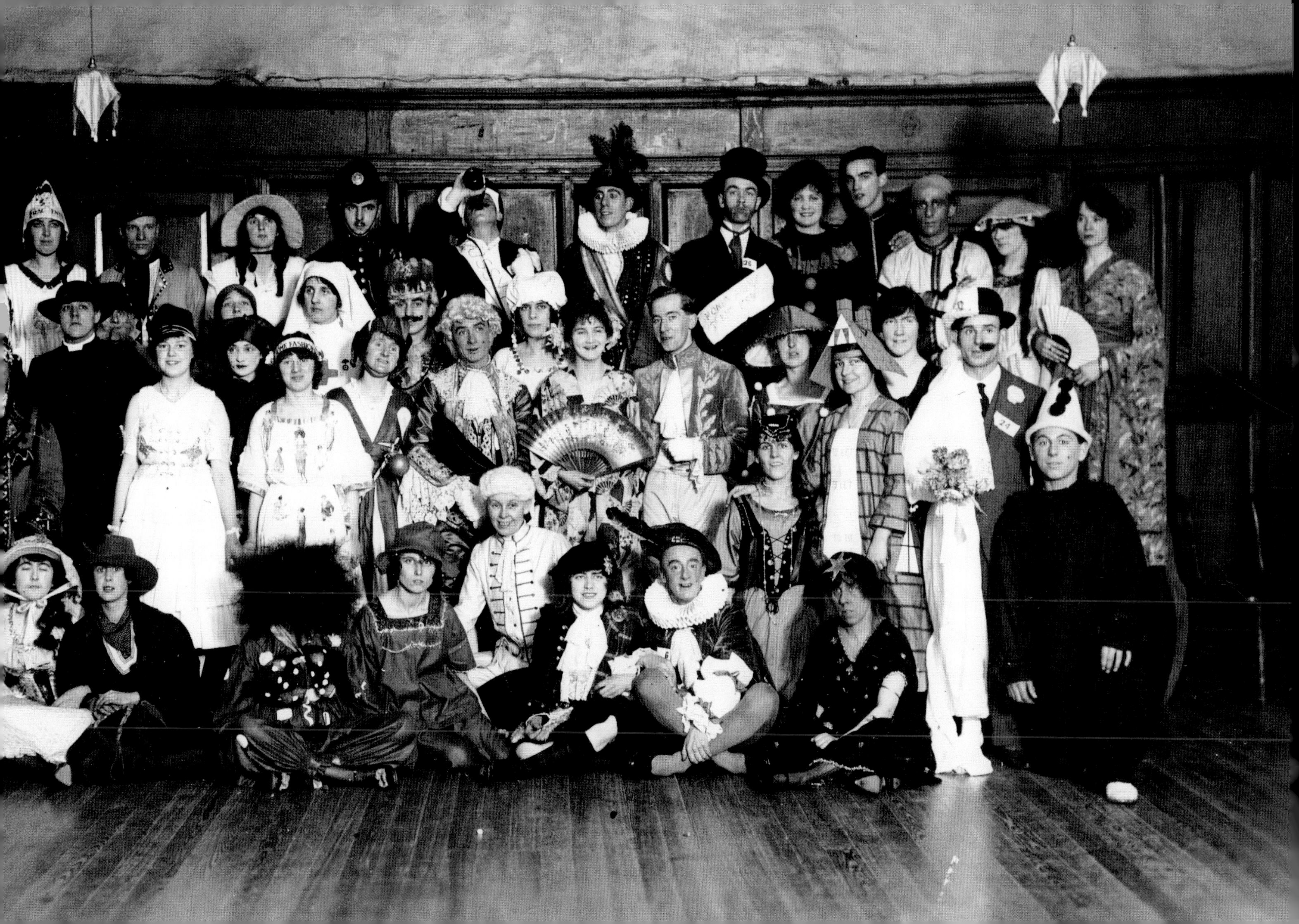
24

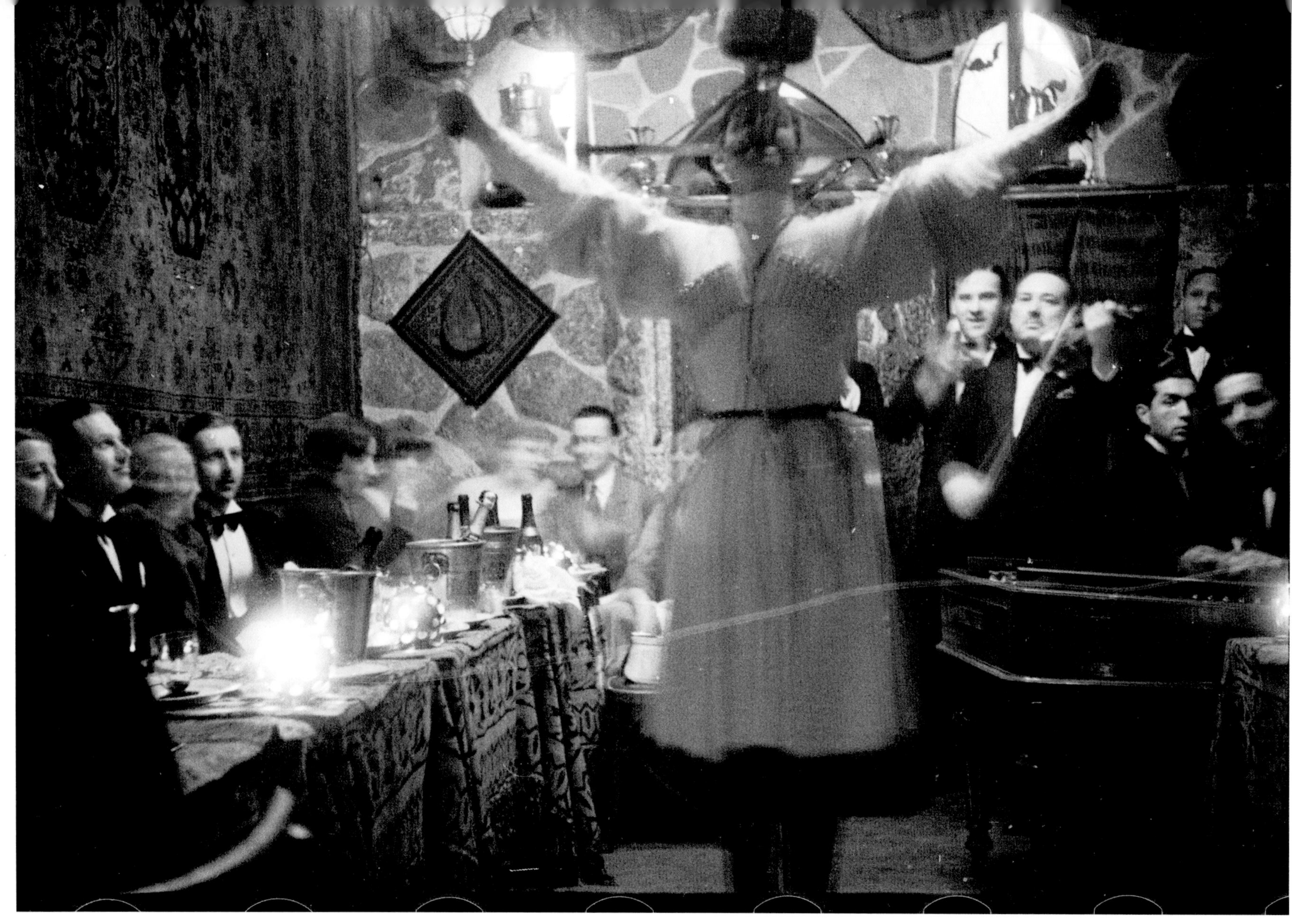

Above and opposite: A nightclub in Montparnasse, Paris, an international mecca for artists, writers, newspapermen, tourists, and insomniacs

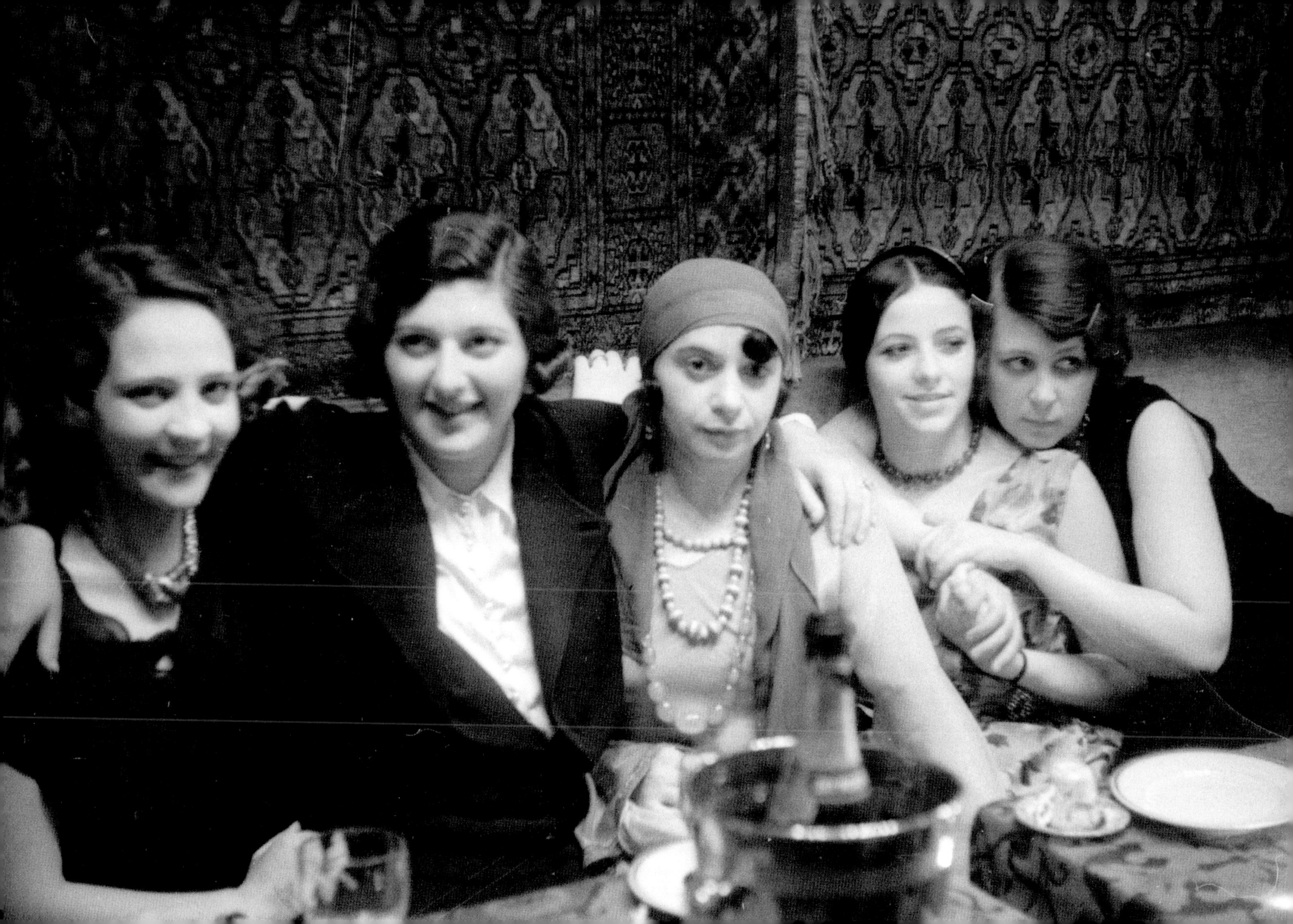

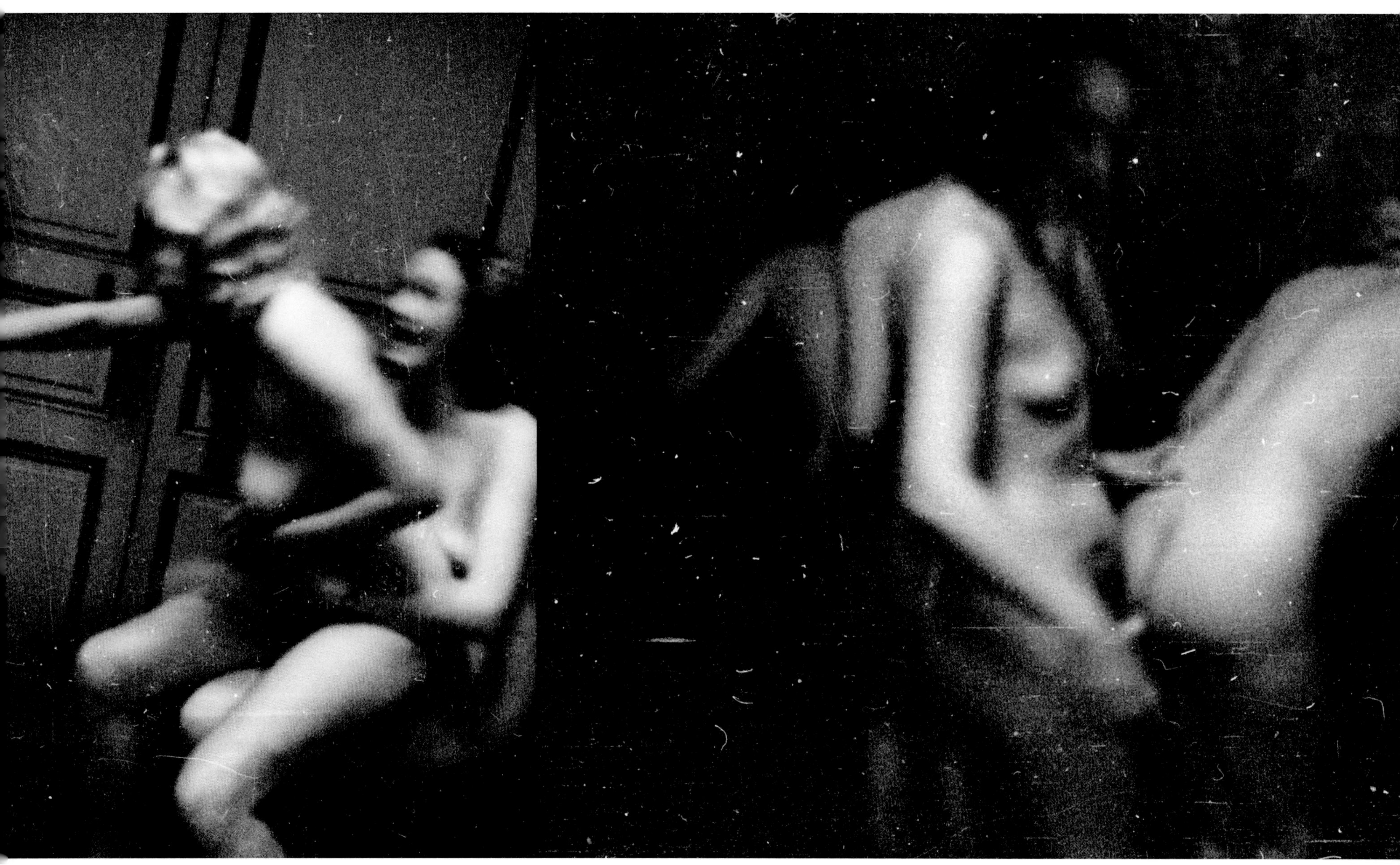

Sex show in a *Bordel*, Paris

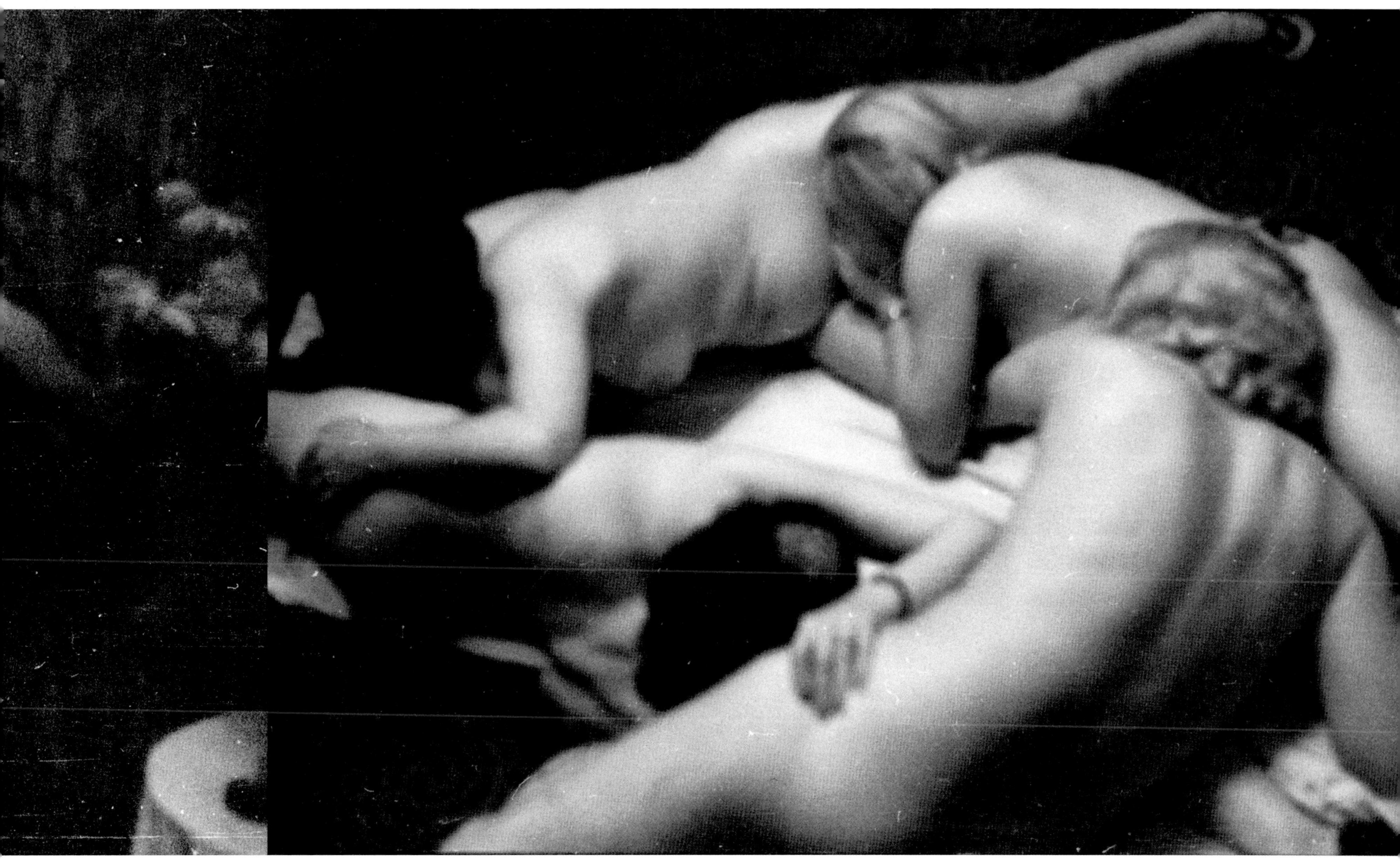

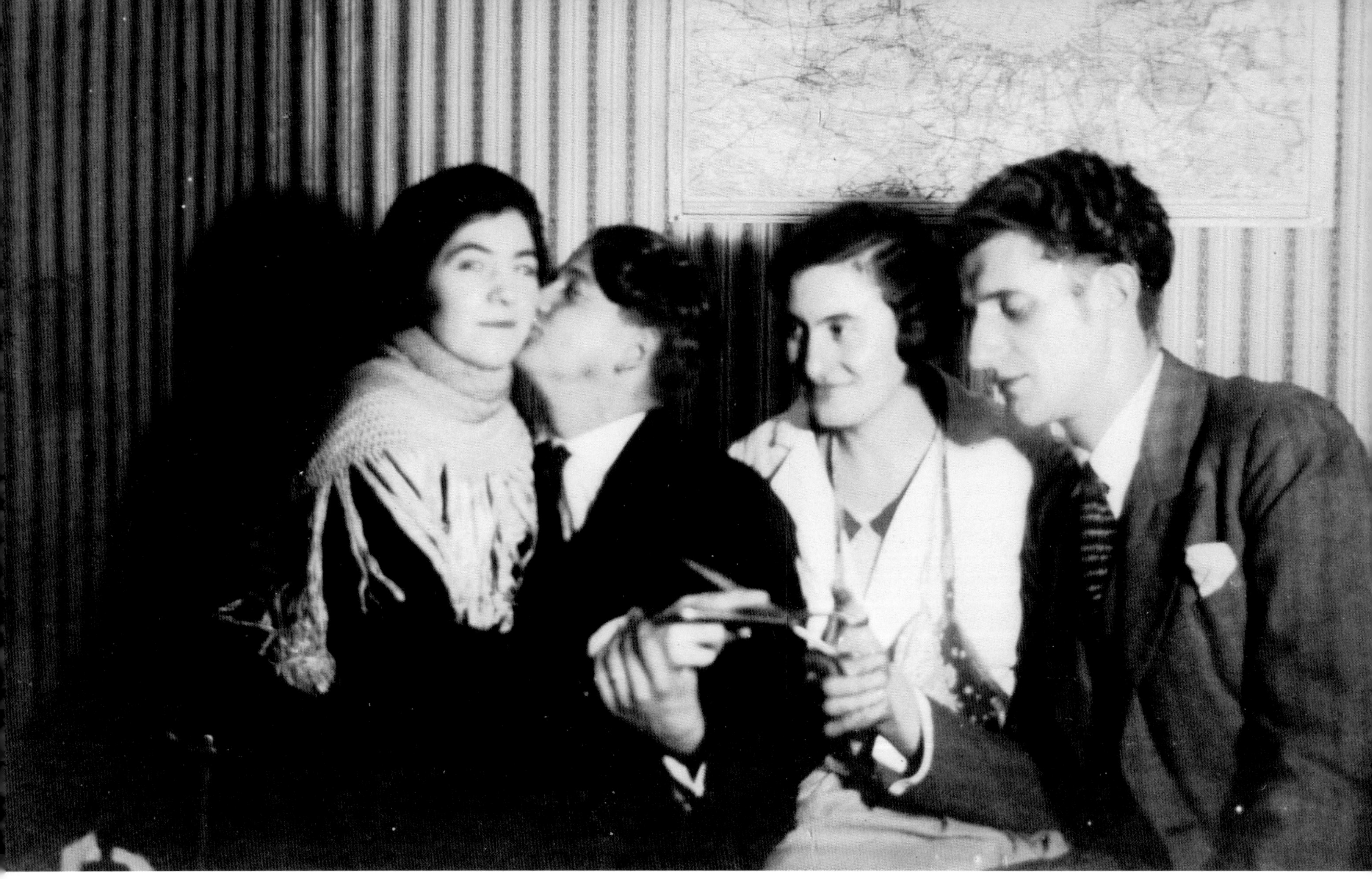

Paris, France

Right: Amsterdam, Holland

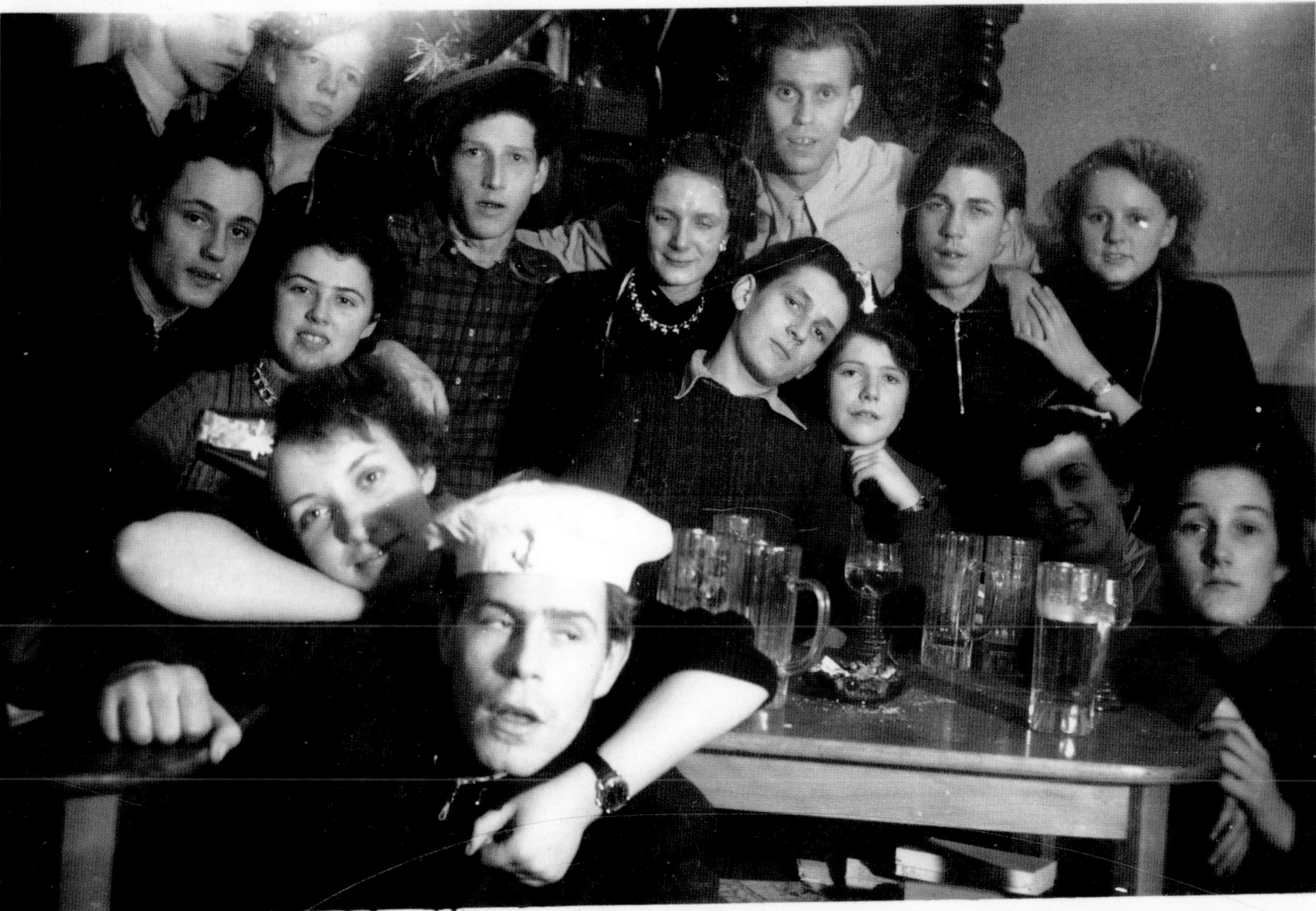

The first quarter of the 20th century saw Bulgaria consecutively fight against the Ottoman Empire and win, lose to former allies Serbia and Greece, then fight alongside the Ottoman Empire and lose, only to emerge in 1920 as a democracy and align itself disastrously with Soviet communism before forging an alliance with German and Italian fascism. Somehow through all of this, the spirit of the age of parties made its mark.

Sofia, Bulgaria

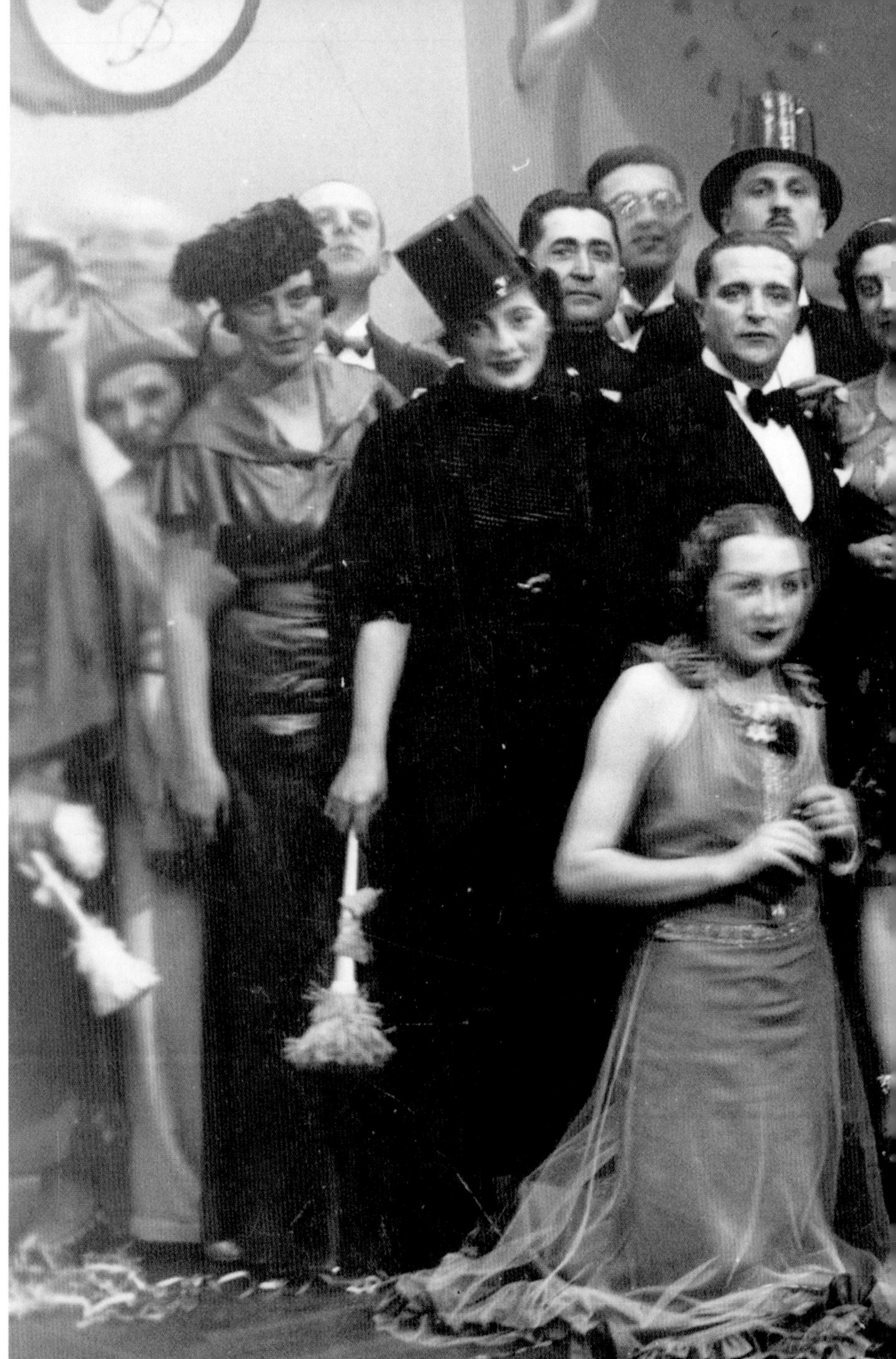

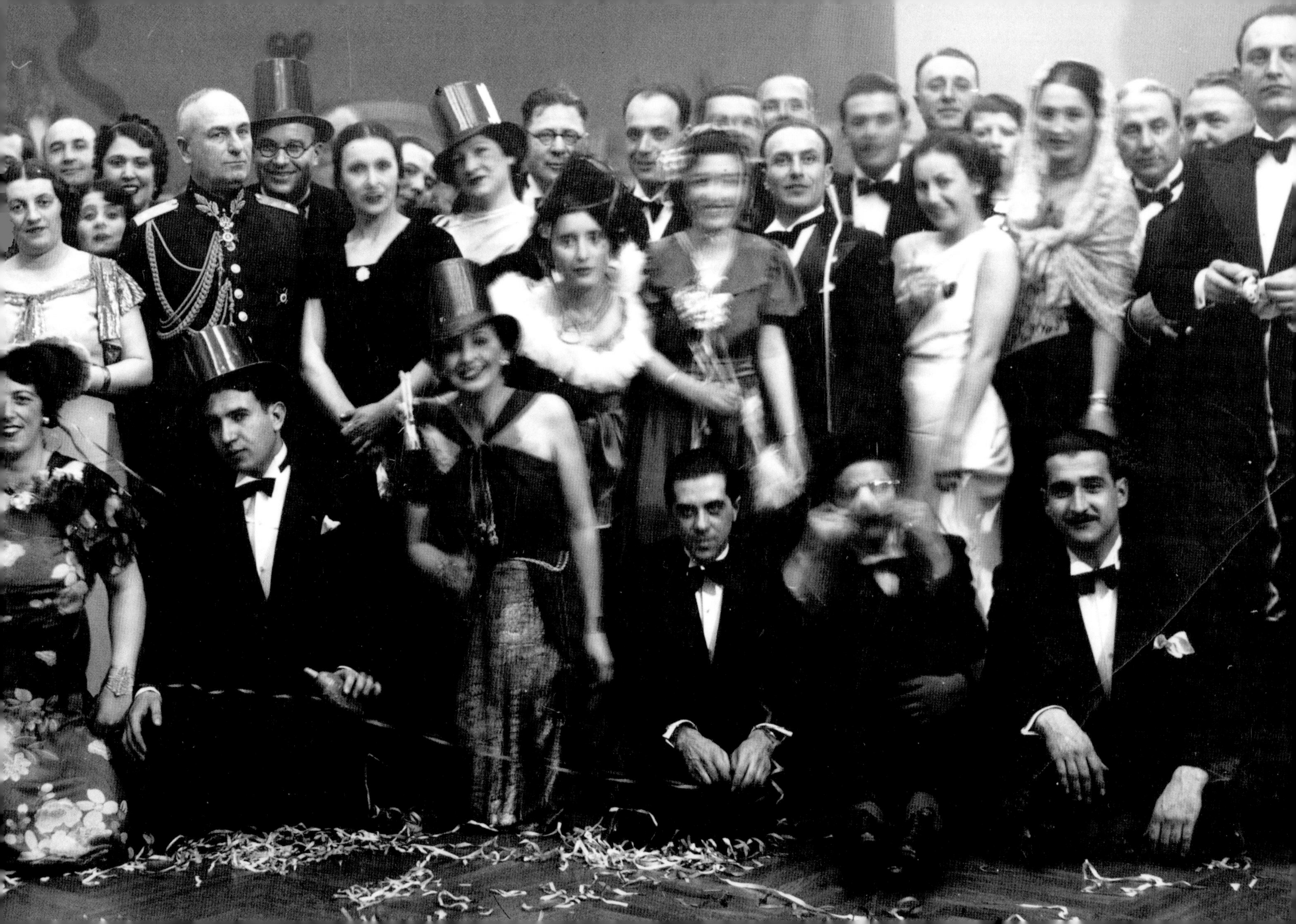

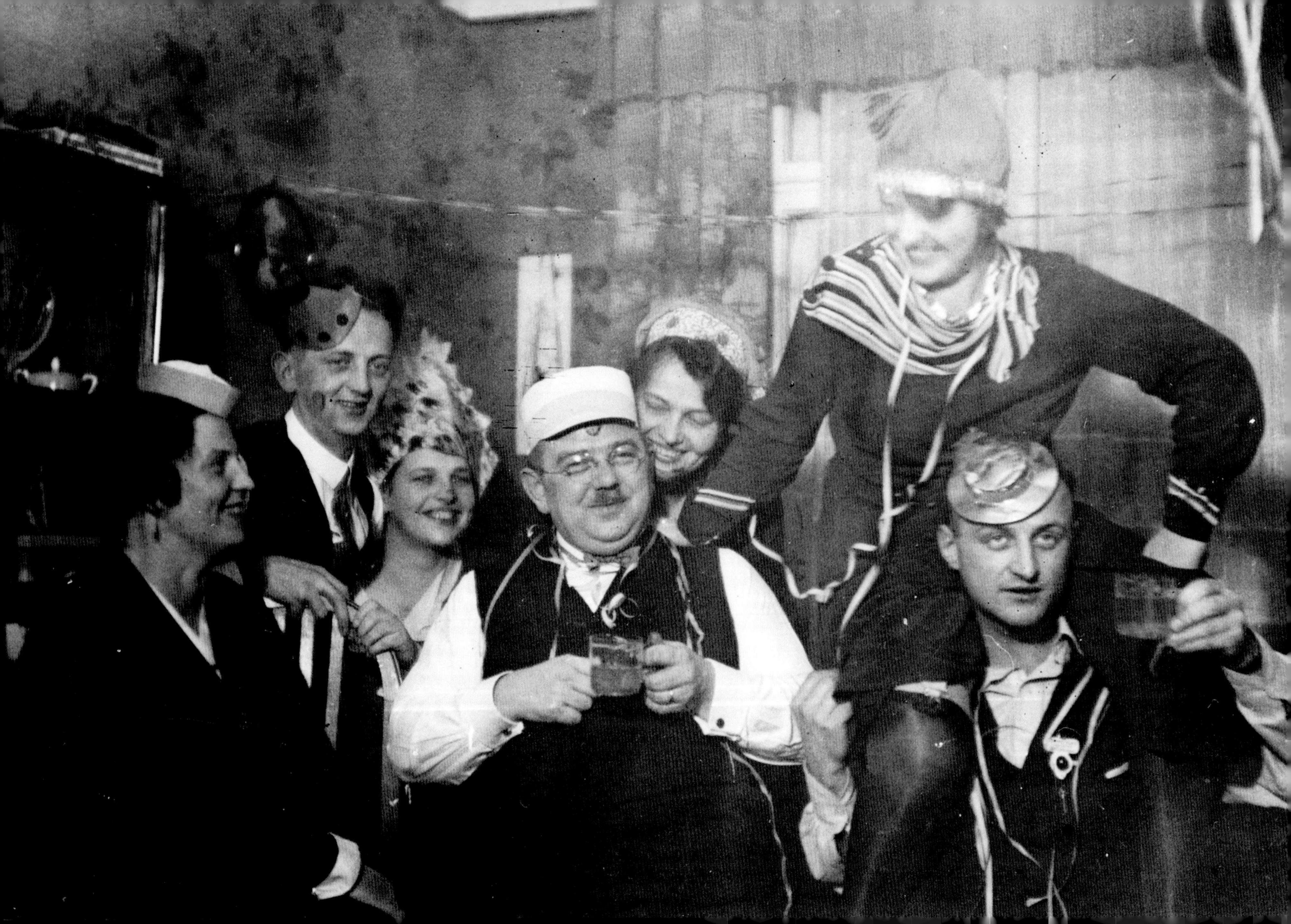

After World War I Latvia was at the centre of a struggle involving the invading Bolshevik Red Army, the remnants of the German occupying army, Polish forces fighting the Bolsheviks, the British trying to maintain order whilst achieving their own political aims, and sundry armed groups who happened to be in the area. This tumultuous period saw the population of Riga drop by half as residents fled, but independence was eventually gained, and the city – along with the rest of the country – re-established itself and began to prosper.

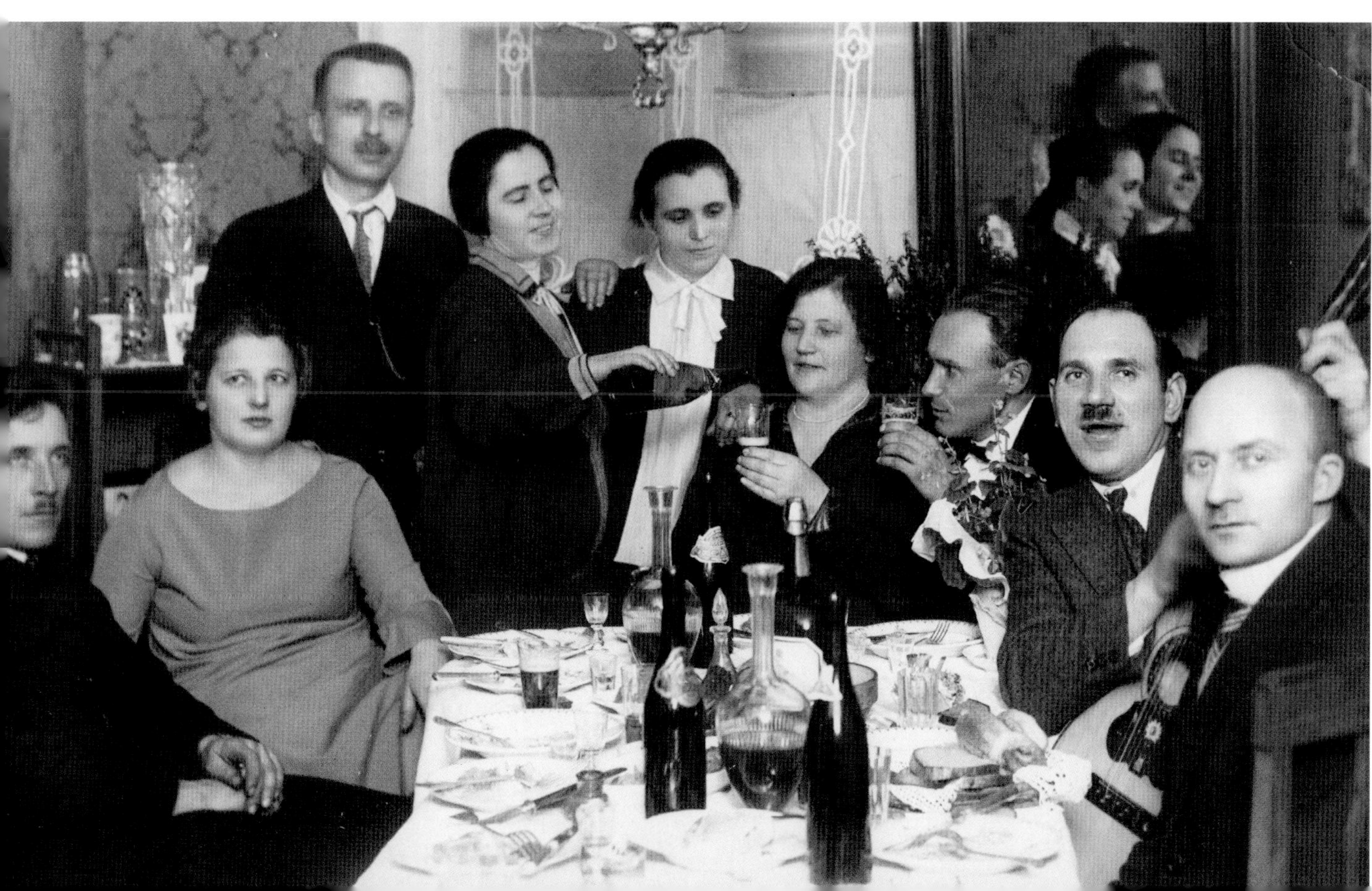

Opposite page: Amsterdam, Holland
Left: Riga, Latvia

part IV

1932
1934

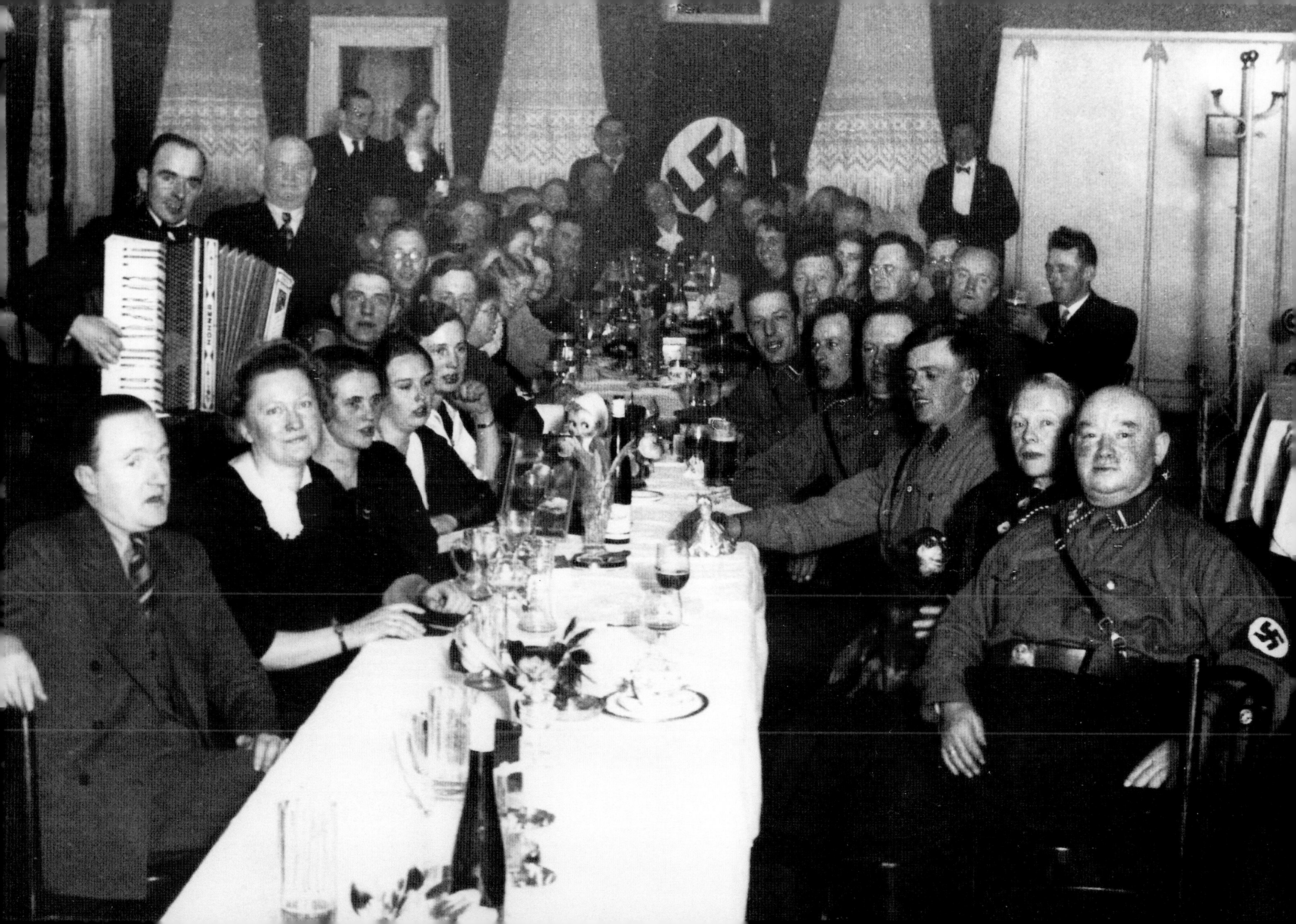

Berlin publisher Willy Sanke's series of photo-postcards showing heroes of World War I become immensely popular, especially those featuring German fighter pilots such as Hans Klein (seen here in the first left card in the first full row from top), Oberleutnant Friedrich Christiansen (third row from top, second card from left), and Oberleutnant Bruno Loerzer (centre card in the first visible lower row). All three men were politically active at the time of this photograph. Klein went on to become a Luftwaffe General, retired in 1943, but died in 1944 under mysterious circumstances (some believe he was murdered). Christiansen became commander of the Wehrmacht in Holland during World War II and was later convicted of war crimes. Loerzer, a friend of Hermann Göring, with whom he flew missions on the Western Front during World War I, also went on to become a Luftwaffe General.

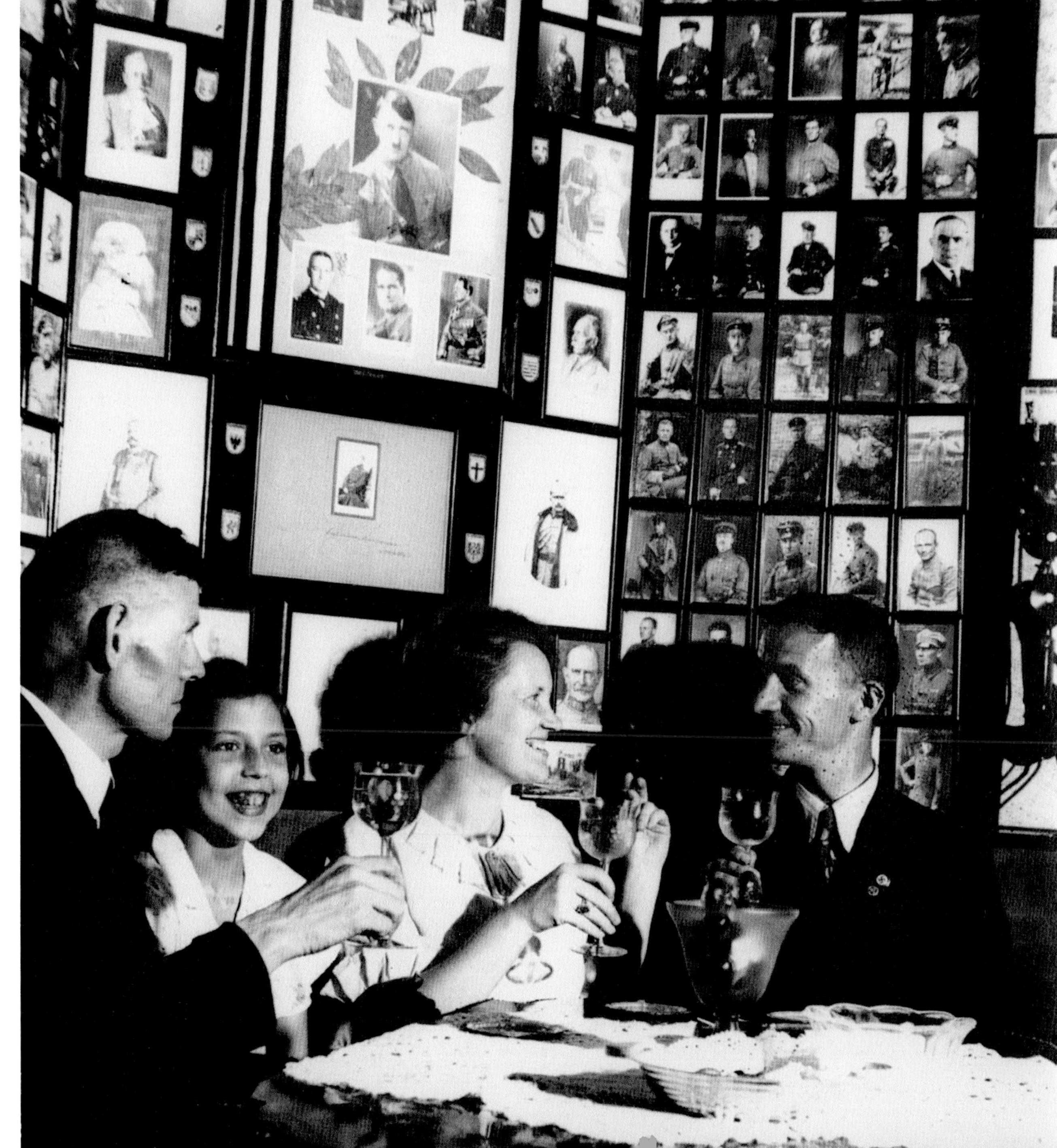

The walls of this restaurant are adorned with a romanticised portrait of Adolf Hitler and an array of Sanke cards

The 1920s was an era of great expansion for the make-up industry, and by the 1930s many pharmacies had extensive cosmetics counters at which women could try the latest products. Lipsticks were particularly popular, especially bright scarlet, and an artistic reshaping of the lips was an important fashion statement.

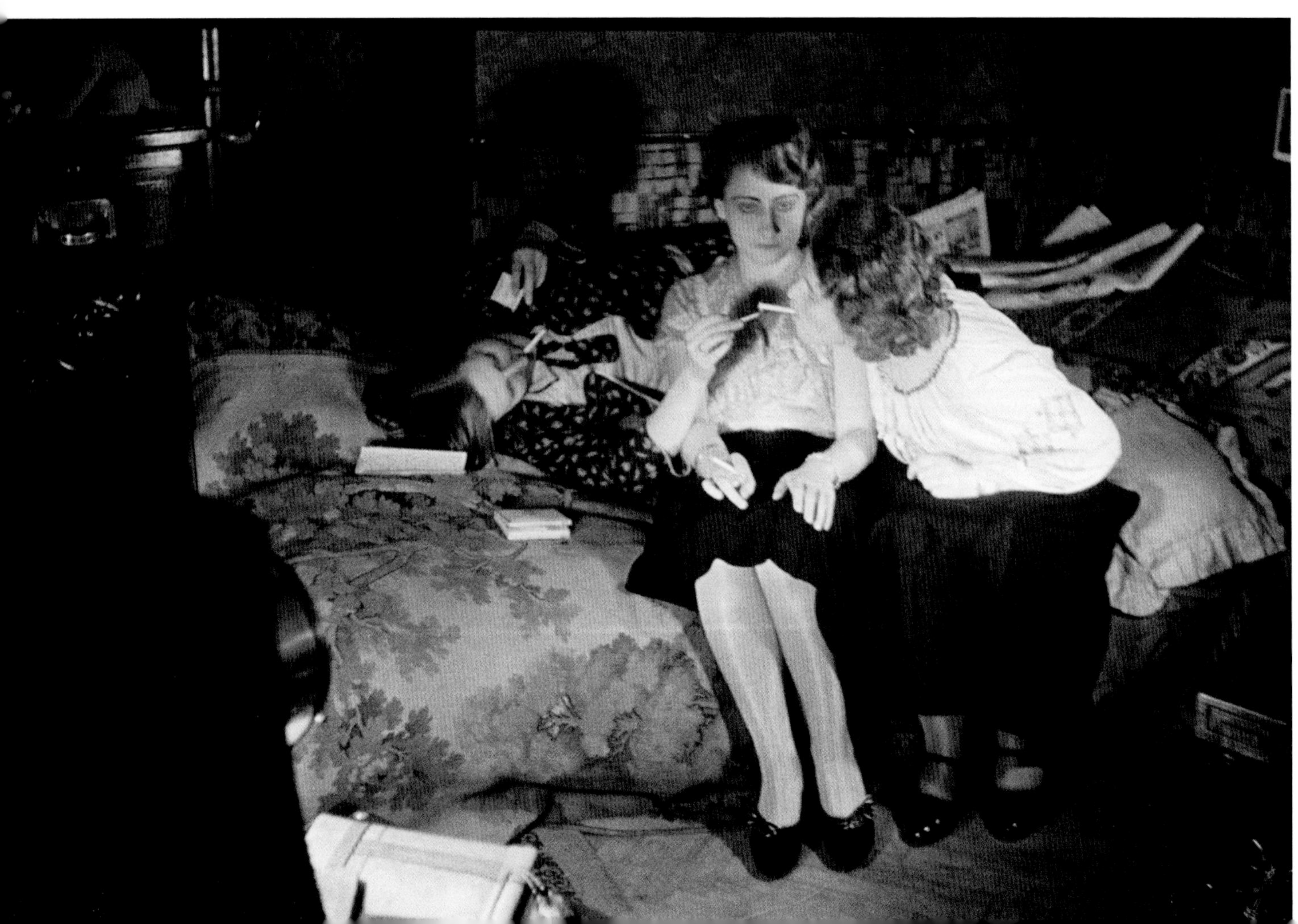

Left: Fritz Scheddin, Annemarie Gurau, and Vida, Berlin. Annemarie Gurau was a dental student whose work included a 1932 publication investigating sugar-related tooth decay amongst bakery and pastry apprentices.

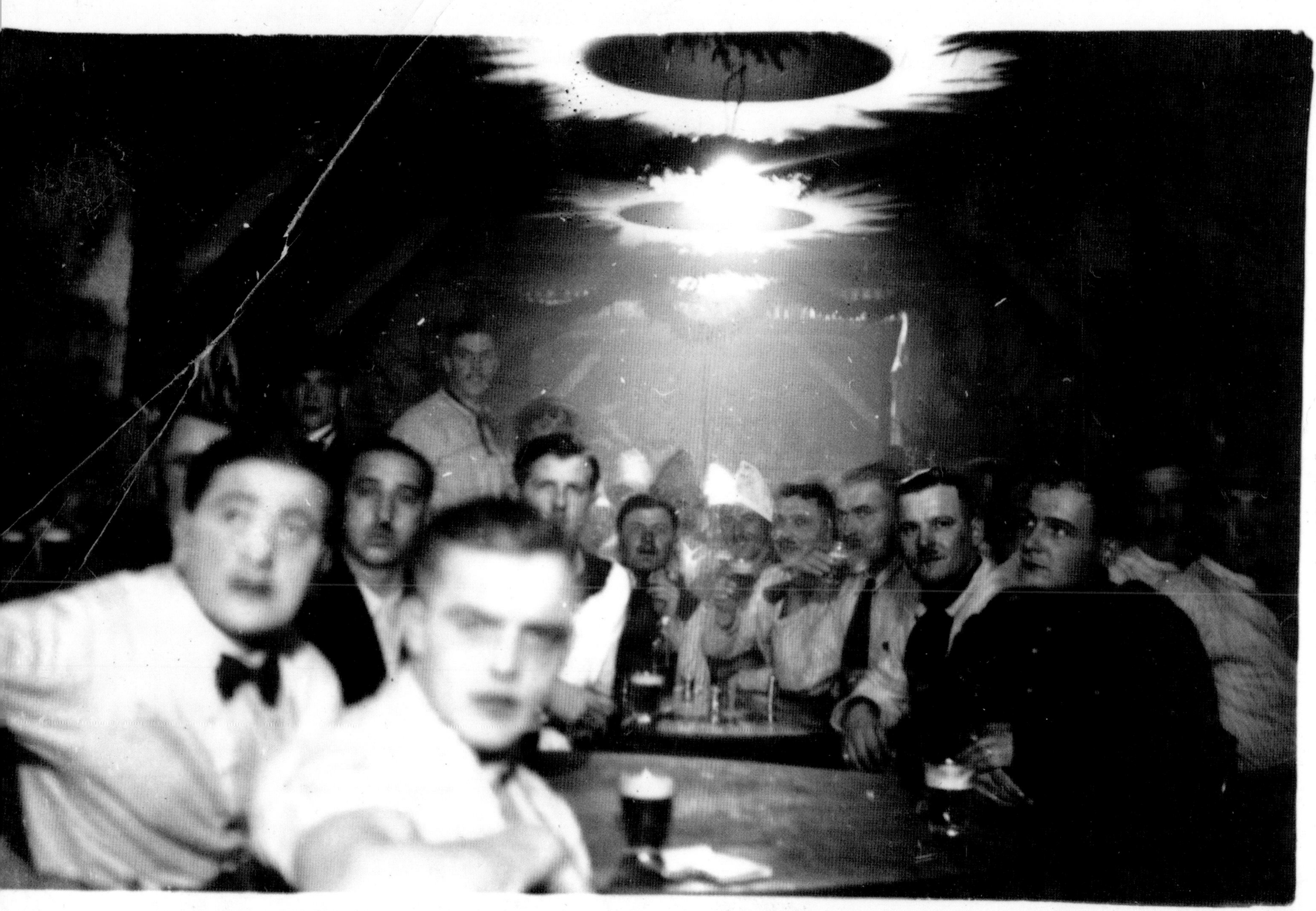

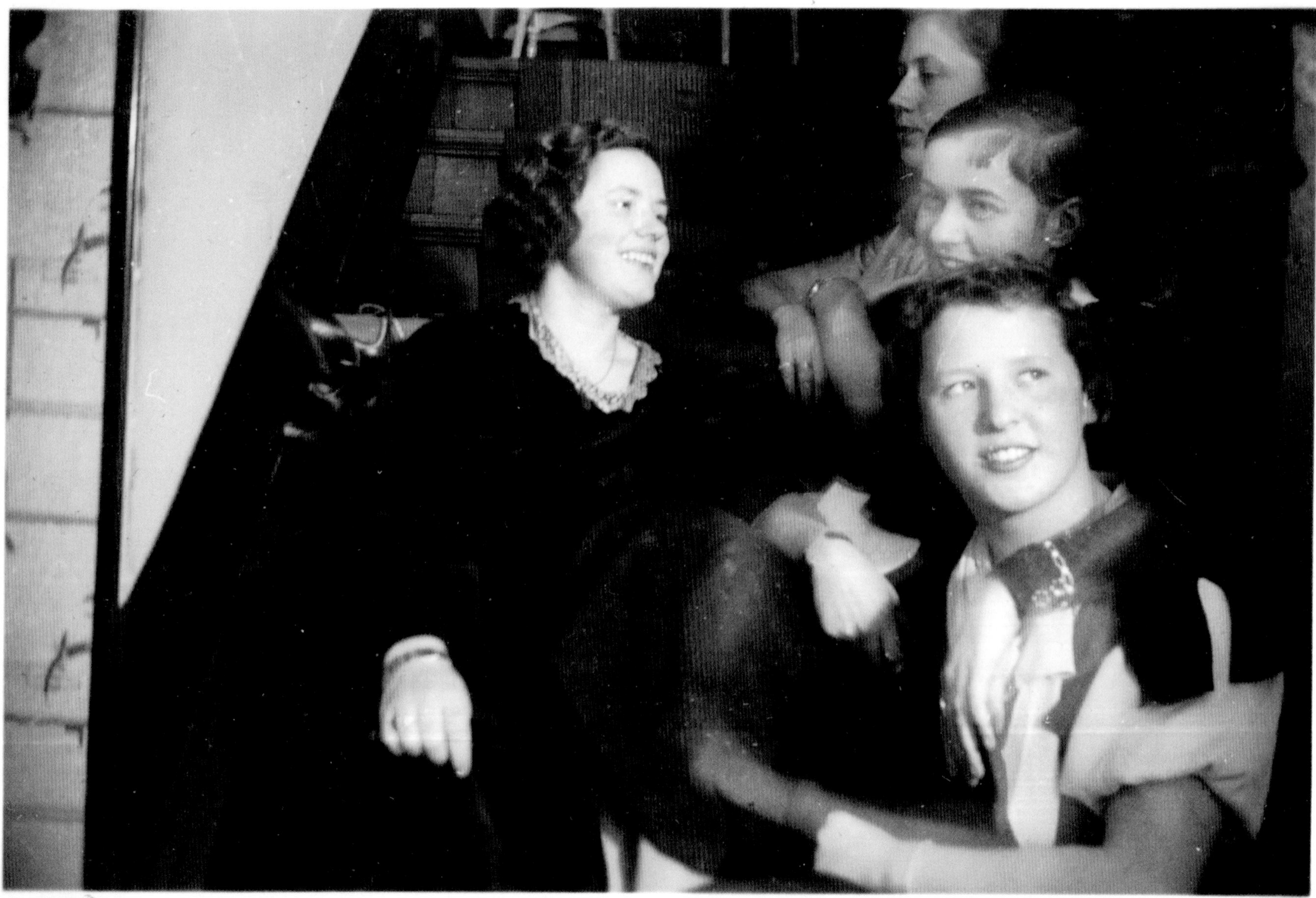

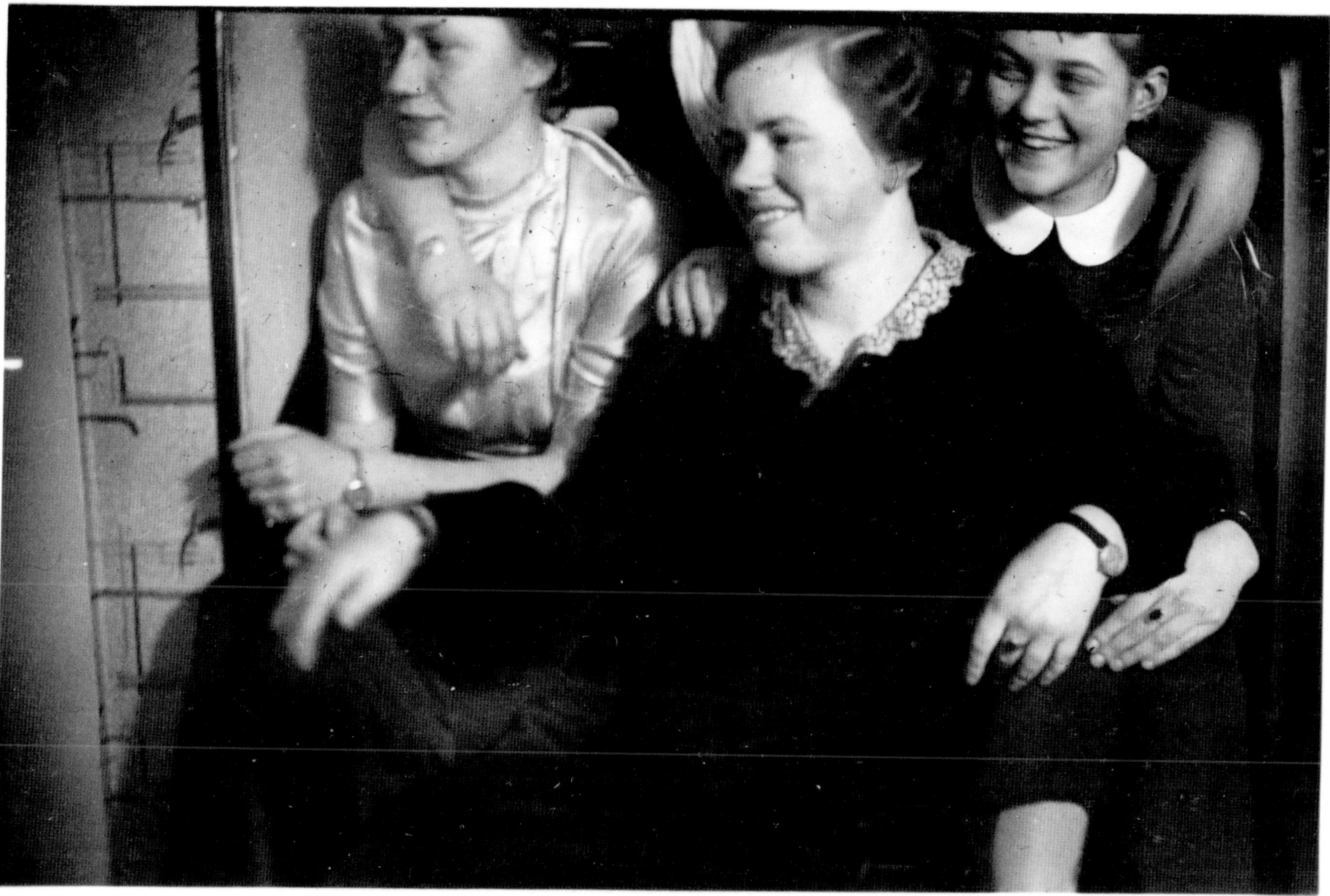

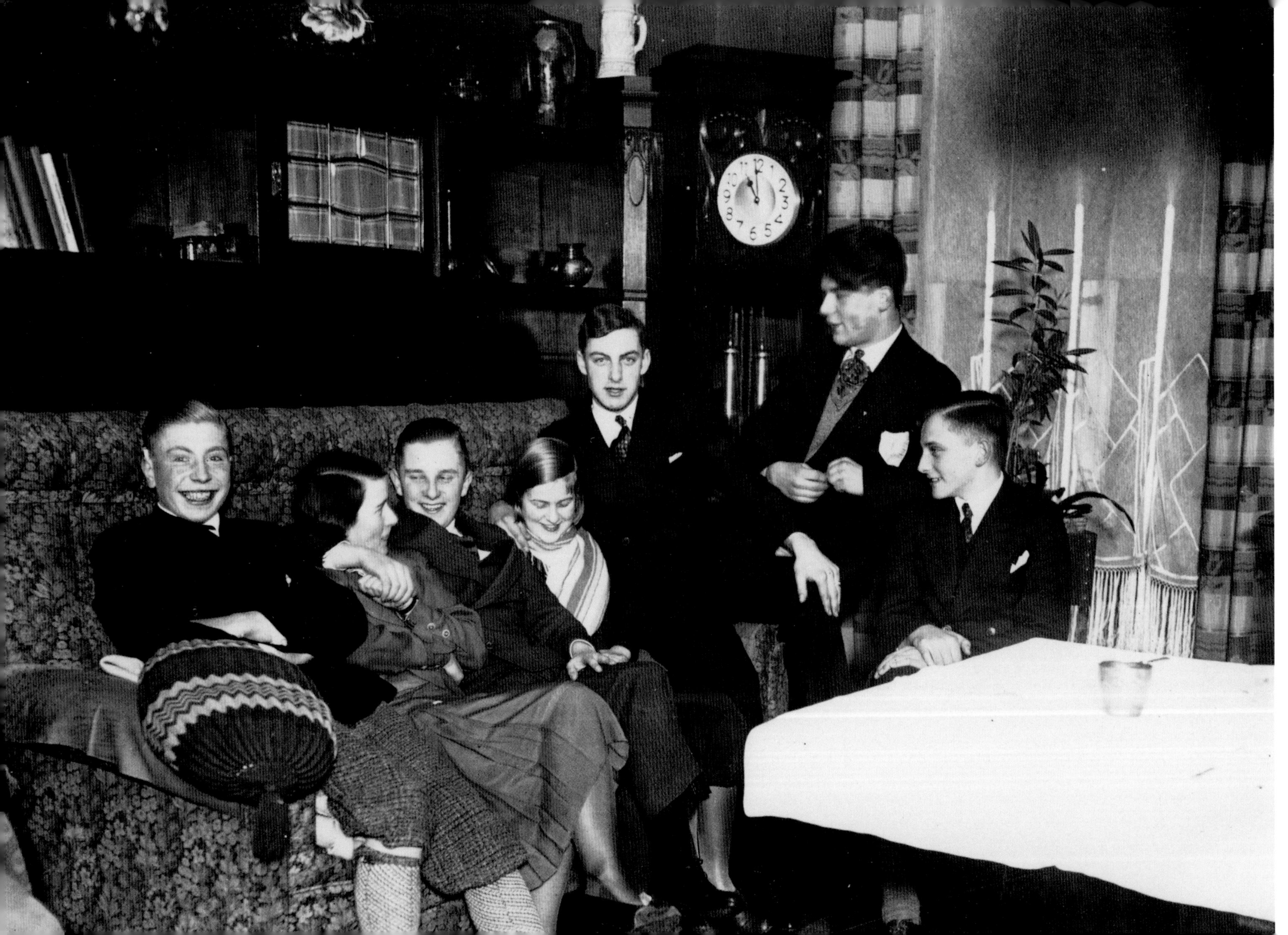

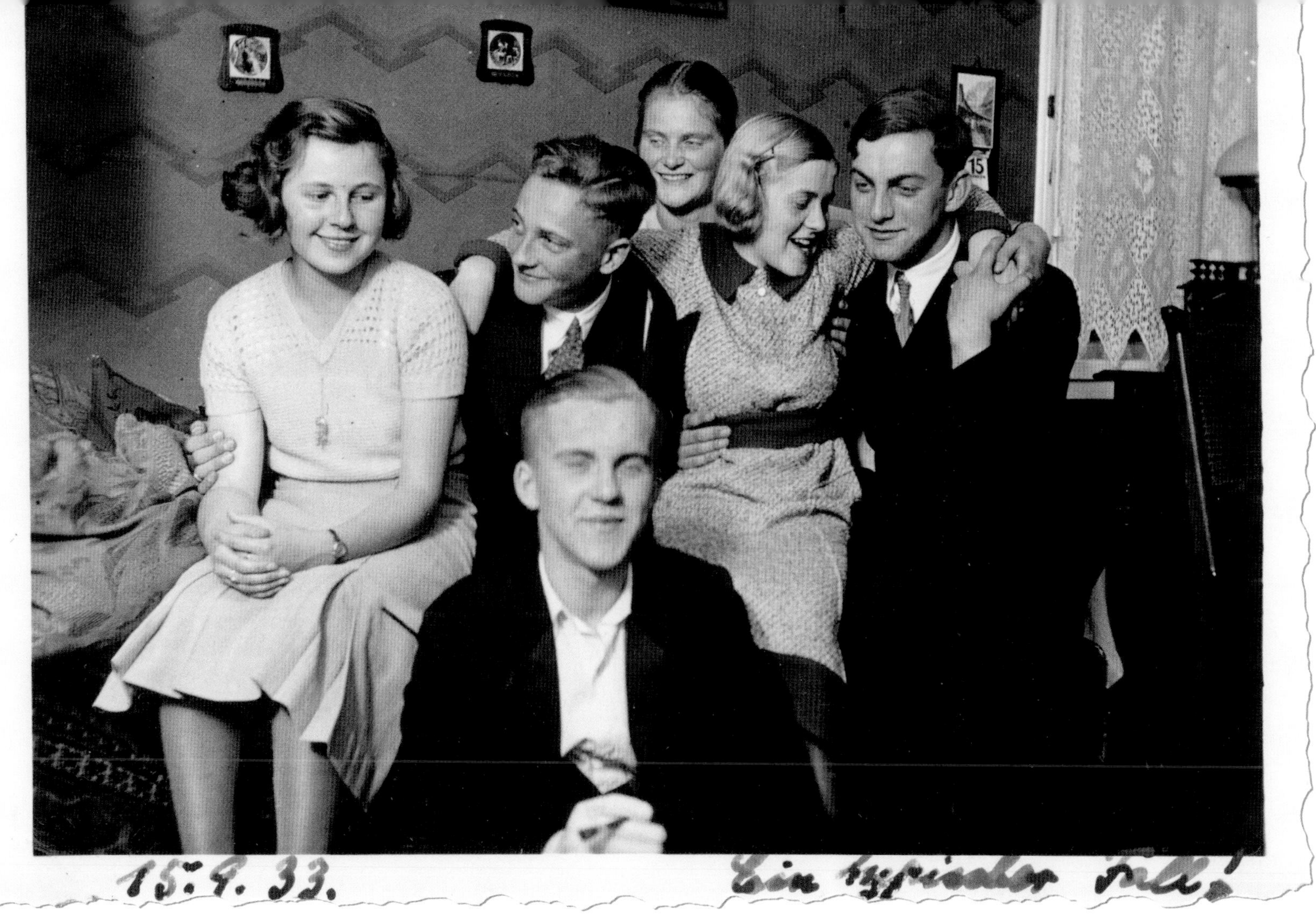

Left: Popular throughout the 1920s and 1930s, the ruralist *Wandervogel* movement embraced neo-paganism and fundamentalist folk dancing, revived indigenous folk songs and encouraged the performance of rituals around roaring campfires. The ruddy-cheeked young man in plaid knickerbockers on the left in this image typifies the sartorial style of adherents to the movement.

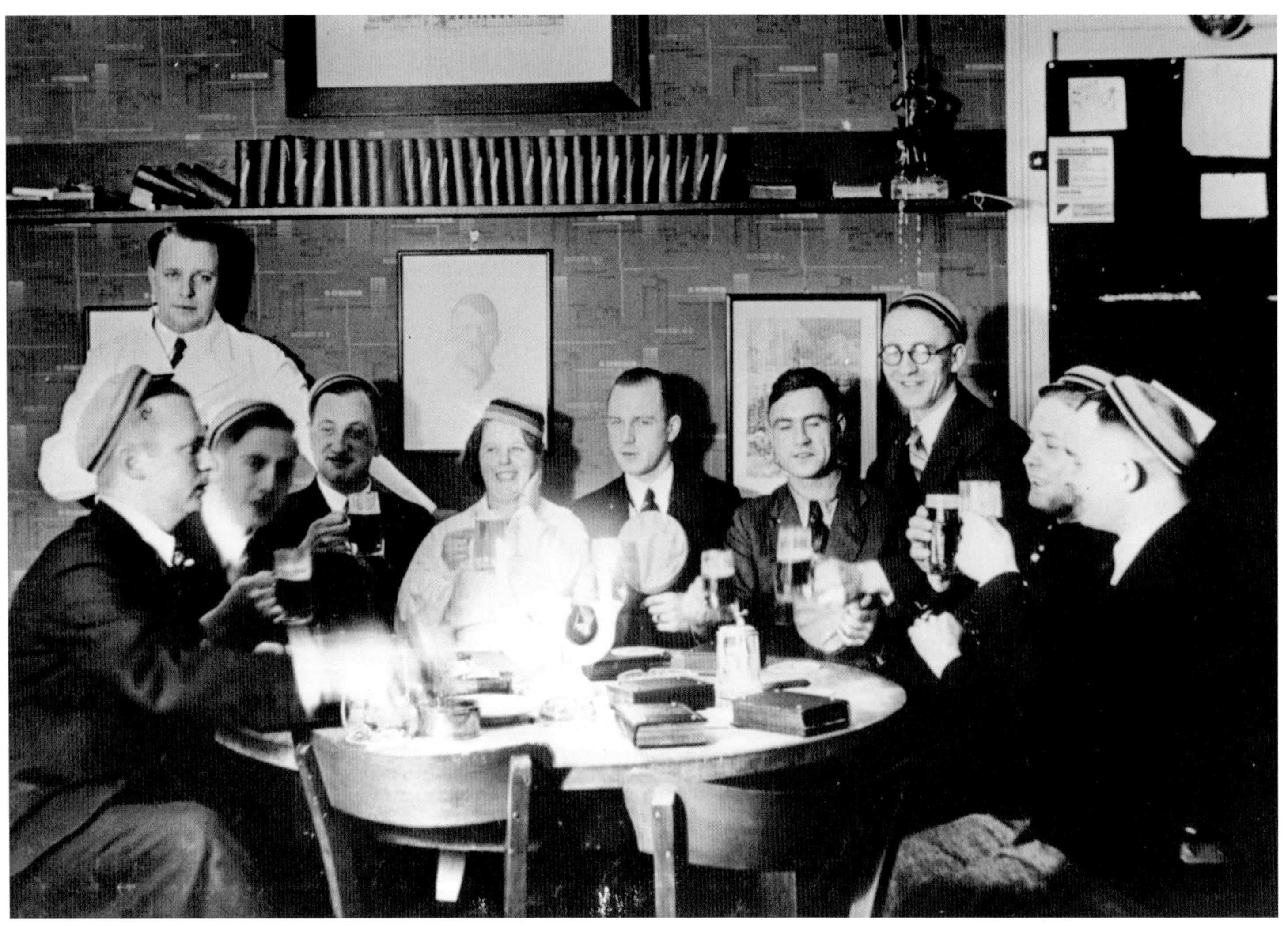

The rise of Nazism made political satire, popular in the cabarets of the 1920s, increasingly dangerous. It was replaced by a safer, more slapstick brand of humour called *Schenkelklopfer*, the German word for an uproariously funny joke, literally a 'thigh-slapper'.

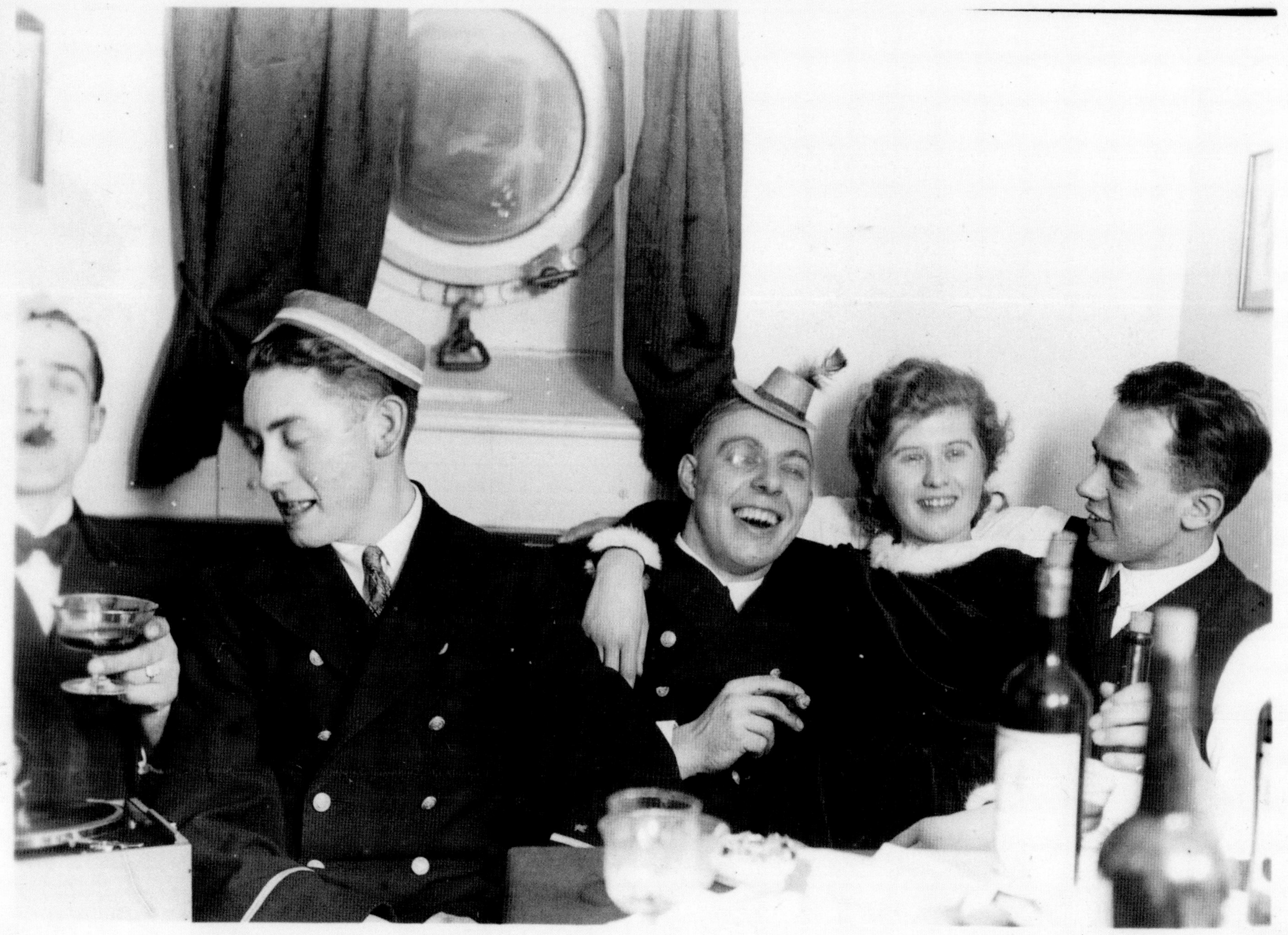

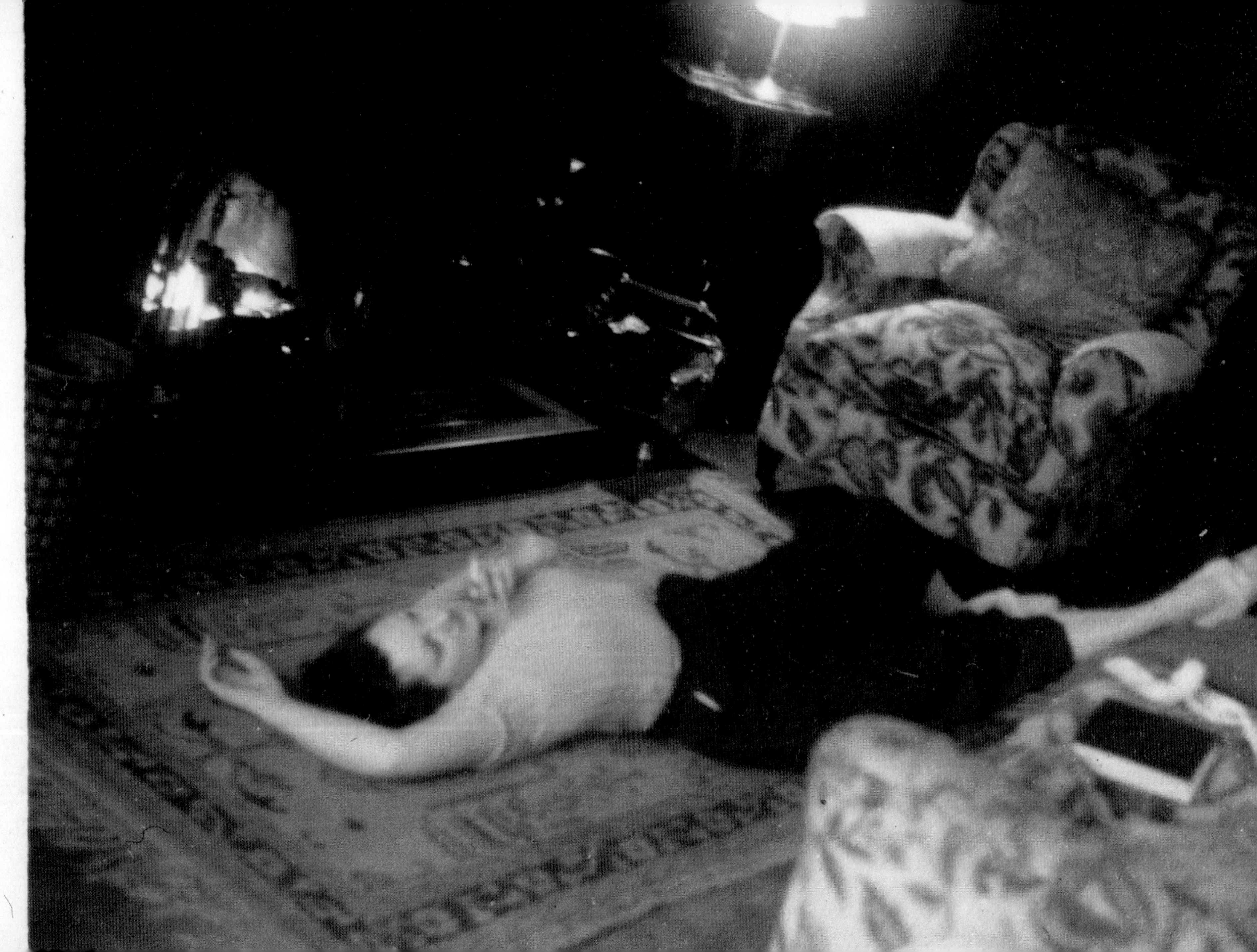

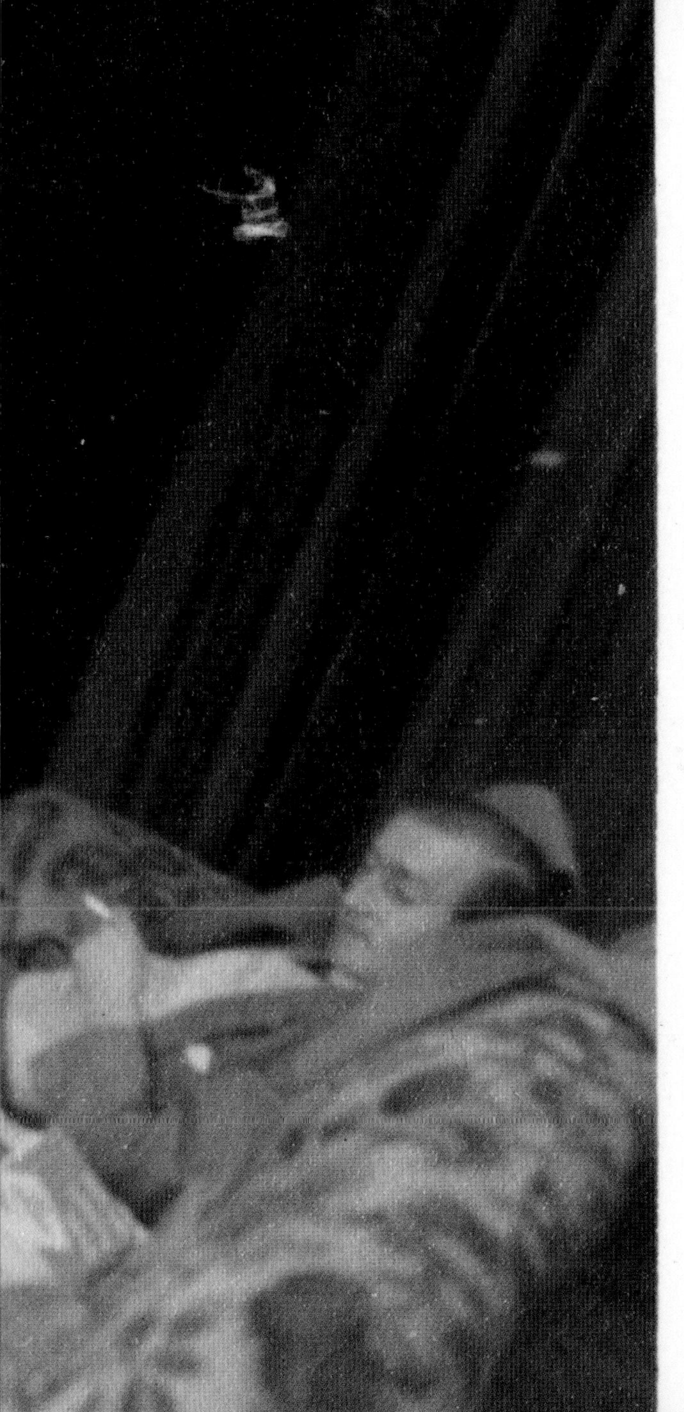

By the early 1930s, Germany had for some time been a fluctuating admix of the cosmopolitan and the parochial, and it was impossible to predict which side, if either, would prevail. Rival gangs from the far left and far right skirmished bloodily in the streets. The numerous, ill-disciplined Nazi SA were a familiar sight in their brown shirts and were as respected by their own as they were held in contempt by their enemies.

Berlin's Institute of Sex Research, founded in 1919 by filmmaker and scientist Magnus Hirschfeld – a sexual rights activist and opponent of Paragraph 175 of the German Criminal Code, which criminalised homosexuality – became a prime target for the Nazi Party. In early 1933 the Institute was attacked by members of the right-wing *Deutsche Studentenschaft*, the German student's union, and the contents of its library, amounting to more than 20,000 books, were burned in the street.

Little more than a year later, leaders of the SA including Ernst Rohm, many of whom were known to be homosexual, were murdered in a government purge dubbed 'The Night of the Long Knives'.

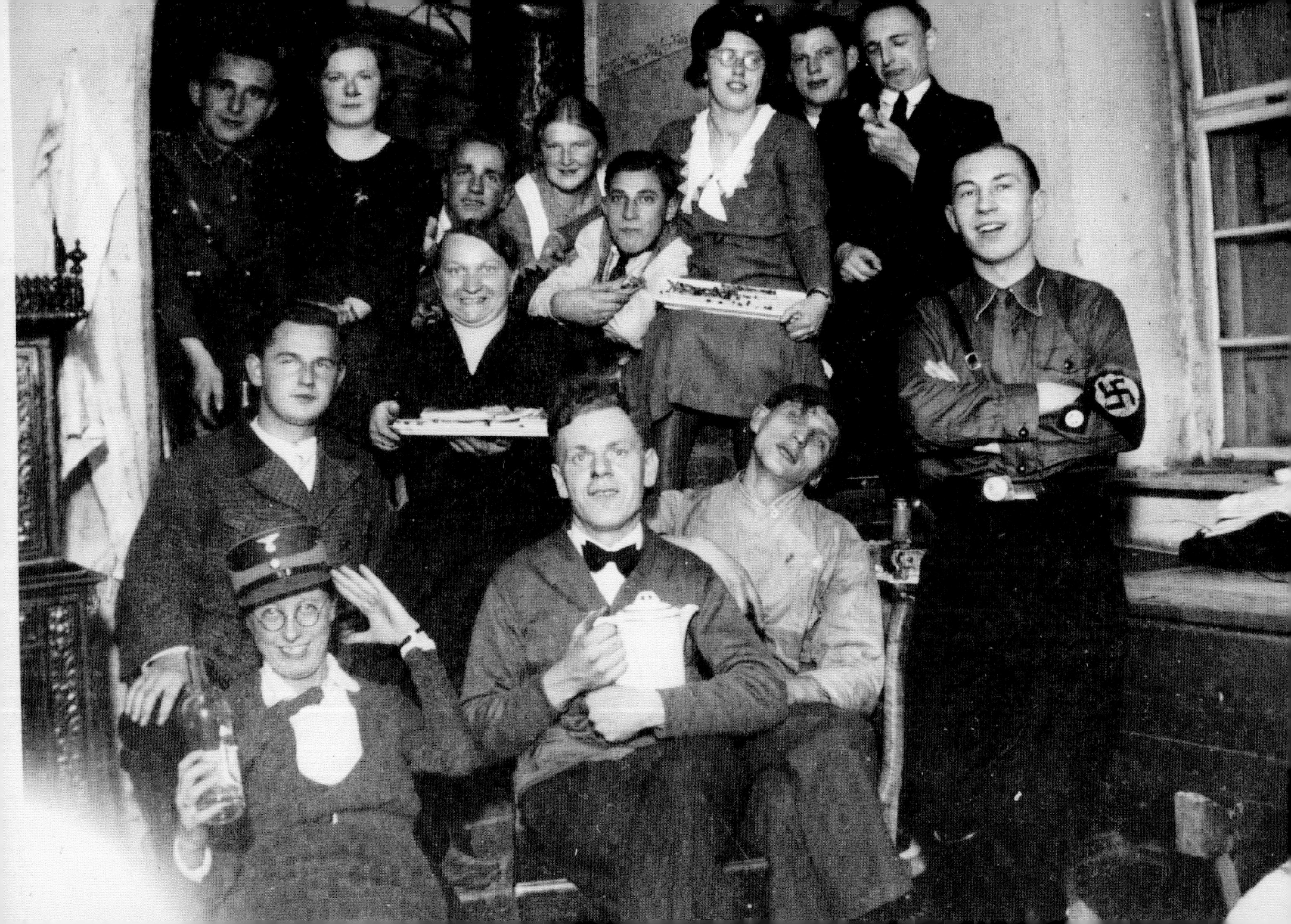

"In Paris, if you can't make your living through dancing, there will be some sympathetic Marquis or American, but in Berlin even God ignores you!"
– Dey, an American Creole dancer celebrated for combining belly dance with the Charleston